JOURNALS, 1939–1977

JOURNALS, 1939–1977

KEITH VAUGHAN

ff

faber and faber

This edition first published in 2010
by Faber and Faber Ltd
Bloomsbury House, 74–77 Great Russell Street
London WC1B 3DA

Printed by CPI Antony Rowe, Eastbourne

A CIP record for this book is available from the British Library

ISBN 978-0-571-26038-6

Contents

Introduction

by Alan Ross

Keith Vaughan himself chose the extracts from his Journals for the years 1939 to 1965, first published in 1966, and I then made further selections covering the years from 1967 to his death in 1977. These appeared in the *London Magazine* in 1983. The complete Journals amount to sixty-two notebooks, so the present selection represents less than a quarter of the whole.

Keith's father died when he was a child, which meant that his adolescence was spent in the company of his mother – tiny, energetic, dominating – and his five year-younger brother, Dick, to whom, during their childhood, he had felt himself more of a parent. Dick had been a nervy, unhappy boy, utterly dependent on him. In due course Keith went to Christ's Hospital, near Horsham, and not long before he left Dick joined him there. Dick matured rapidly, became physically strong and, unlike Keith, good at games, and eventually went into the R.A.F.

Keith, now working for Lintas, the Unilever advertising agency, rarely saw his brother from then on, though they came together occasionally over their shared interest in old cars. When war broke out Keith registered as a Conscientious Objector and joined the St John Ambulance. Dick was by now qualified as a pilot. In June 1940 his squadron went into action and within four days of their last parting at Trafalgar Square tube station he was dead.

In 1941 Keith was drafted into the Pioneer Corps, in the latter part of the war working as an interpreter in a camp for German P.O.Ws. Up till now he was only able to paint in his spare time, but after demobilisation he soon began to establish himself as one of the most gifted painters of his generation, part of the Neo-Romantic revival whose leading figure was Graham Sutherland and whose members included John Minton, Michael Ayrton, John Craxton, Robert Colquhoun and Robert MacBryde. Vaughan's first two shows were at the Lefèvre Gallery in 1944 and 1946. In 1946 John Minton took a lease on two floors of a house in Hamilton Terrace, St John's Wood, which he shared with Keith (and myself for nearly a year).

Apart from the fact that they were both painters and homosexual they had little in common. Johnny was mannered, frivolous in speech, compulsively gregarious, open-handed. Keith was reserved, self-contained, tidy in habit and mind, grumpy. Johnny behaved wildly and without inhibition, alternating between high spirits and physical exhaustion, always generous with his time. He liked to appear unserious, as though the whole art business was a lark. Keith, on the other hand, was miserly with his time, cross at distraction, but, as the day wore on, he mellowed. Once work was over he was the friendliest and most rewarding of companions, serious in the best sense, sharply observant and critical, but also funny. Not surprisingly, as the one grew more and more a creature of the night, attended, particularly after the money rolled in, by a larger and larger retinue of 'students', and the other remained selectively domestic, they came to see less and less of each other. I cannot remember them ever going out together.

While Johnny enjoyed social and commercial success, travelling each year to the Caribbean, North Africa or Spain, and filling portfolios with succulent drawings and watercolours, Keith dug himself in. He taught at the Camberwell School of Art from 1946 to 1948 and then at the Central and the Slade. He painted a large mural for the Dome of Discovery, the centrepiece of the 1951 Festival of Britain. His various romantic attachments seemed to cause him more distress than pleasure, though, unlike Johnny, he was naturally attracted to homosexuals rather than heterosexuals. Whereas Johnny made light of everything, Keith brooded, rather old-maidish in his habits, confiding his resentments, fantasies and general observations on art and life to his voluminous notebooks. From time to time he did break out, cruising Soho and returning drunk, with or without bedfellow. But these were rare occurrences, and when later a longstanding relationship developed it brought frustration and irritation rather than contentment.

It was impossible to be in Keith's company long without becoming aware of his natural gravity and critical intelligence – the latter of a wry, dismissive kind. Once warmed up he was full of speculative humour, jokes and self-mockery. He was more widely read than Johnny, and more questioning, and when he talked about painting it was as someone who thought long and hard, not only about technical problems but about the relevance of art to every aspect of living.

After I moved out of the boiler room at Hamilton Place, I rarely saw Johnny except at parties. As an abstract international style began to develop and figuration of any kind tended to be regarded as obsolete, Johnny increasingly found himself in a limbo between the avant-garde and the academic. Those who held their ground like Francis Bacon and Lucian Freud came through, and so, of course, would Johnny have done. But his nerve failed him, his confidence evaporated and his plunge into drink and tranquillizers became more and more hectic. Aptly, his last public work was his set for *Don Juan in Hell* at the Royal Court, done shortly before his death in 1957.

With Keith I never lost touch. When, after our son Jonathan was born in 1953, we moved to Sussex, he frequently came down for weekends, beetling along the lane under the Downs in his open Morris Minor. He kept this car until his death, by which time it must have been twenty years old. He came and stayed with us in Ischia one September, a fellow guest of Cyril Connolly. The pair of them sat in total silence in the back of my open car, staring ahead or outwards like bodyguards, each incapable of small talk or of making the first move. 'What a nice person Keith is,' Cyril typically remarked later, not having addressed a word to him for two weeks.

From Ischia Keith and I slowly drove back north, hugging the coast. Johnny would have wanted to stop and draw, but Keith had no such inclinations. We spent a night in Turin, dining in the magnificent restaurant of the Principi di Piemonte, and another at the Poste et Lion d'Or in Vézelay, after visiting the great Basilica Ste-Madeleine, a vision that drew from Keith a reluctant grunt. We lunched in autumn sunshine on the banks of the Yonne and I dropped him off in Paris.

Another year Keith joined us in Aegina before he and I drove round the Peloponnese. Travelling with Keith was agreeable, although there was little he did not view with asperity. He rarely made drawings on the spot and when he did they seemed, in comparison to the virtually realized sketch that Johnny used so rapidly to do, rather feeble and fumbling. He had no great facility, but when he was drawing in earnest – as in his Iowa river drawings and those he made in Donegal in 1958 – the impress was firm and the structure solid.

I had never found Johnny's homosexuality obtrusive when I was abroad with him. Keith, however, was always on the look-out, which made me feel vaguely uneasy that my presence might deter potential lovers. It never affected his manners, but I became aware on our various travels together that after we had said good night he would slip out of the hotel, returning later with some boy he then had to smuggle in. I was apprehensive, because there was a sadistic as well as a masochistic streak in Keith, which his later and more private journals made only too clear. When I tackled him about the risks he was taking he made light of it, but I continued to have visions of an officious manager turning him out of the hotel in the middle of the night and probably me as well.

In 1962 Keith had a large retrospective at the Whitechapel. The Hamilton Terrace arrangement had come to an end some years before Johnny's suicide and Keith was now in Belsize Park, sharing his flat with Ramsay McClure, who, at that time, was designing window displays at an Oxford Street store. I remember Ramsay as being nondescript in appearance, slightly built and balding, his voice gentle with a faint Scottish accent. He appeared on the surface undemanding, unobtrusive and placid, but the honeymoon, such as it was, did not last. Before long Ramsay, either by his very presence or because of his acquiescent, dependent nature, was visibly getting on Keith's nerves.

Soon they acquired a cottage at Harrow Hill, in Essex, a small village to which Michael Ayrton and his wife had recently moved. Ramsay was banished there for most of the week, joined sometimes by Keith's mother, who increasingly became another source of irritation to him. Keith referred to his mother in his journal as a 'controlled hysteric', but as far as one could see she was simply overprotective and managing, though possibly bird-brained as well. Ramsay, in his exile, took to cooking and gardening, but left alone so much he also took to the bottle. Aware that he annoyed Keith, he came to behave so unnaturally that it was impossible to be in a room with them both and not feel the strain.

The Whitechapel show, organized by Bryan Robertson, marked perhaps the high point of Keith's career. The example of de Stael in the mid fifties and the effect on Keith of certain American abstract painters – hitherto much despised – had suggested how figurative painting could come to terms with abstraction, gaining tension and compression without compromise. Keith never lost his preoccupation with the male nude, depersonalizing it to such an extent that it became an integral part of its background, but after his visit to America in 1959 and his term as Resident Painter at Iowa State University he shed most of the neo-romantic mannerisms and symbols earlier associated with him and others of his generation.

Of all those who moved in and out of abstraction Keith made the most successful transition. He lost nothing of his identity, simply merged it in pictorial compositions every one of which was as demonstrably his work as the bathers, wrestlers and fishermen of the '50s. His landscapes – empty beaches, untenanted orchards, rocky valleys, bare cliffs – acquired a new strength and ruggedness, reflective not only of solitude but also of defiance.

Keith was by nature a stoic and fatalist. A stocky figure, he was immensely strong and also attractive, even though he began to lose his hair in his late forties and ended up looking like Verlaine. If Johnny Minton's physical characteristics were reflected in his painting, then certainly Keith's were as well, in a less obvious way.

The Whitechapel show was a revelation to most people, though, as Bryan Robertson observed, Keith lacked a clearly identifiable public, a situation to which he contributed by his own reclusiveness. His paintings of male assemblies and studies of adolescents naturally provided him with collectors as much attracted by their subject matter as by their manner and formal quality. But such paintings also shut him off from others who, with more perseverance, might have found reward in the power, complexity and suggestiveness of his technique. His landscapes were no obstacle, and some of his smaller gouaches, whether of English country scenes, the American Midwest or North Africa, are as seductive and accessible as any pictures of their period. But in the oils there is always – in a way rarely evident in a Minton painting or in the work of other contemporaries – a sense of drama and conflict, of the painter struggling to impose himself on recalcitrant materials. The completed work had to be wrestled into submission, the painter being in no doubt as to the arduousness of the process or the gravity of the issues.

This concentrated brooding over philosophical and technical matters gave all Keith's work a highly-charged atmosphere, so that one had the sense of being present at crucial and momentous deliberations. Yet there was nothing portentous or pretentious about him; rather the reverse. The essential seriousness of the concerns that were at the heart of his work was offset by a dry, no-nonsense manner and a total lack of illusion. The sweetness of character indicated by his own particular smile and the charm he exuded in his lighter moments – which were many – may not often have got into his painting, but the sensuousness was always evident. Few modern painters, in any case, convey whatever gregarious and sociable characteristics they may possess, the act of painting being a solitary one and usually more reflective of interior tensions than of general good will.

In 1964 the Whitechapel held another exhibition, the New Generation Show. Returning from it, Keith had a horrifying inkling of what it felt like to be superseded. 'After all one's thought and search and effort to make some sort of image which would embody the life of our time, it turns out that all that was really significant were toffee wrappers, liquorice allsorts and ton-up motorbikes ... I understand how the stranded dinosaurs felt ...'

The Journals up to 1965, published in 1966, reflect a time of hope. As he said of the forties, 'Real things were happening and being done. People were alive. Nothing seemed impossible or too vast to attempt.' This sense of adventure is rarely present in the Journals of the last years, often not at all. What dismayed his friends was the picture these suggested of the miserable existence he thought he was leading while his life appeared to be agreeable, prosperous and successful.

A relaxed, contented journal might make for entertaining reading but it would be unlikely to have the extraordinary effect of these descriptions of a descent into hell. The published volume was of especial interest to students of painting and to anyone curious about the working and thinking habits of a contemporary painter. The extracts from the unpublished journals were less to do with art and more to do with the chronicle of a decline. Keith felt he had worked out ways of dealing with technical problems and after 1970 was just going through the motions.

Most journals tend to reflect on depressed moods and moments and to that extent give an unbalanced picture of the writer's life at any particular time. Keith's are no exception. Mostly they were written late at night when, rather drunk and having failed as usual to make any social arrangement, he found himself alone. He persisted, at much cost to himself, in the belief that social life was scarcely ever worth the candle, that the effort of seeing people, even close friends, far outweighed the rewards. None of this would have mattered if he had enjoyed his solitude, but it was quite plain that he did not. After all, he had been alone the whole day. It was the more misguided in view of the fact that I cannot recall a single evening when, cajoled into coming out, he did not appear to have enjoyed himself.

The routine in Belsize Park over the years covered by the journal rarely varied. He painted, or at any rate was installed, in his studio from about 9.30 to 12.30, after which he had a drink, a snack and a siesta. After tea he worked for another hour or so, read, and then at about seven o'clock had his first whisky. He took trouble over preparing his solitary dinner, chose a bottle of good wine, and, after he had eaten, watched TV. He worked spasmodically at his journal, usually reflecting on the news of the day, on what he was reading, and regretting the lack of human contact and sexual incident in his life. As the number of whiskies increased so did he tend to become obsessively introverted and morbid. The last sentences of the day often petered out into an incoherent scrawl. By the time he was ready for bed and his assortment of pills – antidepressants, tranquillizers – he was fairly drunk. He may not, on non-teaching days, have spoken a single word all day.

At the time of the first entry to these later journals Keith was fifty-five, had recently been made an Honorary Fellow of the Royal College of Art and been awarded the CBE. He had returned a few months earlier from a visit to North Africa, a journey that resulted in a rich haul of gouaches. He was teaching part-time at the Slade.

It is not surprising, given the lateness of the hour at which it was written and the amount of alcohol Keith consumed, that the journal paints such a one-sided picture of his life. The reason he wrote so little here about his work, Keith himself explained, was because he had been physically involved in it all day. His journal was the record of the left-over part of his life, much of it taken up with discussing food and wine, his tax affairs (which had got him into some trouble) and sexual fantasizing.

In bulk the journals are repetitive and extremely depressing to read, but their frankness, spleen and dry humour, together with the fact that Keith's comments on books and painting are nearly always original and to the point, redeem them. They may be preoccupied with thoughts of failure, illness, suicide and death, of life going by pointlessly, but they are not self-pitying.

Although a natural hypochondriac – he diagnosed the onset of cancer in himself twenty years before it arrived – Keith had enough real trouble in his last years. He had no sooner recovered from an operation on his kidneys, which had caused him pain for months, than the first real symptoms of cancer appeared. The surgery was not successful and he was faced with a further course of debilitating treatment. The cancer would surely have killed him within a year if he had not got in first.

Despite the wretchedness of all this, it was only in the diary entries of the final eighteen months that the battle was shown to be lost. Never once, either in hospital or convalescing at home after the two operations, did he complain aloud. Whenever I went to see him he was smiling and joking, quite different from the brooding and grumpy creature of Hamilton Terrace mornings thirty years earlier.

Keith's diaries are of unique professional interest, not just for his comments on fellow painters and the art of his time, though these are usually slyly valuable, but also for the insights they provide into the life of a particular kind of contemporary artist, in Keith's case a homosexual. Had he been heterosexual, his life and painting would have been quite different, though whether he would have been any happier or a more fulfilled painter is another matter. He was absolutely what he was and though in his first abstract works the influence of others such as de Stael are recognizable, for the last twenty years of his life no mark that he made or line that he drew could possibly have been made by anyone else.

Having grown out of his one attempt at a domestic relationship which he yet felt obliged to honour, Keith spent most of his life in a state of acute sexual frustration. His forays into the homosexual underworld were spectacularly unsuccessful, and such encounters as led to sexual consummation of a sort were rarely repeated. Though quite tough in his dealings with 'rough trade' he was often exploited by criminals or near criminals. His diaries are only too explicit about what did or did not go on.

As a last desperate resort he rigged up for himself some kind of masturbatory contrivance that, though depressing to read about and imagine, appeared to give him pleasure. The device was not always a success and the causes of failure are as carefully monitored as if he were embarked on experimental orchestral recordings. Conducted as they were over several hours to the accompaniment of wine and music, the sessions were immensely time-consuming, but they provided physical if not emotional release and appeared to have done no damage. They are perhaps sadder for those who were fond of Keith to contemplate than they were in reality. His own typically matter-of-fact comments on surrogate sex have a scientist's detachment.

Keith's tone of voice comes off every page as if he were standing beside me – his pleasure at certain bits of music, at male beauty in art, at the boy King Tutankhamen. Most of all I hear the caustic comments that his reading provoked. For all the melancholy implications of the journals they provide evidence in every entry of love of life, love of beauty, love of humanity, hatred of injustice, hatred of falseness, hatred of hypocrisy.

Once what Keith called 'the Cancer Era' had begun, he prepared for death. He claimed that it did not worry him but that he wanted to make a graceful exit. In the hot summer and early autumn of 1977 he was often in pain, as well as suffering from radiation sickness, and he brooded daily on the best methods of suicide, on the questions of how and when. The idea of a ceremonial suicide in the presence of close friends appealed to him. It was not like that in the event. Yet the last entry, so evocative of character and of Keith's attachment to truth, is not really sad either.

The cremation at Golders Green, on a cold, blustery day, was about as gloomy an affair as could be. A few friends huddled in coats – Patrick Procktor, Leonard Rosoman, John Synge among them, and Ramsay in a state of collapse, propped up as if he were a sandbag – and then out into the rain. It was bleakly in keeping, as if Keith himself had washed his hands of it.

In thirty years, except for brief holidays, he had rarely left North London, moving a few miles only, from Hamilton Terrace to Belsize Park. In those years the art of his time had altered out of all recognition. Through all changes he remained dourly observant but unaffected, an unwillingly heroic figure.

Preface

When I began writing this journal in 1939 it was certainly not with the thought that it might be published and possibly even read. Its purpose was therapeutic and consolatory. Faced at the age of twenty-seven with what then seemed the likelihood of imminent extinction before I had properly got started, it was an attempt to analyse and understand a state of total confusion and defeat. The people I knew then were mostly too concerned with getting actively involved with things to have much time for inner states of mind, and in any case I tended to form passionate relationships rather than mature and stable ones.

When two years later the expected gas bombs and typhus-bearing lice had still not dropped from the skies and I was in the army and unexpectedly alive, on the chance suggestion of a friend, I copied out an entry I made during the Guildford period and sent it to the editor of *Penguin New Writing* who, I was told, was interested in contributions from totally unknown strangers. The episode dealt with the unloading of ambulance trains from Dunkirk during the summer of 1940. It was received with sympathy and encouragement and to my amazement published. Other extracts appeared subsequently in the same magazine and also some drawings which attracted favourable critical comment. Thus protected from all harm by the army, and under the kindly auspices of John Lehmann, was effected the unforeseen transition from an anonymous private chrysalis to a damp, bewildered but public moth.

The journal thus begun has continued with intervals to the present day. But introspection is a luxury which can be indulged in only when the framework of one's life is reasonably ordered and secure. Such conditions were admirably provided by the army. Writing became a substitute for living and the output was prolix. But when on demobilization there seemed the opportunity of actively pursuing the career I had always wanted the journal was packed away with my Soldier's Release Book. For this reason almost nothing appears in the notebooks from 1946 until the end of the decade.

In selecting from the forty-eight notebooks the present text I have tried to hold a reasonable balance between repetitious introspection and objective recording. I have not suppressed opinions I no longer hold, or attitudes of mind which are now embarrassing, if they seem true of their time. I have omitted passages which would clearly be offensive to other people (as against merely rude) and those which would be better confined to an analyst's consulting room. I used to hold the view that the truth could be revealed simply by telling all; consequently the notebooks are nothing if not indiscreet. I no longer see it as quite so simple, and do not believe that an accumulation of facts necessarily add up to a truth unless they can be correctly interpreted.

Keith Vaughan 1966

1

1939–1943

25 August 1939 I have endeavoured all my life to find my own solution to the problems which confronted me and to maintain a standard of values which seemed to me right in spite of the prevailing standards and values of the society in which I find myself. By misfortune those standards have never coincided with my own, and so I have had to go my way without very much help from other people. As a result I find myself in my twenty-seventh year quite alone, with no very great liking for life, without much ambition for the things most people pursue, but simply a dumb and mule-like persistence in continuing the struggle. If I have achieved nothing positive, at least I hold to the belief that a truth does exist, and that it is within my power to find it.

For fear of missing this truth I have refrained from accepting many doctrines which had the appearance of being right because I could always see the case for the opposition. The danger of an open mind is that a crisis catches you without an anchorage. And that is my position now. But I have no alternative. I always imagined that complete loneliness could only afflict a person who deliberately sought and desired it. But I find this is not so. I find myself alone in spite of the fact that my dearest wish is to be on intimate terms with my fellow men. I want more than anything someone I can love and trust and who is willing to return the same. But I cannot find that person, nor do I know any longer where to look for him. Am I asking too much of life? Few people ever achieve such a relationship completely yet most people achieve sufficient happiness without it. If so it is a pity – because without it I do not think I can go much further.

30 August 1939 We wait still; war or peace. The governments have locked themselves in and continue exchanging letters; only we no longer know what they are saying. Tension has relaxed, simply because it was impossible to remain at that pitch of anxious fever for long. But the situation is the same. One hopes blindly for some miracle, but one dare not speak about it. People seem resigned, almost cheerful. 'I think we're going to have a slap at him this time.'

Sand everywhere. The weight of London must be increasing steadily by hundreds of tons an hour. The Heath is blighted by a plague of bull-dozers, their grinning steel faces burrowing into the sand like diabolical ostriches. Moist caverns yawn beneath the glare of paraffin arc-lamps as the frantic digging goes on all through the night. The familiar worn paths, the dry grass baked and trodden by countless feet, the hummocks and bushes which I have passed by since childhood, never questioning their permanence, are torn up and scarred by the steel caterpillars until the landscape is a nightmare filled with the shriek and clang of pulleys and chains and dim in a mist of dust and smoke. Groups of people hover in the shadows. Cyclists, workmen, young couples, gangs of excited youths, solitary old men, stand and watch and discuss the merits of different kinds of explosive and protection from direct hits as though they were already familiar with these things. The boys look proud and confident in their sleek blue uniforms posing gracefully on the backs of the new grey fire-engines. They wave and are happy. They are part of something, vital and important; appointed to positions of conspicuous importance. And how absurdly easy. Just call at the office and sign your name and immediately you're somebody instead of nobody. The diabolical deception of war. How can they help but be disappointed now if it doesn't come.

3 September 1939 At eleven o'clock this morning England declared war on Germany. The insane calamity whose fear has overshadowed most of my conscious life has happened; has become actual, real and present. And it takes all my will to convince myself that it is so. The moon is high and full and the sky is starred with stillness. There is a peace over the land more profound than anything I can remember. I have just driven Max home with Harold and we sat and talked a long time in the car. A soldier passed. We sat and joked and laughed. It felt as though a shadow had been lifted from the earth and everything was clear and clean again. I cannot understand this feeling. Every sense is quickened and full and I feel alive. There were cows in the next field, stirring and pulling at the hedges, the shapes clear against the moon.

A few hours back I was in London and the first air-raid warning went and I knew for a moment the suffocating weight of terror. A futile, helpless fear in which we waited, idle, concerned with silly trifles – should the windows be shut or open, which was the safest room, trying to gauge the strength of walls against blast. We waited and nothing happened. The dull familiar street was empty. Wardens patrolled in steel hats. I removed the lens from my enlarger and put it in a drawer. One wondered how loud the first explosion would be, tried to anticipate the shock, wondered how much the nerves could stand before they cracked, but all the time silence. I cannot remember a single sound during those minutes; only a smothering sense of fear and the effort of maintaining the conviction that one was not dreaming. M. [K.V's. mother] was strained and pathetic with fear, tearful because her gas-mask didn't fit – 'I've never tried it on'. It was so agonizingly improbable, so ridiculous. I suppose it takes a little time to adapt oneself to so uprooted a change. I suppose there will be some agony to come, though all the laws of natural continuity now seem suspended.

I have joined the St John Ambulance and am expecting to be called at any moment to a life which holds I know not what, except that I imagine it will be something like going back to school again. I have left Lintas and do not know how much money I shall have. But all these things seem not of the least importance. They are mere facts which glide easily off the mind and leave no trace of their significance or consequence. I have never lived in such a heightened sense of unreality. For a week I was battered by the prospect of war, feeling all the time a net closing in around me and seeing no way of escape, yet always visible was a thin ray of hope born of uncertainty and desire that it might not be. Then a small puff and the lamp was out and it was darkness. My throat went dry for a whole day and I found it impossible to eat a mouthful of food. That was 1 September.

Then I came to the country and the war was no longer a reality, but just something one talked about. Only the country was real. The sky and the stars and night wind carrying the prospect of rain. The smell of the earth rich and heavy with harvest. That was real and unchanged. Then London again and the nightmare reality of war, the feeling of undergoing an anaesthetic, fear of a reality one couldn't see. Then Shere again and immediately the 'raid' became history, so that one seemed to be living an event and then reading its history at the same time.

If I force myself to think I am aware that the future must hold much misery. But peacetime living was not worth the living to me. What is wartime living to be like? I only know that this morning and evening of the Second World War have given me an abundance of peace, that my spirit is drunk with it.

5 September 1939 The third day of the war and it feels more like the third year. I've sat all day in the noise of ping-pong balls, the tap of billiard cues and incessant vulgar music on the radio. Reading about severed arteries, fractured femurs, dislocated shoulders in the aloof impersonal prose of a first-aid manual. And listening to the stories of the last war by the decrepit old veterans who have suddenly become leaders again. Sitting and waiting. Waiting and doing nothing. The sun has been hot and the sky blue and innocent. Where is this war? If there is a war let us see it and know it for what it is. If there is no war let us stop playing these idiotic parlour games.

30 September 1939 All the week the moon has been climbing to fullness. Each night was radiant and cloudless and still. Today we went out to our first accident. A boy on a motorcycle. He was sitting pale and shaking on the settee of a neighbour's house. Outside was the crowd and the motorcycle twisted in the gutter. One steels oneself to see something horrid, and prays one will not lose one's presence of mind. 'There's nothing much the matter with me. I don't know why they sent for you fellows.' He was badly shaken, his hands cut and trembling. His foot and knee had been crushed, but the bones did not seem to be broken. He wanted to walk. Reluctantly he allowed us to pick him up and carry him to the ambulance. We drove him to the hospital to be X-rayed. Usual red tape first of all, filling in forms, while the injury is completely ignored. I suppose it would be different if the case were serious. Sensing the general lack of concern he tries to adopt the same detached attitude and jokes about his injury. 'How old are you?' 'Twenty-one today.' Fair-haired with soft blue eyes. He was mostly anxious that his mother shouldn't know. She would worry if she knew he had been in an ambulance. They painted the wounds with iodine. At each dab he winced and his face went moist. The nurses laughed and dabbed again. I went home with him in the car. He became talkative with relief from the shock. He was worried that his mother would forbid his cycling, yet he seemed too big and grown up to submit to maternal orders. I saw her and tried to reassure her, knowing I was making no impression. Ambulance men are simply porters. I helped him in and he smiled and hopped to the sofa and said good-bye.

15 November 1939 The days pass with an even measure. Nothing is demanded from me but inaction and the acceptance of mild discomforts. The hours of my waking and sleeping are fixed, and I have not the responsibility of ordering much of the day. We continue to play games. Ping-pong, billiards, and first-aid, bending intimately over each other and feeling for arteries and pressure points through thick clothing. Tying each other up with splints and bandages.

There is warmth and toleration in my associates. If there is not friendliness it is only because of my own awkwardness and inability to share my life with theirs. I envy the ordered simplicity of their lives, but I remain a spectator and never a participant.

5 March 1940 At the top of the hill the earth had been newly turned over. The soil was rich and chalky and dry. The whole hill-side had been ploughed up, not very deep, six inches perhaps. But the whole high back of the hill now slipped away in a single ochre-white sweep down to the green valley with the cluster of farm buildings and red sandy tracks. Beyond it rose again in a bank of woods and then over in wave after wave of blueing hill lines and clumps of woodland. The air was violet and banks of cloud filtered the sun in slanting shafts of light which lay in pools over the distance and drew slow veils darkly across the foreground. Some plover turned over slowly like scraps of paper; nearer, a flock of crows, sharply black like soot against a broken segment of pale sky. The clear and clean sweep of the foreground dropping steeply down to the massed trees gave a sense of vast space, and the dry turned-up earth an illusion of heat and the south.

A boy was loosening the harness from two horses. He had drawn them off the field towards the low hedge which ran down one side. A light harrow dragged behind, sending a white dust down into the valley. He stood by the two horses pulling at the harness and trail ropes. He came level with their backs. He had on a grey jersey and loose cotton trousers; blue down to the knees, then bleached out into a grey-white where the dust had risen and blended them off into the earth. He had fair golden hair which the wind drew out straight from his head. When he moved about two trails of dust blew out from his feet. I heard him calling at the horses and the thin chink of metal and the slap of harness, his body bending strongly inside his clothes and his hair pulled forwards and backwards as he turned in and out of the wind. His voice and the dust blew straight off the open field like a white scarf down into the valley.

When he had finished he led the horses down the hill. The dust went on ahead in a rising cloud, and they followed silently getting smaller until they reached the farm and went in behind a building. The low sun was burnishing the crests of the distant hill lines and filling the hollows with thick blue mist; and the hills piled up behind each other in layers of blue into the sky. Smoke curled up from points in the valley and lay about like puffs of breath. The dry turned earth came in a clean unbroken sweep to my feet.

The curtain is ready to rise any day now on the last act of the Decline of the West. It was only a question of waiting for the spring, they said, then the great showdown could start. The Maginot and Siegfried lines are equipped and manned and each can withstand an attack three times as strong as the other is capable of making.

10 April 1940 Norway and Denmark invaded. Oslo bombed. The compositors reach for their two inch san-serif, the sub-editors rap out their hot staccato captions and all the screaming hysterical machinery of the press gets going. Most people seem joyful and invigorated by the thrill of action after the tedious months of waiting. All today and yesterday a battle has been raging somewhere off the coasts of Norway about which we know practically nothing, except that throughout long hours men are being killed and smashed and broken and drowned quite deliberately and scientifically. But that one certain fact is not mentioned. I feel myself being pushed further and further towards the very edge of life beyond which lies total isolation and loneliness.

14 April 1940 Canadians have arrived in the town; simple looking clumsy boys with gentle faces and soft eyes and a ready smile. They have come voluntarily to join in the mad house. Why? I cannot believe they want to kill people any more than I. Which is one reason which makes it impossible to be a CO. I do not want to be superior and isolated, to act as though I were morally better and cleverer than these men. The war seems now more of a monstrous folly than a crime. I would rather be foolish with the herd, just for once, and enjoy the easy comradeship this would offer. I cannot say whether I could bring myself to kill Germans, but I suppose I could manage it all right in company and at long range. It is more my reason that is offended by the war than my conscience. I can still postpone the decision a little while.

14 June 1940 'The organism which begins to dismiss actual experiences because these disturb the simplicity of its explanations is headed for that ever narrowing awareness which ends in presenting itself with a world in which it can no longer live.'

Perhaps there is only a little time in a man's life during which he can keep himself in this state of open suspension. Then the need for security, for a foundation, becomes so acute that he has to assemble hurriedly whatever he has gathered and make of it a basis and creed for living. Thereafter he must shut his mind to disturbing experiences and ideas. Or he treats them playfully, as things to talk about but finally to put on one side and forget.

To me there is a sad sense of failure in admitting the extent of your limitations. Yet to imagine yourself with unlimited capacities is absurd. A man needs to be very strong to rebuild his life more than once after the age of 25. But simple explanations are part of adolescence. Why then do I make such a fuss if all that is happening is that I'm growing up.

19 June 1940   It was long after midnight when the train came in. Word had come through earlier that the first casualties from France were expected that evening, and we were told to stand by. Time lay heavily, dry and still over the hot afternoon. About nine we drove the ambulances down to the station and lined them up along the far siding where the cattle were usually unloaded. We prepared the stretchers and blankets, and then stood about in groups, talking and smoking cigarettes. A small crowd collected on the bridge and looked down on us, idly, to see what was going on. Traffic moved carefully about the town as the light faded. Then the searchlights went up and gleaned the last thin clouds out of the sky and went out and the crowd wandered away one by one and we were left alone with the night and the tiny points of our cigarettes pricking the darkness.

The moon was high and full and clear and the night still. We walked up and down the tracks, past cattle boxes, and looked out beyond the signals and sheds trying to distinguish the first signs of smoke against the horizon. For a long time there was nothing but the empty moonlit rails and a dull stain in the sky where the sun had set. People yawned and kicked at the rags of paper and rubbish lying about the tracks.

As soon as we forgot to think about it the train was there, a long shadow creeping quietly, carefully up the siding, avoiding hurry. The first windows slid past, over-crowded with heads like family photographs. Sparks of words caught at us out of the darkness and drew us to them. The engine closed against the buffers with a soft compressed sigh, then greetings and the click of buffers broke thunderously about our heads. Hands reached up and met hands, exchanging cigarettes, matches; faces were lit here and there in momentary smiles; questions, shouts, laughter, poured over us from the windows; but some kept silent, leaving others to speak for them, content to rest their faces against the glass and gaze out on a night miraculously free from treachery.

Further down, the carriages stood immensely high above us, steel walls without windows, the red crosses dim beneath layers of soot and dirt. We talked and waited with our attention narrowed to the paper edge of light beneath the doors; to the buried murmur and hurrying within. The doors swung back suddenly, and doused us in light, as though a portable aseptic heaven had opened in the darkness. We drew in like moths, blinking at the whiteness. Hands helped us aboard and we climbed from the night into a warm smell of wool and urine and sickly sweet flesh.

Three tiers of bunks lined the white walls, each with a face that stared out quietly and expressionless, like the eyes of an animal caught for a moment in a car's headlights. We felt strange and helpless with men remote from us in experience. Some turned to look at us, visitors out of the night, from another planet. Others were still locked in their prisons of pain, where we had no admittance. No one spoke. We drew on our stretchers and began the routine of unloading, glad of the work that would let us forget our awkwardness.

The stretchers were held up level against the bunks and the men coaxed, like animals, to brave the crossing on to their steel meshes. They dragged across those parts of their bodies they were able, the rest we carried for them, grotesque shapes of wool and splint and bandage, joined to them only by pain. Some moved suddenly and clumsily, hoping to make the journey before pain had observed their going. Others, like children impatient to show their ability, would begin lowering themselves gleefully before we were ready, their white woolly feet swinging down everywhere from the white ceiling. As each stretcher was filled it was lowered to the floor, arranged with blankets and launched out into the sea of arms and anxious upturned faces waiting below in the darkness.

In the bunk near the door was a mild, timid youth of eighteen or nineteen with thick lenses roped to his face with black string. He was a German. His eyes followed each stretcher as it went out, a smile behind his lips ready to be released at the first hint of friendliness or recognition. 'Leave Fritzie, – there's a special ambulance for him later,' an orderly said. We took the boy from the bunk above him.

He watched our approach with an open, curious gaze. He was so pale that it seemed to be only a pair of eyes that looked at us from the white pillow. When he saw we were coming for him he turned his face away quickly. A nurse came up and leant over him and whispered something in his ear and wiped his forehead with some wool. We asked him if he could ease himself across a bit. He tried and couldn't and looked miserably at us. 'It's his leg, poor laddie,' the nurse said and gave him a quick little pat and a smile. We drew back the blankets and saw that his arms finished at the wrists in two logs of yellow stained wool and bandage. His right leg was a shapeless embalment of bandage and lay supported on pillows. He worked himself across slowly on his elbows, balancing the pain precariously to his endurance while we gathered up the leg gently to being with him. He moved a little way and then froze suddenly rigid and we lowered the leg quickly on to the pillows. He lay back a moment with closed eyes and lips trembling on despair. Then drawing together the last fibres of courage, forced himself too quickly on to the stretcher so that the leg twisted in our arms and broke open his face into silent tears. We reached for the pillows, quickly, to take the weight of the leg, but the nurse came up and told us no pillows could leave the train. We looked at her helplessly, holding the bones and flesh and bandage in our arms. 'Sorry, it's an order.' She picked up his kit-bag and neatly patted its lumpiness into place where the pillows should be, 'There, try that,' she said, her cuffs clicking with authority. Obediently we lowered the leg, knowing it was cruelty. But he had no strength to protest. Pain too long endured bent him backwards like a strung bow, fretting his face with sweat. We covered him up, miserably; there were others waiting, and he went out over the dark shoulders of the bearers into the subaqueous glow of the ambulance.

As each carriage was emptied we moved to the next, leaving the orderlies dazed with sleeplessness leaning on their brooms amidst the white ruins of bedding, and lighting up the stub ends of cigarettes. We worked on through the night, through each intimate and infinite tragedy, not noticing when it turned to day. Above the last stretcher the sky was already blue and adorned with morning. The doctors made a last round of the ambulances, checking forms, adding signatures – final instructions. The train lay behind us, a hollow, picked carcase, the whiteness of the carriages now grey and dirty in the morning light.

We started out through the town, through the early traffic. Women with perambulators stopped to gaze anxiously at the frosted mystery of our windows. Newsboys shouted the morning news, the Cabinet was hopeful, the line held near Châlons – enormous losses had been inflicted on the enemy – our own casualties were not large considering the numbers involved. The drivers sweated with anxiety at each scar in the tarmac that might hold a fresh pocket of agony for the men behind. We left the town and moved on into the country; beneath the mounting sun, between fields heavy and still with the green abundance of summer.

22 June 1940 The inevitable news of Dick's death came yesterday from Geneva: F/O Eric Richard Dennis Vaughan 65878 mort. Even M. through the tearful wreckage of her grief could see the grim irony of that one word, understood in all languages, telegraphed across the battlefields of Europe. All I could think of was that I drank my first

Pernod there on my birthday at a little café by the lakeside, watching the red and white sails skimming across the shadowy water.

If you drop a bird with an injured wing from the top storey of a high building so that it breaks itself a little more against each stone balcony on the way down it is no use saying that you only launched the bird into the air so that it might learn to fly.

A soldier sits opposite you in the train, his eyes turned sadly on the green country slipping past. His rifle slips forward all the time and has to be pulled back. His face young and strong and sad. His mouth always open a little. Lips that were never meant to feel each other. His hands that you keep looking at – big and straight and generous. His body big and strong, harnessed over like a circus horse with brass and khaki. You felt you could love him? An impossible yearning to protect him – to put yourself between his clean body and the savage mechanism of destruction. Just to save this one fragment of the earth's springtime from being stamped out utterly. But who are you to think you can interfere? A stranger sitting in a grey flannel suit with the *New Statesman* and a service respirator. A bit of a toff – with suede shoes. 'Are you come on leave or just going back?' (not that it matters to you – but it makes a contact. Not a real contact because it is not you speaking but a young toff in grey flannels trying to be pally with one of the fighting boys.) 'Just back – come from Narvik.' 'Oh really – what was it like – pretty awful?' 'Only there a day. Lay out in the boat for ten days. Got three days leave now.' 'Oh yes.' 'Lucky to be back at all.' – 'Yes I expect you are.' No fields of Amaranth. 'So long.' Three days – then back again – then you can wipe the sweat off his face when you move him on to the stretcher and his arms are gone.

1 July 1940 For days on end I live in a lethargic trance which seems to lie on the other side of sleep. Beyond the first tiredness of not sleeping you cease to desire sleep. Sleep when it comes at odd hours of the night and day is only an interlude in a world of deeper unconsciousness. I wake, not refreshed, but to the same insensitive existence of a chrysalis, only the biological routine continuing inside. All day the sun shines through a mesh of fine spun gold in which noise and dust and silence are intermixed. The mind feels wrapped in hot wool. I sleep and wake alternately throughout the day without any clear sense of the difference. Only in the evening the mind frees itself from its anchor of heaviness and becomes conscious of a present and future that staggers the imagination.

Day follows day in gentle secure monotony and it is impossible to steel the senses to an agony which is incomprehensible. One goes on saying with feeble monotony that such things cannot happen, but everything moves with inexorable purpose towards its end. Life is like a desert where only the sun lives. There is neither joy nor pain but a timeless flow of apathetic existence. It is not unpleasant. No values belong to it. It is like the time before one was born. Its only colour is that of a pale and heavy fear. An ominous sense that at the given moment the silence will be splintered like night at the cock's crowing. And it will break easily; fear is very near the surface.

It has been too long this waiting. Ten months now. Fear has gone sour and the weapons forged against it rusty. Inaction forms a scab over the first wound and hope breeds inside it like maggots.

'But let us not think of things which we hope will be long in coming.'

2 July 1940   The faces are bronzed now and at night blend in equal tone with the khaki. Hair sprouts in bleached tufts from forage caps. They stand about in the sunlight with hay sticking to their trousers, little groups of spirited cocky confidence. But away from the herd you can see in their eyes all the tender hopes and fears, the high and hopeless courage, the banners of love unfurling as they touch the checks of their girls. A solid phalanx of youth passes by. Studded boots crunching the gravel. Clear voices ringing in terrifying unison.

This is the target.

An iron door opens and a tongue of flame leaps a hundred feet into the raftered ceiling. Sparks fall in showers as though the heavens themselves had collapsed at the blast of a trumpet. Men step backwards and shield their faces against the intolerable heat. An iridescent pillar of steel moves slowly across the arena of fire. Cold hammers drop a thousand tons from the sky and stamp on the white metal, flattening it like stiff butter. Flakes the size of a palm sweat off the tormented metal. Rollers squeeze and drag out its length like pastry. It passes through each thundering apartment of the giant inferno built by man and takes shape exactly to his calculations. Cools. Passes through lathe and drill rooms. Is polished, turned to micrometric exactness. Becomes a gun barrel, recognizable, docile in chains.

Arms (not human). Small arms and large arms. Tapping, jiggering, humming and chattering. Little levers and pistons and pinions and bearings (too many to count like the coins of sunlight on water) but each for its purpose. A thousand a minute. Three thousand a day. Guns like felled pine trees. Little bullets like hornets, only tougher.

This is the instrument.

Man the creator and man the victim. Man destroys man like a rat eating its own limbs. Unparalleled in nature? Prometheus the liverless continues to steal fire from heaven and perishes in its flames.

Mr Scott Kennedy talks about some insect nuisances on the radio.

A girl turns her shining eyes towards the orchestra at the entry of the solo violin.

An old woman ties the tails of a white apron behind her back and says – 'he got the DSM at Narvik and went all through Dunkirk you know – all through.'

A youth pushes away the plate of his half eaten supper and wipes his mouth. There is a far-away look in his eyes. All over him rays of motherlove, ever-puzzled, ever-questioning, never doubting, never understanding bounce and flutter like sunbeams.

Mr Churchill maintains a loud and clanging commentary on the heroic performance of all concerned. Members of the House rise and give cheers, then sink into leather armchairs with a whisky and soda and the latest casualty lists.

Mme Verdurin dunks her croissant in her coffee.

12 August 1940 Went to Reading for my tribunal today. I had rehearsed so many different roles for all possible situations that I felt confident that nothing could catch me off my guard. But in fact it was a complete anti-climax. It all happened so quickly that I hadn't time to feel anything. My name was called first, a minute after I got in. I walked up feeling like the first man to step on to a new continent. The four of them sat on a dais in high backed chairs looking magisterial and untouchable. The president took a copy of my statement and another copy was handed to me. He began to read it out in a flat expressionless voice, getting the sense wrong in one or two places. I had spent so long writing it that I knew it by heart, and wondered vaguely whether I was supposed to correct him. When he had finished there was complete silence while the members looked at each other with inscrutable expressions. I steeled myself for the attack. Then he looked up with a kindly smile and asked very politely whether I would consent to serve in the RAMC. I said yes, then immediately regretted I had not said no, but it was too late. He said he would recommend me for the RAMC if I liked, but pointed out that it would excuse me from having to carry arms, as though I had been pleading to be allowed to carry them. He regretted that he could not guarantee that his recommendation would get me in, but that in any case I would not be called up for combatant service. It seemed unreal that this new status could be conferred on me so casually half way through a sentence. The others asked me a few questions about my life and work in the respectful tones one employs to someone in reduced circumstances whom one recognizes nevertheless as being a gentleman. In five minutes it was all over.

All the way home I felt as though I had been cheated of something. I had got what I asked for too easily. I should have asked for more. But I realized this would not be a conscientious request. I tried to console myself with the thought that I had given evidence of moral courage, but I remained quite unimpressed. I pictured, too, how unimpressed the RAMC will be with this unblemished soul who must not soil his hands with weapons. All I seem to have done is to earn the right to join the army without the one thing that would make it attractive – solidarity and companionship. What I remember most from the day is the boy with vivid red hair who was drinking bright yellow lemonade from a green glass while I was trying to coax a sandwich and coffee into a stomach which refused to relax.

15 August 1940   Earlier this evening I went into the Lion for a drink. I hoped I might see the person I had seen there two nights ago, but there was nobody of any interest. The place had the usual air of an officers' mess, loud and caddish. I drank my beer and stared past everybody out into the hall where I could see the green baise notice board covered with letters. Suddenly I remembered the last time I had seen it was with Dick and he remarked as we passed it: 'Wouldn't it be funny if you found a letter addressed to you there.' The reality of his death came home to me when I realized we should never again be able to exchange those inconsequential sort of remarks which showed a subconscious awareness of what the other was thinking. Ever since the news was confirmed from Geneva there has been a climate of grief about me, but my mother's excessive suffering made it impossible to feel. Because it didn't touch my daily living at any point it seemed a distant and abstract idea which could be thought about later.

I want to remember now all I can about Dick: about our childhood together and the casually intimate attachment that grew in later years. As we got older we changed not only in our relationship to life, but in our accepted attitude as brothers. We retained a certain curiosity about each other which kept our relationship fresh and rather adventurous. After he left school we saw each other only rarely and at each meeting there was something memorable and unexpected. I was always far enough ahead to watch and understand the stages of his growth, but a real understanding only began with the war in the long letters that crossed to and from France. We were almost at the moment when we could have become friends.

As children I had been more of a father, and felt for him an unwilling sense of responsibility mixed with tenderness and exasperation. To him I was absolutely necessary and he looked on me with complete trust. People called him a difficult child. He was nervy and often unhappy. He lived much in a nightmare world of fear. Fear of the dark – of other people – of noise – and of 'pricky-men'. I remember particularly during the long summer holidays his fear of all places of entertainment, cinemas, theatres. And because this fear seemed to everyone so unnatural he was never allowed simply to stay away from them, but endless arguments were used to persuade him why he ought to like them.

Whenever a new film arrived in the neighbourhood I would first have to go off and see it by myself and report whether it was suitable and free from 'bangs'. He would wait at home with my mother, pale-faced and anxious for my return. As it was the time when cowboy films were popular this was often a difficult condition to satisfy. Provided it was moderately quiet, or if I had been particularly carried away by my own enjoyment, I would report it was all right. Then, after much persuasion, an afternoon was decided on when we set off together hand in hand. It might have been to the dentist rather than a place of entertainment that we were going, so anxious and fearful were our faces. 'There won't be a bang will there, Kee?' he would ask and I would reassure him patiently and repeatedly. But half way through the film, even if it had been comparatively noiseless, the strain of anxiety would be too much and he would turn to me in sudden panic, his face screwed up for crying, and implore me to take him home. I would hurry him home angrily, holding his hand tightly and too high, and he whimpering along behind miserable at his fear and lost pleasure in the harsh afternoon sunlight. The only picture I have of him at that time is his pale thin face turned up towards the screen and the corners of his mouth squaring up on the edge of tears.

The first film he saw through to the end was *The Covered Wagon*. It was a succession of crises. At each moment of excitement, the galloping of a horse, a chasing figure, the drawing of a gun, he would turn to me with his face full of accusation and fear. And I, feeling doubtful and slightly guilty, would have to admit that perhaps there might be a small bang, but would try desperately to draw his attention to the outstanding merits of the film and strive to tide him over until the crisis had passed. It must have been an exhausting experience for both of us, but afterwards the sense of victory was bright and rich as we stepped out into the sunshine and hurried home to break the good news.

From then on he could think of nothing but repeating his triumph. No other film would do. It always had to be *The Covered Wagon*. We followed its release through every cinema in London and must have seen it seven or eight times. And each time I had the satisfaction a trainer might feel in seeing a nervous horse taking a difficult jump. It was our first successful campaign together.

But the ill-fitting rôle imposed upon me prevented any natural companionship between us in those days. There was not the influence of real grown-ups which would have narrowed the gap of five years between our ages. The games we played were always those I had grown out of. I joined in with the conscious condescension of an adult and enjoyed them only through his pleasure. It was not until he joined me at school during my last two years that he began to develop an independent life apart from me, and this was forced on him by the rigorous conventions of a public school.

There was a period soon after I left and he was still at school when we were both too busy developing our own lives to notice each other much. I remember noticing, with slight alarm, the rapid increase in his size and physical bulk (he became very good at games) and the day I discovered to my humiliation that I could no longer overpower him by physical force. Then later, when he joined the Air Force and our meetings became even less frequent, we began to discover the points at which our lives still met.

Our greatest interest was in old cars. I bought a 12/50 Alvis for £20 and for days afterwards the engine was distributed over the kitchen table. We worked silently putting it together. He knew more about it than I, and so for the first time was able to take the lead. We could go for whole days without speaking and never felt the need for words. We could throw our opposing views together and know they would never jar. We never had to tolerate each other as so often happens between members of a family. We would drive off together without any particular destination, sometimes driving all night, and find ourselves the next morning on the Welsh coast. We fixed a wire basket on to the exhaust manifold into which we put tins of pilchards and kipper snacks and these we would eat sizzling hot half way up some mountain in the middle of the night.

The circumstances of war gave shape to an understanding which had always existed beneath the surface, and we could say in letters things which it would have been impossible to talk about in speech and were never referred to again afterwards. Our relationship would have struck others as casual to the point of unconcern. We hardly ever talked about the war and I never knew what his attitude was, though he accepted without mention the fact that I had registered as a CO. He liked Germany and had many friends there, but he realized they were beyond his reach and did not grieve for them. The technique of flying was sufficiently absorbing to prevent his thinking about wider issues, and he was not given to introspection.

We took leave of each other at the entrance to Trafalgar Square tube station. A casual wave of the hand and a smiling glance was all the ceremony, although each knew it was unlikely we should meet again. I knew his squadron was going into action although he was not able to tell me this, nor was it necessary. The following day news came of the invasion of Holland and Belgium and four days later he was dead.

3 September 1940 The desire to make this journal grew out of the sense of my failure to live a life. When war came I felt that all further hope of success or achievement was over and that there remained only one task, to keep a log book of the last remaining days of the stricken vessel and try to discover what went wrong. If I could do that I felt that failure would lose some of its bitterness. From the rather melodramatic conception of war current at the time I thought it unlikely that I should have very much longer to live. I didn't consider the span in terms of actual weeks or months, but I thought it unlikely that I would see another birthday. The fact that I now find myself alive does not appear extraordinary, nor would it appear extraordinary if I were to die tonight. Life and death are concepts of equal probability. Expectation of life as a natural birthright is something we seem to have outgrown. Announcements declaring the value of War Bonds in 1950 seem rather ridiculous, like taking a house on a ninety-nine year lease. Time in the future is as difficult to comprehend as interstellar space. One lives in an extending and dimensionless present.

My desire and pursuit of the whole has all but lost me my sense of values and the capacity for taking sides in any question. I seem to be a neutral spectator of life. My mind is like the surface of a lake which takes its shape and colour from the changing environment. I seem to be shaped all the time from the outside. I realize this is probably an illusion and that to other people I present a more or less consistent quality. But this is unsatisfactory as I know that the person I present is not me. This might also be an illusion. I have considerable powers of self deception. I walk out of a cinema always in the rôle of the most admired character, supremely confident that I could deal, then and there, with any circumstance that life cared to present. Dispersion of energy over too wide a field has left me almost impotent without diminishing the corroding urge to create. If one only knew what things one should never even attempt. I do not think I should have made a painter even if I had had the chance. I lack the dogged onesidedness. All my failures I feel to be due not to congenital incapacity but to the misfortune of circumstances, or through sheer stupidity on my part from having exiled myself from the place where I belong. And often in bed at night I feel the desire to live and think and feel in terms of paint with an intensity that is almost sexual.

September 1940 (written in Guildford gaol)   Between pages 73 and 76 of Proust's novel I 'came to' as it were and found a measure of equilibrium in body and mind. It was a physical change rather than a mental one – a settling of the stomach. But states of mind follow each other so rapidly now that it is difficult to know at what point to halt their progress so as to maintain the necessary consistency of viewpoint to write about them. Consistency is about all I can hope for at the moment. Objectivity can only come later when these days have receded into the relatively painless landscape of memory.

It was also the same time that the dog stopped howling from somewhere at the end of the long hollow corridor; a noise which, coming unchallenged hour after hour out of the silence, became slowly identified with the sensations I was trying not to notice inside myself while I drifted on the tide of Proust's prose, wavelets of panic lapping at my feet. There are people who cannot stand being shut up, I said to myself – claustrophobiacs – they go mad. And instantly I felt that the very fact that I was shut up was sufficient in itself to make me a claustrophobiac, and it needed a violent effort of will to prevent myself falling in a faint from off this wooden board.

But all that and a day has passed now. I write twenty-four hours later. Despair returned in a sleepless dawn. A state of impotent misery which seemed to come not from the mind so much as the turbulent writhings of the stomach. The first impression of a prison cell is of a defiant and absorbing neutrality. Not only does it isolate you completely from all sound and contact with the human world, but it seems to absorb into itself your own natural vitality and cohesion so that you are left in a state of loneliness so extreme that the binding fluid of your personality is slowly dried out and you begin to fall apart, like heated crystals, into uncoordinated fragments of thoughts, feelings, memories, fears, all meaningless and incoherent because they lack a centre of reference.

After a while the walls become saturated and soften to a more benevolent neutrality. You begin to examine them more closely. Along each strata of mortar which separate the white glazed bricks are pencilled the names and addresses of those who have been here before me. Some are repeated over and over again in different places, each in the same meticulous writing, as though as much time as possible must be used up in the writing. And when there was nothing more to write, and still time to be used up, there follows a series of signatures, monographs, initials, until the end of the seam is reached and the ritual can start again on the seam below. At one place there is a message, something more than the compulsive reiteration of identity, the words – 'Love to any young cocky who happens to be placed in this cell – E. Wade.' – Pray God that neither time nor the renovators will ever efface that tiny flame of consolation from the glazed masonry. Others who had nothing to say have picked the mortar away, presumably with a match or pin, into small deep holes which look as though they had been made with a drill.

My cell measures about eight feet by six and contains a wooden plank with a thin mattress and blanket and a large WC. When the cover of the WC is lowered it forms a table on which food is placed at regular intervals. The table is too low to sit at, and anyhow there is nothing to sit on except the bed which is too far away. Every so often someone goes along the corridor and pulls the chains of all the lavatories, since they cannot be flushed from inside. There is no window or daylight, but high up in the centre of the ceiling a single sixty watt light burns continuously night and day. I can hear the hours strike on the church clock, but it is not always easy to know whether it is am or pm. The roof of the cell is vaulted which has the effect of amplifying all sounds which come in from outside. It is mostly from the amount of sound that I can tell whether it is night or day. Not that it matters since I spend the whole time reading Proust. It is perhaps the ideal situation for reading his novel.

Now, at night, after the bombers have passed overhead and there is no more sound or movement, this cell takes on a complete neutrality and becomes a perfectly acceptable place to be. The fact that I cannot leave it does not matter because in any case I should not want to. It is during the day when the noise of iron-shod boots rings along the corridor, keys jangle in the locks, iron doors are opened and slammed shut, that its essential and intended hostility becomes apparent. One of the most distressing things is that although I am only here on remand everything I do or say is automatically regarded with suspicion and mistrust. It is this incessant suggestion of guilt which undermines one's spirit and makes one wish one really were guilty of what they suspect.

Sounds are amplified and distorted to such an extent that it is difficult to connect them with the actual occurrences that produced them. For instance when I fill my pipe and scrape up the last shreds of tobacco from the bottom of the pouch, the sound this makes is like the sea searching out the crevices and rocks in the innermost recesses of a cave. And the grains of leaf that fall back from the bowl sound like the fall of shale or pebbles. My heart beats as I lie on the wooden bed are as clearly audible as a metronome buried in a coffin.

A strange fear creeps over me at times that this is only the beginning of a long and endless succession of disasters which regardless of my deserving them, and regardless of any law of justice, have simply been set in motion, and nothing I can now do will alter or prevent them. It is perhaps like being part of Greek drama. One knows such things do happen to people, but they are always other people, remote and anonymous. For oneself one feels certain there is some clause in one's contract with life that would make such things impossible. It is obviously quite silly to try and arm oneself with the special weapons appropriate to some situation, the nature of which, even if it comes about, is only speculative. All one can do is hold together the natural strengths and weaknesses of one's own character and leave them to withstand as best they may whatever strategy the enemy choses to employ. And since the nature of the unknown is invariably quite different from one's anticipation one acts, when the time comes, by instinct and improvised judgment in a way which is quite uninfluenced by previous resolutions.

Note in retrospect 1965   The situation came about as follows: I was walking in the country near Guildford one afternoon when I came upon a deep square trench which had been dug along the edge of a wood and across the nearby sloping fields. Its sharp, geometric lines contrasting with the gentle undulating lines of the landscape interested me and I resolved to return during my off-duty period and make a painting of it. When I got to the site next day a group of soldiers were working on the trench, with a young lieutenant in charge. I realized of course that the trench was for some military purpose so I asked the lieutenant if it would be all right for me to work there. After a few polite questions and a glance at my Identity Card he said he saw no reason why I shouldn't. So I set to work. It was a warm sunny September afternoon.

After half an hour or so a policeman came cycling slowly along the Gomshall road near the site where I had set up my easel. He saw me, seemed rather surprised, and came across. He asked what I was doing and I explained. His manner was friendly and I imagined he might perhaps be an amateur painter himself. I pointed out the particular interests of the motif. I also mentioned that I had, of course, obtained permission from the lieutenant in charge of the digging. 'How long will you be here?' he asked. 'About an hour or two,' I said. 'Don't go away just yet,' he said. 'I don't intend to,' I answered. With that he went off on his bicycle, not in the direction he had been going previously, but back towards Guildford. I noticed that he seemed in a great hurry all of a sudden. I went on with my work.

Half an hour later a small black van came bouncing along the road, stopped suddenly, and three policemen hurried across the field to where I was working. One was the policeman I had already spoken to. But the atmosphere was now quite different. I was ordered to pack up my things and come with them. I protested, argued, explained the situation all over again and was met with stony silence from all three. The order was repeated. Could I not finish the painting I asked, and then if they wished I would bring it into the police station that evening and they could see for themselves what I had done. 'You're under arrest,' they said. 'Get your things in the back of the van and look sharp about it.'

I was driven to the police station, brought before the sergeant in charge, and charged with making a drawing or photograph in the neighbourhood of defence operations, contrary to section x of the Defence Regulations. I was cautioned, searched, and told I would be held in custody while further investigations were made. I was allowed to keep my tobacco, matches, and a pencil and paper, but my sketch book, letters, and all other personal documents were taken away, I was taken to my cell and locked in.

Although stunned, I remained confident that at any moment they would realize they had made a mistake and would come with smiling apologies and let me go. But slowly the truth of the situation became clear. They would not come back and they had not made a mistake. For weeks the papers had been full of stories of fifth-columnists. They were dropping from the skies dressed as nuns. They were lurking in woods dressed as gamekeepers. They came in crates of bananas. They came in coffins disguised as corpses. And at last they had caught one, and at Guildford of all places, disguised as an artist and caught red handed in the act of making a plan of a tank trap.

That same night, at 2 am, the CID called at my mother's flat in London, informed her of my arrest on suspicion of fifth-column activities and that they had a warrant to search her flat. She responded with her usual spirit. Putting no obstacles in their way, answering no questions, she followed them from room to room during the search keeping up a placid, stonewalling non-cooperation the withering effect of which I know only too well. 'What's in that cupboard, madam?' – 'I've no idea. Why don't you look and see?' And they would proceed to turn out her linen cupboard, and then be obliged to replace everything precisely to her instructions. 'What about the loft, madam?' – 'There it is. There's a pair of steps in the kitchen if you want to get up.' Similar searches were made at the ARP station where I was employed in Guildford, and the house of some friends nearby where I used to stay.

Each morning in my cell I was visited by a friendly plain-clothes detective. We would sit together on the bed and he would chat to me about my life, my friends, my visits to Germany before the war. He would show me passages in my private letters or journals and ask me to enlarge on them. They were all passages which contained some mild political comment or dealt with the problem of becoming a conscientious objector. At first I welcomed his visits. They were a relief to the neutrality of my surroundings. Then as I was consistently unable to supply him with the sort of information he clearly was seeking I began to dread them. The less I was able to tell him, the more he regarded me with suspicion. I was obviously going to be a hard nut to crack. His friendliness took on a more and more menacing aspect. If only I would tell him everything he would do his best to help me. But there was nothing to tell. Already he was in possession of more of my secrets than any other living person.

After eight days of this my case came up and I was brought before the bench of magistrates. I remember the sudden pleasure of seeing the sky and daylight again. Also the surprise of seeing my half finished painting propped up on an easel in the centre of the court, as though it was about to be auctioned. It was the first picture of mine ever to be publicly exhibited. It was a fairly large canvas and as I had only worked on it for about an hour it was almost completely abstract. It looked rather like a late Cezanne watercolour (or so I hoped). It was scrutinized by each member of the bench in turn. They nodded approval. 'I think there can be no question at all what the picture represents,' announced the chairman and the bench agreed. This surprised me. It seemed unusually perceptive. Would they have been so certain, I wondered, if the picture were being considered for the local Art Gallery? It was not a time when abstract art was very popular in the provinces.

I had been told by my lawyer that I must plead guilty to the charge and this I did. I noticed with pleasure the young lieutenant from whom I had asked permission to work near the site. He corroborated my story and was told in no uncertain terms that he would do better in future to mind his own business. I felt sorry to be the cause of his embarrassment. 'The penalty,' said the magistrate, 'for the serious offence which you have committed can be a £100 fine and six months imprisonment.' My heart stopped but my mind clung to the tiny word 'can'. 'Nevertheless we are prepared to take a lenient view in consideration of the circumstances and the time you have been kept in custody. You will be fined £25 and the picture will be confiscated. Your other possessions will be returned to you.'

I sometimes wonder what happened to the picture. Does it still decorate some waiting room or canteen in Guildford police station? Was it destroyed, with ignominy? Or does it repose in the Black Museum at Scotland Yard along with the effects of other convicted criminals?

22 December 1940 The first post ever to be delivered on Sunday brought me my calling up papers for 2 January, and a bottle of scent for Christmas from H. The first thing I did was to have a hot bath, and viewing the situation from a blanket of warm steam the prospect does not seem to alarming. There is some comfort in certainty. Also I'm getting accustomed to the fact of constant change and impermanence. And knowing nothing about the Pioneer Corps helps to give it something of the allure of the unknown. It is disappointing that I shall not now get the job in camouflage which I was coming to believe might after all be possible. But I am not greatly concerned with what I do but only with whom I shall do it; who I shall meet. There is always a slight excitement about this.

I certainly shan't mind leaving London because I'm beginning to get too conscious of the raids. There is little that I care about leaving behind. I have forgotten the time before the war and I cannot visualize the time when it will have ended. I am sometimes aware of a slightly stimulating sense of chaos.

2 January 1941 The countryside was brushed over with white, like the first coat of icing on a cake. The afternoon sped quickly past the train, cold, clear and silent. At Ilfracombe a wind met us off the sea like the blade of a sword, also a lieutenant and an orderly corporal. We fell in and marched in dishevelled ranks of three, which surprised me, having marched in columns of four at school. The lieutenant marched at the head. He made one remark during the journey. He said to the man who happened to be walking nearest to him, 'What time did you leave town.' He pronounced 'town' in the round water-melon voice of an officer. He seemed satisfied that this discharged the full burden of his social obligations, and we continued the journey in silence.

The faces of the other recruits in the train were like houses with the shutters down. Their eyes were eloquent with memory and fear, sometimes almost tearful from incessant yawning. They ate sand-wiches out of paper bags without enthusiasm and with dry mouths. Now we are here there is no more fear, but some of them have a lost look and are unhappy.

3 January 1941 Cold misery on waking and unwelcome return of consciousness. Wandering in sheeplike herd through darkness and cold in search of water to wash. Too cold. Too many people. Luke-warm porridge and bacon for breakfast. Some contentment as the routine shape of the day takes shape. Lectures, talks, orders, fatigues, nothing very terrifying. Uniforms and kit in the afternoon, an over-burdening mass of stiff new khaki. Warmth again. Walking on smooth black stones. Renewed contact with the sea. Boats, rope, sand, sails, tar on wood, but in the unfamiliar atmosphere of an ice cold wind that skins the face. Rows of empty hotels, clean in the winter sun. I feel a little uneasy at not feeling more discomfort, at the thought that the real pain may not yet have penetrated my numb exterior. But the big surprise is that I can make contact with others. No effort is needed, no pretence.

12 January 1941 There are nice looking people here; people I would like to know. But my eyes follow them only from habit. Too physically tired to think or feel at all. Painful feet destroy one's self-confidence and poise. Life is wearisome and stupid, but I am not afraid of it, nor am I interested in it. I cannot identify with the person I am here, strutting up and down the parade ground. To drill properly is no effort to me, I did it for years at school. Most of the others find it incomprehensible and regard me, not altogether approvingly, as a born leader.

20 January 1941 Today we have hauled and hugged and staggered with sacks of coal through continuous rain, the dirt and wet working miserably into one's skin. It was too wretched even to offer the simple excitement of physical exercise. There is nothing exhilarating in breaking one's nails on wet sacks which are too heavy to lift and feeling the black slush working its way up the inside of your sleeves. The only consolation was to know one shared it with others of the same opinion. This at least was a new experience.

28 January 1941 Handling cast-iron stove pipes gives you a certain appreciation of their texture after the second hour. Yesterday the ground was hard with ice and later snow fell covering everything with white dust. The sheets of corrugated iron were stuck together with ice and made a crunching sound like a small boat against waves when we moved them. Ice lay in hard lozenges along the corrugations. Bright red water ran in parallel lines over the metal as we tipped them. Each one had a different pattern of rust and frost and oily discoloration. The air was crisp and clean.

6 February 1941 We were taken off by lorry this morning up on to the downs above Salisbury. Naturally we had no idea where we were going or why until we got there. There was fog on the ground which made the world small and featureless. We started filling sand-bags with white and ochre clay. After some minutes Ron enquired what the bags were going to be used for. It turned out that they were to reinforce a pill-box nearby. Whereupon Ron decided that such work was against his conscience. He went up to see the lieutenant. The question was not disputed at all. He was told to 'look after' our kits instead. The rest of us were more concerned with keeping warm than with our consciences.

March 1941 Most of the people here are younger than I and better read. University students, school masters, young dons from Oxford and Cambridge. The daily routine of coolie labour keeps our bodies occupied but not our minds. Talk is mostly on the Big Subjects, art and life, literature, truth and philosophy. The only ones with whom there is no contact are the religious groups, Plymouth Brethren, Four Square Gospellers, Jehovah Witnesses. They form an entirely separate group to themselves, and spend much of their free time in prayer. Kneeling by their bedsides in long new woolly pants they look like new-born elephants. It is very much a society of individuals and eccentrics. Consequently I feel more at home than I have ever done before. I am accepted with no difficulty as an 'artist'. A year ago at Guildford such a thing would have seemed impossible. There is no need any longer to use this journal as a refuge and escape. The war is something remotely distant. Private life and its problems seem of no importance. There are days when I feel more alive, vigorous and happy than I can ever remember. If only one had more time and leisure and the work were not so physically exhausting.

June 1941 Codford. The rank smell of grass and canvas and warm men. Misery and discomfort of living in tents. Everything covered with dust and ants. The eighteen mile march from Bulford was not as bad as we imagined. Sore feet. Country of wooded hills and lush valleys and grey stone houses set deep in trees. No chocolate or cigarettes, the mainstays of our existence.

Piles of soft hay covered with pink chestnut blossom. Yellow bellied horses with glistening flanks. Bronzed arms brushed with golden down. All day reaping, turning, lifting in the steamy heat. Hair full of straw and nostrils coated with pollen. Arms aching, shirt sticking, lips dry, mouth sticky with saliva. Draughts of cold water from the pump. The sun spins up through veils of mist, crosses the sky and sinks in cloudy gold. Rough cider brought to the barn by the farmer in the evening. All this during a summer's day while the panzer divisions are marching against Russia, and Arthur L. sang the *Dichterliebe* accompanied by the fair haired youth from the north on the canteen piano. 'It's the biggest battle in the history of the world, more Russians killed in the last few days than all the British since the beginning of the war,' said D., curling his toes and munching chocolate. 'I'd like to see every country in the world,' said little John, meaning the world of a fireside, a girl, a radio and a safe job.

But the army sees to it that we do not become too contented. Every few weeks the groups and sections are split up and one's companions, on whom the whole of life depended, are sent off on detachment, leaving us miserable and helpless as abandoned children. Meaningless fatigues and kit inspections after the day's work keep the nerves tense and exasperate one.

July 1941 Melksham. We are here to quarry gravel. After the full summer of Codford we have moved to a suburban landscape dominated by the Avon Rubber Company. The camp is in a field strewn with derelict and rusty machinery. Life requires no thought and the future no forethought. One swings a pick and eats and rests and sleeps. I pine for lost companions and fear the strain and anxiety of making new. But with each move and breaking up there is usually one who before was only on the fringe of one's life who now becomes the centre. Here it is Bill G.

Two latrine buckets stand filled to the brim each evening. All our bodily functions are performed communally, a gesture of privacy being offered by a sheet of thin canvas. Often in the morning I wake with a sense of terror at the sequence of mornings that lie ahead and from which there is no escape. One longs to sink back into the oblivion of sleep. The mood passes as the day's routine begins with the bearable monotony and mental coma of navvying and the short brief freedom of evening when for a moment one has the sense of being alive. But I live with as much purpose and enthusiasm as a cow. A belly-filling existence. Driven and chivvied all day by NCOs we have no idea of the beginning or end of a job or what its purpose is. This more than the labour itself is what makes it exhausting. Day follows day with no more change then the date on the calendar.

28 August 1941 Talk is now all on the question of transferring; giving up our protected status and joining a combatant unit or volunteering for bomb disposal. Everywhere there is restlessness and exasperation with the boring and trivial routine of daily life. Bill has been offered an attractive job in the RE, Cosmo could get a job in intelligence which would take him to a training depot in Oxford where he would be among old friends. People are being worn down by the daily humiliation of going about with NCC flashes on their shoulders. There have been one or two unpleasant episodes with combatant units in the YMCA, though curiously not with the Guards regiments. I resist this with every argument that I can muster. Partly because I think it is a definite policy of the authorities to try to break up the Non-Combatant Corps, but mostly because I cannot bear the thought of losing this society and these people and being thrown back once again on myself.

About nine o'clock C. and I walked across to the cookhouse to see if we could find something to eat. It was full moon and the wind was pulling at the guy-ropes and the marquees were swaying like galleons. Inside, Bill was sitting in his shirt sleeves at the table writing. The lantern in front of him lit his face and arms and a strip of his shoulder with a deep bronze radiance. Other figures sat around in the shadows. The air was warm after the clear windy night and everywhere was the hum of conversation. We made tea and ate sausage rolls out of a box on the floor. The box was quite invisible and everyone tripped over it as they passed, but it never seemed to occur to anyone to pick it up. Presently Bill got up and stood away from the table by the fire and out of the light of the lantern. I stood near him drinking my tea which C. had brewed. C. moved about quietly collecting bread and bits of jam from various tins while the others sat around the table talking. I did not listen to what they were saying but looked at Bill once or twice and he smiled – the smile one gives when one has nothing particular to say but wants to acknowledge the other person's presence. When the conversation began to get animated I walked towards the door so as not to be drawn into it. I was aware of that sense of magic, of something unique and unrepeatable that such moments can sometimes hold. Bill followed me and we walked out into the sudden lustrous moonlight and fresh warm wind. The tents were like geometric impressions of mushrooms, hardly distinguishable from the colour of the dull grass. Clouds were mounted over the horizon, the rest of the sky was clear and star-lit. I put my arm round his shoulders, and he put his arm round my waist and we walked across the muddy grass back to the tent.

October 1941   As we march back from work in the evening lamps are being lit in all the little cottages along the lane. Cattle and farm implements are shut into the barns and a farmer stamps his feet on the stone flags with his finger on the latch of his door. Inside the kettle is boiling and tea is on the table. A boy lifts his bicycle into the garden shed. A woman talks to her neighbour at the open door. Mist creeps up the valley from the river. Children are going to bed to the sound of bath water. A day is finished in the lives of the people who live in the country. A day which will not have been quite the same as another day, and in a village which to them is different to any other place.

Our day too is finished as we stream out of the camp gates singly or in groups and move down towards the village. But we are the exiles. We descend on this place like a blight; like a plague of insects. We live here but are not part of it. We bring our own special paraphernalia of ugliness, iron huts, smoking cookhouses, tents, latrines, and spread them over the fields. And in the evening we descend on the village like wolves, crying for food, comfort and affection. Each one of us has his home and roots somewhere but not here. We know nothing of these people or their society. They give us their church hall and barn which we fill with tables and benches and urns of weak tea. Whether this village or another it is all the same to us. To them we are the tommies – the exiles in khaki. Every town and village in England has its share. A homeless nomadic tribe of men and boys, dressed alike, feeding alike, thinking alike.

November 1941 At six o'clock the guard's cane smacks the taut canvas of the tent. It is pitch dark. Nobody moves but everyone is instantly awake and weighing the agony of getting up against the penalty of staying in the warm cocoon of blankets. The guard can be heard in the distance thrashing the canvas of the other tents. Presently a tremor passes through the tent like the disturbance of sediment at the bottom of a heated flask. A hand emerges from its blanket and gropes for matches to light a candle. Sleepy but emphatic curses break out. When it is already late everyone gets up together and fights their shivering way into clothes, burrowing into the ruined heaps of kit to find their belongings. With practised skill we knead the blankets into the regulation mould and crawl through the opening, forgetting always the hooks which hoist us back again by the loops on our trousers. Outside the moon is still high and we start the perilous journey over slippery mud and through the minefield of guy-ropes and tent pegs to the marquee. Black smoke pours from the cookhouse chimney and we line up with tin bowl and plate while the orderlies bring in the heavy dixies of tea and porridge blanketed in steam. We shovel the hot stuff quickly into our bodies. It is too dark to see what we are eating but we bend over the tin bowls letting the steam pour over our faces and thaw out our fingers on the mugs of tea.

We sit pressed tight together like cattle, wrapped in scarves and leather jerkins, and nobody speaks or wakes up more than is necessary to take in the hot mush. The tables are at all angles owing to the uneven slope of the ground. If anyone moves carelessly eight mugs of tea slop over and a dark stream rushes to the end of the table where the bread is piled. When we have finished we dip our plates and mugs into a bath of luke warm water which removes the larger particles of food and spreads out the rest in an even layer of grease. Another day begins.

January 1942 After the slush and misery of half the winter under canvas we now live in the luxury of Nissen huts. A shining steel tube with two rows of beds six inches off the floor. By candlelight the ends of the huts are invisible and the tunnel seems to stretch indefinitely in each direction. Some people are already rolled in blankets quietly asleep in the dark shadow. In the centre of the hut the roaring stove glows red to the first joint in the chimney pipe. Doug sits on the edge of his bed eating some heated up liver on toast. The liver is from breakfast. He wears only a greatcoat and his pink and glowing legs and chest show beneath, freshly bathed. His feet lie in the ashes of the stove along with boots, mud, billy cans, cups of coffee, crusts of toast, cans of boiling water, firewood, cement dust. Ken and Arthur sit at the table around a complicated spread of food. Cosmo is propped up on his bed with folded blankets, greatcoat, bolster, with a wooden board across his knees like a tray on which are balanced a neat array of dainties. He has the knack of always looking supremely comfortable. He leans across with a long toasting fork from which the bread drops on to the glowing top of the stove and bursts into flames. The hut is crowded with beds, blankets, people, piles of kit over which people step hazardously if they want to move about. I sit at the table with Ken eating cold trifle out of the same plate. This is the moment of the day when life becomes worth living. From being separate closed-in units of manpower, numbed with cold and wet and fatigue, we expand into a warm argumentative contented scrum. Each part of the hut has a different atmosphere created by the occupant around whom the others cluster. Outside the snow is crisp and clean beneath a sky bright with stars. Inside a spontaneous ever-changing ebb and flow of life laps round the warm centre of the stove; toast making, water boiling, coffee brewing, boot cleaning, dubbin melting, clothes drying. All our hopes and anxieties are momentarily forgotten – the forces that brought us here, the reasons that will draw us apart.

The best of the army is in the relationships which could only exist under these conditions. We are a mixed and weirdly assorted lot with no common bonds or interests, except an unwillingness to kill strangers to order. Our community is formed simply by military law. We have no choice in it. In an atmosphere of tolerance, which since we sought it for ourselves we do not find it difficult to extend to others, and with living reduced to its animal essentials, one after another people flower into individual personalities. Contacts, confidences, intimacies are formed too briefly to be complete or to grow stale. Since nobody is seen as part of their social environment, their class, their profession or their job, and since the environment is equally anonymous and hostile to each one, personalities burn with a particular individual brightness which is both more intense and more unreal than in a freely formed society.

Nobody here can be easily classified or seen as part of a unit larger than ourselves. We were all more or less misfits in the societies we left. An evening's conversation can cover modern painting, brick making, existential philosophy and diesel engineering, each person drawing on the store of their own memory and experience and contributing to a shared enthusiasm. There are moments when this can seem better and richer than anything I have ever known.

June 1942 The days go by like water running out of a tap with a gauze over it. Everyone is getting restless and exasperated at the aimless repetitive existence. What would happen if we all had to restate our claims again before a tribunal, or public sentiment changed towards us and our conscientiousness had to face the test of persecution? In desperation many people have already gone over to a combatant unit. But what is the point if one has no conviction about fighting the war either. The only solution seems to be to find somewhere where one is least interfered with and where conditions are sufficiently stimulating to keep one's faculties alert. So far as I am concerned the eighteen months in the army have not been so much time wasted as the years before. All I want is to hold on to the best things here – the personal relationships. I have no convictions one way or the other. But as always I am trying to hold on to a reality which is no more than a projection of my own desires.

Freddie was blowing bubbles in the washhouse this evening, and like everything he does he blew them with a fanatical concentration and absorption. One hand was not enough. He used both hands. His thin white torso bent over the basin and both fists full of suds he blew them as quickly as he could, to left and right, his glossy black hair falling from side to side and his eyes darting like swallows. When I spoke to him he didn't answer. When someone tried to get past he took no notice. Only when ten or twelve bubbles were simultaneously in the air did he suddenly relax, gazed at them with the wrapt attention of a child, then hugging himself with delight made everyone stop whatever they were doing and count and admire them.

One of the best things about Freddie is his sudden inspired clowning. This afternoon when we were all exhausted by the heat, nerves frayed and on edge, dragging about one behind the other beneath the heavy loads of timber, suddenly, summing up the whole situation and transposing it into farce, Freddie flings himself on the ground, drags his body along the railings hanging from the arms and cries – Water – water – and sprawls full length in the dust. Everyone laughs. Everyone's spirits are suddenly lightened. The situation is robbed of its power.

He has the gift of real spontaneity. He follows an impulse with the simplicity of an animal without forethought or regret. I asked him the other evening why he had got married so young. He said he had never thought of getting married at all. But one Christmas he was alone in the house, his parents were out, and he was listening to the *Christmas Carol* on the radio. Suddenly he saw himself as Scrooge. He felt certain that that was what he would grow into. The thought terrified him. He went straight out and round to the girl he was going with at the time and asked her to marry him.

July 1942 Fatigues today. I volunteered eagerly, certain that nothing could be worse than the dump in this driving rain. So I spent the day washing down the ceiling in the cookhouse. The paint was caked with the grease and soot of years, and washing it down with an abrasive it came up 'like new'. But it was exhausting washing a thing all the time above one's head and having to press upwards. It caused quite a disturbance among the colonies of flies up there. From the beginning of time they must have regarded this territory as theirs by sovereign right, and this sudden human intrusion utterly inexplicable. Right from the start they were on the offensive. Unable to conceive any danger to themselves at that altitude, they buzzed angrily around and settled on my hands and face and mouth. A thin black snow fell down all the time on to my head from between the boards of the ceiling. The ATS chirped and twittered away below and took no notice of me. As the afternoon wore on I got rather tired and depressed. The woodwork was covered with little brown dots everywhere from the flies which were hard to get off. I felt I no longer belonged to any world but the flies' world with its dirts and soot and the weary smells of cooking. I consoled myself that it must be very much worse on the dump in the relentless east wind that has been blowing for days.

1 August 1942 I spent the whole morning painting round the bottom of one of the Nissen huts which face on to the road and I got up to stretch my back at the moment when a boy was passing down the road on his bicycle. There was nothing else moving in sight at the moment and I watched him pass the short length of the street, approaching, receding, and finally disappear round the corner. I experienced what I can only describe as the reality of the situation; of becoming absorbed in, and finally identified with, the passage of that cyclist. I was aware simultaneously of his independence and his basic similarity to myself; of his strangeness and the fact of non-recognition and the fact that I alone of all living people was observing him at that moment. I was aware of a purpose before him and an impulse behind him which had combined to set him in motion. I was aware of his existence subjectively in the strain and flexing of muscles, the hardness of saddle and the coolness of handlebars; objectively as a figure in movement against the row of stationary houses; aesthetically as the pattern of his limbs against the geometrical framework of the bicycle. I was aware of his existence in time – about ten seconds, and in space about fifty yards.

If one could sustain the welded sensations of that complex moment throughout the time necessary for painting, one might succeed in painting the subject of a boy on a bicycle.

29 April 1943 *Re: Arthur Koestler on Richard Hillary* 'In search of a redeeming emotion; a credo that is neither sentimental, archaic, or vulgar, whose words one can say without embarrassment or shame.'

So Hillary goes into the air with patchwork face and hands, to be burnt with clear premonition a second time. Lawrence buries himself in the anonymous ranks of the RAF. Search for the delusive companionship of the simple. Lawrence knew it was a delusion. 'I was a fool to think I could ever become a man again.' Hillary too knew this part of it to be a delusion. The Mystique of flight, closely akin perhaps to Existenzephilosophie. The weakness of the cleft personality, the man divided against himself, the 'Lost Generation' in search of its leader, the psychological flaw of our time that feeds Fascism.

The point at which their self-awareness breaks down is just on this question of redemption. They preserved their cynicism immaculately in all else, in love, in patriotism, in success, in glory, but not on the question of redemption. Belief in the possibility of this must have existed for them to have gone the way they did.

It is a comparatively simple matter to discover a bond between people when they are reduced by circumstances to their minima. The emotional tension of RAF messes, the 'shared tyranny' of Lawrence, in all cases of hunger, extreme danger, because all the qualities which give them their difference, and their real status as human beings, are over-ridden by the primary instincts common to all. But what satisfaction can such a relationship give to persons of intelligence and sensitive perceptions. It is surely degrading to find unity with others simply through the baser elements in one's make-up. Under all conditions of war men are something less than their true selves, are artificially confined to a pattern of intense stimulus, fear, anxiety, strain. It is through these conditions commonly shared that one imagines oneself at one with them, but it is an illusion. Remove the conditions and the bond vanishes. Meet the same people in different circumstances and they are strangers, each complete and compact and exclusive. What then constitutes the redeeming emotion. The purely physical stimulus of flying. If so, then this also is a delusion.

Hillary was deeply influenced by the life of Lawrence; so was I, so I can understand that. The question is what is this quality in Lawrence that attracts. It is primarily a negative one. No man surely has achieved a reputation which depended so little on his actual achievements. It is perhaps his strength of will and self-discipline which attract those who find themselves at the mercy of conflicting urges. But neither Lawrence nor Hillary found the redeeming emotion. At best they found moments of simple animal contentment, merely in the release of their bodies from physical strain. Lawrence lying on the airfield awaiting the return of 'kites' 'pillowed on each others' softnesses'. There is something shocking in the idea of a man of Lawrence's calibre wilfully allowing himself to be subjected to such conditions that in the mere momentary release from physical oppression he finds his fullest happiness. 'I always took my pleasures downwards because there is a certainty in degradation.' Really it amounts to an attempt to escape the responsibilities of that position to which by nature and education they are inheritors. Not artists enough to find themselves completely in their art, they still have to pay the price of the artist, loneliness and isolation. They envy the seeming completeness of the simple, the naturalness of simple tastes, ideas, actions. But it is their particular perceptions as artists that reveal, what to others remains totally unremarkable, the rare beauty of the commonplace and simple. And it is precisely the possession of these perceptions that bars them for ever from entering the ranks of the simple. Lawrence found this out and yet remained in the ranks. It is always easier to remain than remove as long as conditions are not too insufferable. Hillary went back to the RAF and flying, largely, he says, as a result of reading *The Mint*, though I think that is more probably a sentimental confirmation of a decision which he would in any case have taken. Both voluntarily preserve an illusion knowing it is an illusion, like a man returns to a drug, loving and hating it.

With both Lawrence and Hillary one feels that they regarded self-knowledge as a final and complete end in itself. The discovery of a weakness gives them the satisfaction of a major triumph. 'I crept back to my hut and cried like a child, much to my own surprise, as I thought I had steeled myself for this.' This is Hillary speaking, but it could as well have been Lawrence. The impregnable armour all through is cynicism. 'Much to my own surprise.' The critical raised eyebrow. Inspecting one's weeping self. The difficulty for such a person, for ever sitting in judgment upon himself, is how to carry out any programme of action at all. Action is undertaken solely for the purpose of self-testing – self-revelation. Success or failure are unimportant, the self-knowledge is the important thing. Thus Lawrence would goad his full talent and energy for the attainment of a single object until it was just within reach, 'until I only had to reach out my arm and pluck it', then he would deliberately let it go, content that he had proved to himself that it lay within his power. The attraction of an organization which enforces a programme of action which is beyond criticism, allowing them just sufficient time as individuals to appreciate their captivity, is obvious, but one cannot escape the conclusion that all this is a sickness. The RAF promises just this and so did Fascism in its early days. It is the iron lung for the psychologically rigid. The support that banishes the fear of freedom. It gives pilots their strange, strained, rather hectic dignity, the 'ethereal quality' Hillary called it. It is the reason why so many people are really happier during a war than in peace time. They are given an artificial armour over their soft shells.

It is unlikely that Hillary any more than Lawrence would have become a great writer. Their continual self-criticism and unwearying insistence on perfection would in the end paralyse the creative spring. The greater their natural talent, the more penetrating and exacting their self-awareness, and the two are all the time tearing each other to pieces. Lawrence produced his two books by reason of the few blind spots in his critical awareness that concealed from him their flaws, and though vaguely dissatisfied, he could never particularize his dissatisfaction, and so could never be certain he had not produced a masterpiece; even then it was a near thing many a time whether the book was published or buried and the very memory of its having been attempted erased. Hillary wrote from the sense of obligation to his companions who had shared his experiences; not, be it noted, from any positive creative urge, but to pay homage to the dead. Lawrence too undertook a military campaign and wrote its history mainly he tells us for private reasons which he could not even bring himself to disclose. Hillary returned to the RAF to 'keep faith', Lawrence's mystical formula. He could not see that his duty to the dead lay in living and not in dying. Only by striving to fulfil himself in life could he really keep faith with those of his generation who had been deprived of even making the attempt.

'A good looking and confident young man,' Cyril Connolly called him. Confident in what, one wonders.

3 July 1943 Journeying north. Everyone in the carriage is reading or writing letters. There are still four hours of rhythmic monotony and time to take stock of one's position. Geographically it is somewhere spinning up the backbone of England. There are fields full of summer and fields of wheat and trees and hedges and fields of fields, rather flat and uninteresting. Sometimes a field of bright red poppies and black crows and then a cluster of red brick cottages appear and are whipped away. An old grey building turns slowly round on the horizon. The towns begin with a fidgeting of the rails. They cross and recross and subdivide and then multiply wildly over a huge expanse of ground until the whole thing becomes hopelessly over-complicated. Gasometers loom up and smutty cottages peep between, then whole mean streets fan out like the spokes of a broken umbrella. Chimneys and tall spires sail comfortably above it all. After that it is black walls and tunnels until we are out in the country again. It all looks dull and rather sad, yet I am reluctant to let it slip by because it all adds to the immense accumulation of distance piling up behind.

I am obsessed with the idea of parting. A chapter has finished before I had time to get to the end of the page and I am forced to start a new one with reluctance. Things are always like that in the army. I cannot realize that there are people I have lived with for the last two years whom I am unlikely ever to see again. There is no sense in this eternal movement without a goal. All values and judgments suddenly become shaky like these rails when they enter the confusion of marshalling yards and it seems as if blind momentum alone carries one across to the other side without mishap. The person now sitting in the opposite seat is one I have known for two years without taking the least notice of. Now he is the most valuable friend I have, but without either of us having changed at all or become in any way better acquainted. Only the situation has changed and what each of us represents to the other.

Kettering – poppies are bleeding through all the wheat fields now. Cows stand knee deep in muddy ponds in the sparse shade. There is a gravelly lane with a pub standing behind a semi-circle of green and a bench and table outside and white posts linked with chains. It reminds me with a sudden grief of the pub Bill and I cycled to last Sunday, where we sat all day in the orchard talking. It is possible to see things almost as a pure negation of themselves. That little lawn with the linked white posts signified only something that was *not* there.

A clearing in the wood suddenly reveals children pinned against the wire railing in attitudes of waving. The speed of the train reduces the wood and the children to equal immobility and one is left with the memory of a sort of tableau vivant. The movement gives one only a generalized aspect of things. One sees just little houses and gardens and people in them. The differences, the colour of the curtains, the size of the ornament in the window, the really important facts that make up the lives of the people in them, are lost.

Sheffield – more and more people crowd into the train. They are stacked along the corridors like patient sweating animals. Not many of them look as though they were travelling because they wanted to.

Sheffield is black and sinister. Black steel and black stone. Batteries of chimneys, kilns, crucibles. An engine snuffing its way into the black interior of a factory. Thousands of little pipes pissing steam and hot water. Steelworks, railway-wagons, roads are in uncontested possession. Men crawl about them like flies. There is something reassuring in the final victory of machinery over nature. The conflict no longer counts for anything. Every trace of nature has been effaced. There are not even those indescribably sad little weeds that grow up through the cracks in poor concrete. This world seems to be part of a natural order of things. It has achieved a perfectly consistent logic of its own.

If only one can keep still in one set of circumstances it is nearly always possible to find some way of accommodating oneself to them. It is this impulsive restless movement that makes any sort of solution impossible. Like a plant which is continually transplanted, one slowly dries up.

Humanity has struck its tents and returned to its nomadic origins. But this time the motive power is fear from behind rather than hope before. And we are overburdened with baggage. The acquired and inherited habits, the memories that seem more and more precious the further they recede into the past. The objects, possessions, and people in which, when we have to part from them, we realize suddenly we have deposited an essential part of ourselves.

Here is a small factory with a yellow brick chimney, some sheds and a little cottage standing in a plot of sour waste ground on the edge of meadows. Traces of organization are still visible beneath the encroaching weeds. A strip of overgrown road can be traced by the sudden change of colour in the grass. The cottage where the factory manager perhaps once lived, the garden laid out so much for vegetables, so much for pleasure. Someone thought it all out, took pride in it. Now the doors and windows are black holes, the brick-work bursting apart, wires and pipes twist like giant briars. Dark nettles grow tall to the level of the lower windows. All around are the fields of fat wheat.

In a small oily stream pearled with the colours of petrol, children are bathing against a background of derricks and shale mountains. The air is the colour of amber. All over Europe children bathe on Saturday afternoon in summer. 'Our day is our loss. O show us History, the operator, the organizer. Time the refreshing river.'

4 July 1943 As we came up the incline from Keighley the landscape became mysterious and exciting. Village cottages are built in rows like slum houses, not mean but hard and clamped into the hard landscape. They break out from the thinly covered rock slopes like vertebrae. They have no individual distinction. Each is the same simple stone cube. At first they suggest rows of village police stations. There is none of the prettiness of the south; no decoration, no trimmings, no striving to be different from each other. The landscape has a tremendous sense of spaciousness. At any point one is standing level with the foundations of one house and looking down the chimneys of others. The sense of strangeness was finally crowned when we turned the corner of the steep winding road and confronted a tiny solitary figure standing in the middle. He seemed to be an official of some sort, but when we drew closer, he turned out to be a dwarf village idiot dressed up as a policeman. He flapped both his arms at us furiously and then shambled off giggling. But somehow the whole thing was less unexpected than it would have been elsewhere.

We reached the barracks about 10 pm. A disused mill clinging to the rocky side of the valley like a mediaeval fortress. There was no sound but the wild rushing of invisible water. Lower down the valley stood another mill whose single tall stack reached to the level on which we stood. I thought it must have been unpleasant here when the mill was in operation. We had marched with full kit five miles up what was virtually the side of a mountain and were feeling tired. First of all we were documented and then fell in to have our haversacks inspected. Apparently it was necessary at that moment to ascertain whether we carried old or new type haversacks. Then we were issued with blankets and were shown our billet. This was an enormously long low room whose sagging ceiling and bulging floor were held apart by numerous slender iron pillars. From the ceiling hung pulleys and shafts and fly-wheels and other pieces of machinery. There were double-tiered bunks which were all occupied and we asked the sergeant what about some palliasses and he said sorry. Then an officer came along to see if we were quite comfortable and said there were no paliasses because the trouble was people had been taking two. He seemed grieved about it and his tone of voice suggested that we ought not to have reminded him of so painful a subject. He said we could each be issued with an extra blanket in lieu. We trooped off again and received the extra blanket apiece and then helped ourselves to as many more as we liked from what appeared to be an unlimited supply. When we had got up to the seventh floor again we were fallen in and marched back to the bottom for a meal of stew and bread and marmalade and tea. Then we went back and made our beds up on the floor and when we were all inside them the officer came back and said anyone without a palliasse should go downstairs and draw one. He told the sergeant he would find palliasses in where the straw was. The sergeant said follow me and we scrambled out of bed and followed him downstairs and along the endless corridors and out along the battlements and behind some boiler houses to a sort of stable where there was a heap of straw and a pile of what looked like old sacks in one corner. He said we were not to imagine the palliasses would be damp because they were not. We dragged them out one after another and found each one had been split open down the side and had obviously been discarded as useless. We told him they were split and he said if we played the game with him he would play the game with us and what did we think we were anyway; couldn't we tie them up with something. Then he had a look at them and saw we couldn't, so he said hold on a minute and he would go and draw some more from the store. After some while he came back and said the storeman was out and he couldn't find the key, so we said really it didn't matter because we were quite OK with the blankets. But he said it was the OC's orders that we had to have palliasses and we would have palliasses and he was there to see that we got them.

In bed I lay awake listening to the strange sad noises from the hundreds of sleeping figures and the ceaseless noise of water some- where outside. I tried to work out the logic of the black iron machinery hanging from the ceiling, hoping none of it would fall. Here and there bits of coloured paper streamers still clung to it from some forgotten celebration.

August 1943 Derby. Saturday afternoon was hot and everyone had either flopped out on their beds in a stupor or disappeared somewhere into the white blazing streets. I had a strong desire to get away from the smell of pavements and dust; to get a breath of the country. After work I changed quickly and hurried down to the bus station. There was a crowd of people and buses stood round in a semicircle each opposite the white painted board showing its destination: Nottingham, Matlock, Belper, Ashbourne, Alfreton. All the buses had long queues of people trailing behind them like the tails of kites, except the Alfreton bus which was smaller than the rest and only half full. I liked the sound of the name and I liked the look of the big sanserif letters standing up on their white board. While I was staring the driver got in and slid open the window of his cab which was just above my head and settled himself to await patiently the time to start. When he caught my eye I said to him, 'What sort of place is Alfreton.' He lent out and said, 'Yes that's right.' I said, 'Can you tell me what sort of place it is, I mean is it large or small.' I had a wishful vision of a small stone village tucked into the hills with a river and perhaps tea gardens with tables in the shade and home-made cakes. He looked me up and down and looked at my cap badge and epaulettes and then his face went extinct. I said, 'What I'm looking for is just somewhere not too far out in the country where it is quiet and cool and where I can get some tea.' The bus in front was blowing out a cloud of smoke and fumes and the yard was filling with noise so that I had to shout above it and the whole thing was becoming ridiculous and I wanted to walk away and forget it. Perhaps the absurdity touched him too, and he wanted to be helpful, because he suddenly smiled and shouted above the noise: 'Try Belper. This is only a mining village. There's some tea gardens at Belper I think. The River Tea Gardens. There's a bus every quarter of an hour. It only costs one and three return. You get out at the Triangle.' I shouted my thanks and hurried to joint the Belper bus.

It was hot and steamy in the bus and with luck I got a seat and we started out through the usual dull suburbs. Then the country began and slowly closed in, folding itself up into two long lines of hills. We drove along the white blinding road of dust past villages and factories and eventually came to Belper. The bus stopped at a fork in the road. There was a triangle of green grass with two trees and an iron bench. I got out.

Straight in front was an enormous red brick factory with rows of broken windows and a single tall stack the purplish colour of raw meat. Some gardens and shrubbery and a high railing separated it from the road. I began to walk in what I hoped would be the direction of the river. A little way along there was a large entrance which was an entrance to the factory though it looked more like an entrance to a seaside pier. There were tall iron gates and over them an arched semicircular wooden board with some faded blistered letters; looking more closely I made these out to be *River Tea Gardens – Swiss Café.*

Inside the path led between shrubberies and flower beds ringed round with large white flints. Everything was laid out with the precisely determined effort that reminded me of those small and unexpected plots of flowers one comes across wedged between the lines at railway stations. The sun blazed down in a fierce heat. There was no one about. The paths and flower beds led down to the river and the factory I discovered was on the other side. A jet of sulphurous coloured water spouted high up out of the wall and plunged into the white frothing river. There were one or two seats facing the factory and further on some more railings with a turnstile and a polygonic green wooden kiosk. On one side was a notice saying *River Tea Gardens – 2d*.

I imagined the 2d was just another part of some long-forgotten past and was surprised to find the kiosk occupied and the turnstile in working order. Inside the kiosk was a woman asleep. She wore a sleeveless black satin dress and a string of pearls intagliated in a fold of flesh round her neck. Her arms and bosom and head lay as it were on a tiny wooden tray which was the counter. The rest of her was invisible. A fly was buzzing up and down one of the panes of streaky glass. I made a small noise with the gate to draw her attention. She rasised her head, stretched her neck, revealing another row of pearls, yawned, and focused me with a look of interrogation.

'One please,' I said.

Slowly her eyes unglazed and her face recognized the necessity of action. Imperceptibly the ranges of black satin unfurled themselves off the counter, swayed backwards. An arm slid silently off the counter, disclosing a tiny aperture, and reached down out of sight. A moment of effort distorted her face. From somewhere deep in the ground came a soft purring noise and a tiny pink ticket was excreted on to the brassy surface. I took it and went on.

The paths and flower beds went on as before. Presently I came to a long low wooden building with a veranda running round it which I took to be the Swiss Café. Inside were chairs upside down on tables and a white painted counter at one end with a large showcard of a smiling girl holding a glass of Horlicks. It looked as though it had been closed for a long time.

I walked back into the town and found a turning which led down to another part of the river, and where the buildings finished in a sheer wall of brick was a small door and a window which said *Teas*. To one side was a gate which led steeply down to the river and a narrow strip of grass with a long green table and two benches. I asked at the window if I might have some tea at the table outside. An old woman said, Yes, in a tone of voice which implied she would like it clearly understood I did so at my own risk. I sat down and looked through the railings on to the ochre-coloured waters of the river below. Presently a waitress came and asked me what I would like. The question was rhetorical because before I had time to answer she said I could have a meat tea, a fruit tea, or a plain tea. Through the open door I could see several tables of people eating meat pies with rather sombre enjoyment. I chose a fruit tea. The waitress had a round amiable face like a harvest moon; small white hairs sprouted from it at unexpected places. She brought the tea on a stout wooden tray. There was a pot of tea for four, a pint of hot water, a sediment of sandy coloured sugar at the bottom of a bowl, a plate of bread and butter, two ginger nuts, and a plate of stewed apple. She set it all out with a great deal of clatter on the table and smiled broadly as though the whole thing was a great lark. I ate it and read for a bit and watched the numerous boats going up and down the river. There were boats of boys straining at the rollocks with groaning effort and boats of girls twittering like birds. There were boats of boys and girls. Long thin boats pirated the river with alert skill and two soldiers came past feathering with professional ease. An Air Force youth came past carefully rowing his mother. The shadow of the steep granite bank lengthened across the water, deepening the colour. The heat and glare slowly drained out of the afternoon. The waitress came back and started to collect up the things. I paid and left and later on took the bus back.

22 November 1943 The idea behind the story of Alfred burning the cakes is, I suppose, that the great man must not also be able to do little things. It is the ordinary man's defence of his ordinariness; the idea behind all the jokes of absent-minded scientists and artists living 'Bohemian' lives and never being able to manage their domestic arrangements. It was absolutely necessary that Alfred should burn the cakes, otherwise people would be uneasy. If Alfred had simply given his mind to the matter for a few moments, which of course he could very well have done, he would appear slightly ridiculous. The whole situation would be embarrassing. It would mean that he was, after all, a human being at the same time as being Alfred the Great, and would therefore offer a perpetual challenge to people to rise above their ordinariness. As it is, the story allows the baking of cakes and the defeating of the Danes to be activities of equal importance, and everyone may remain satisfied with the littleness of their achievements.

2

1944–1946

22 January 1944 Further evidence of the way things are going was offered by the MOI film of air service after the war. Here is the smooth totalitarian efficiency of the large air port. The control tower with charts and panels and clipped conversation. The flare path, the runways, and the liners arriving to the minute from all corners of the earth. The poker-faced pilots with their brand new clothes and old jokes. Breakfast in Leningrad, lunch in Le Bourget, and on in time for the evening show in Madison Square Garden. This, we are confidently asked to believe, is the answer to world organization. Getting about. 'Because,' as one earnest baby-faced American pilot puts it, 'it seems to me that when folks get to know more about each other and understand each other better wars just won't happen.' Maybe. But has it occurred to anyone to wonder how much one will get to know the Russian people through a succession of breakfasts in Leningrad, or how much experience can be gained at the pilots' bar at San Francisco or Los Angeles.

In fact, of course, the technicians and pilots and the managerial revolutionaries will take with them their own world, culture, and values. In their specialized cosmopolitan society they will be insulated from the people wherever they settle as a thorn is separated by pus from the flesh in which it is bedded. They will no more prevent wars than the international capitalists who had 'friends' in every country. Far from getting to know different countries, these people will immunize themselves from all contact by sterilizing wherever they alight a small territory of airconditioned desert. There they will meet their counterparts of all nations, equally conditioned and sterilized.

The future they tell us is in the air. The prospect dismays me. Why is it that merely to extend the area of man-made confusion into regions hitherto unconfused invariably gives people the illusion of achieving order. I suppose because the inherent order in nature delays the confusion long enough to conceal the inevitable results of the process, like polluting large rivers but not small ones.

It is as well to know where one is going before one leaves one place for another. It is essential to know if one travels fast. Travelling slowly one comes upon interesting things by the way which were not foreseen. So that even if one arrives finally at the wrong place the journey was not wasted. But the greater the speed the more accurate must the aim be. Fast travel eliminates everything that lies by the way. There is only the beginning and the end – least satisfactory of positions. Only the very sure should travel fast. Our dilemma is that the speed and facility of travel increases in inverse ratio to our sense of direction.

24 February 1944 People who adapt themselves completely to the demands of their existence are no longer aware of being untrue to themselves. The young man who sat in the café in his smart uniform playing with his pipe, going through all the actions of a man of the world, was just such a completely adapted type. How did I know he was adapted? Because he looked ridiculous, and no human being should look ridiculous when being true to themselves. Children never look ridiculous no matter how absurdly they behave. The deception can be perfectly well kept up throughout a whole life. It gets more difficult though as age advances and reality wears continually against the fabric of pretence. But the difficulties are explained in terms of tribulations, external misfortunes beyond the power of prevention. The difficulties can be accounted for precisely: 'the war' – 'the depression' – 'the problem of employment' – 'hardening arteries' – 'change of life' – 'death of a loved one' – 'loss of money'. Or they can be accounted for vaguely: 'difficult times' – 'human nature' – 'original sin'. The extrovert adapts easily because he is aware only of the demands of the situation. The introvert cannot adapt because he senses the true nature of his own potentialities and the falseness of the demands made on him by the situation. Self-consciousness is used to mean almost the exact opposite to its literal meaning.

The Lie now lies over life like a hard unbroken enamel. There is not even a crack to tell people it is a lie. But the cracks will appear after the war. You can make one lie cover the whole surface when there is one purpose. When there are several purposes one lie will not do. You need many different lies and then some of them will accidentally approach the truth.

There must be many deaths for each person before he can begin to live again. Each false adapted self must be cast off and the rawness endured until the new tender skin grows again over the spot. The last, not the first death should be the death of the physical body because there is no resurrection from that in this life, and anyhow there is nothing more for humanity to learn about that sort of dying. Perhaps after all 'except ye die ye can in nowise be born again' refers to the death of the false self of adaptation and has nothing to do with a life after death. 'Except ye become as little children' – note the *as*. You cannot revert to the primary ties but you can grow towards true and not false secondary ones. 'Except ye become as little children' – 'Si le grain ne meurt'.

4 March 1944 Bernard: 'Non, mon vieux, non; je ne sais pas si j'écrirai. Il me semble parfois qu'écrire empêche de vivre, et qu'on peut s'exprimer mieux par les actes que par les mots.' 'Les oeuvres d'art sont des actes qui durent,' hasarda craintivement Olivier; mais Bernard ne l'écoutait pas. 'C'est là ce que j'admire le plus dans Rimbaud; c'est d'avoir préféré la vie.'

The question is an old one, a naïve one some will say, but is the answer so simple? It is not of course a question merely of duration or longevity. Christian art endured longer than Christendom. The value of the lives of conquerors, kings and princes seems to lie in the living rather than in the achievements; in the spectacle of their lives as something complete and rounded off. Their accomplishments, when they amounted to anything of consequence, can seldom be said to be the work of one man. Rome was built, Christendom existed, but Charlemagne and Hadrian were items in a long chain of circumstances which brought about their inception. But the ultimate significance of the life of a Charlemagne or a Hadrian was that they fulfilled their potentialities as men. The life of an artist seldom shows this completeness. They are destroyed in their creating, or perhaps their creating is an alternative for a life from which they are in some way disqualified. We see them at odds with themselves and others, perpetually lonely and ailing, carved out with wretchedness, their manhood falling to pieces about them and only the bright jewel of their creative rage burning in the centre of the wreckage. Was it this that Rimbaud found insupportable? – that he could only write as a poet and not live as a man. It is not a question of what is ultimately of more value to humanity, but what is properly fulfilling to the individual.

The more individual, the more art becomes a compensation for life. As society becomes more cramping so the art of individuals burns with a brighter and more feverish flame. But when we look back, beyond the fifteenth century, to the time before the individual had emerged properly from the womb of society, the art is anonymous and the artist seems more complete, more fully human, less self-concious. And it was at that moment when the individual first sensed his aloneness, yet was still held on the pinnacle of a living and vital society that mankind achieved its greatest moments, the early Renaissance. Thenceforward art was a protest against non-art. Art became the brilliant personal discoveries made at the expense of life. It is natural that now when the isolation and chaos is complete we should seek first the individual significance in art, recognizing a fellow-traveller rather than the impeccable flower of a civilization.

We come to them as lepers to be made whole and comforted, clinging desperately to our belief in the miracle. But the men who worshipped at Chartres or Wells saw only the cradle of their own religious aspiration. They did not draw nourishment and sustenance from a world alien and more exalted than their own. They entered a cathedral as naturally as a man enters his study or sits by his fireside. From the potters of China, the negro carvers of Africa, the monks of Lindisfarne, the masons and carvers of Chartres and Vezelay we turn to a world remote and almost incomprehensible. We get a glimpse of the life and thought of a whole people and epoch, of a growth as natural and inevitable as a flower.

Koestler: *Arrival and Departure*.

'They are the eternal adolescents through whom the race matures.'

The final conclusions seem to be that artists, at any rate, should leave their neuroses alone; that art is in fact the manifestation of a psychological problem which is barred from solution in living. The little fable of Pythagoras on the sands is very convincing. Peter, after being freed from the inhibitions of his past, is left in an empty present with an uninviting future. 'Where the dead are left to bury the dead, the living remain alone.'

Most psychoanalysts admit that some such state usually follows analysis, but it is only temporary, until the person has gathered together the true threads again. It does not entirely discredit the therapeutic value of analysis. But there seems some truth in the neurotic foundations of artistic activity. Finally K. accepts the relative value of psychology. It gives a true picture, but not a complete one. But if he objects to the psychological view as representing the whole case he must show what factors it cannot account for. He mentions Napoleon's career as being the result of the activity of the pituitaries, and Leonardo's Giaconda as the manifestation of an incestuous dream as though such accounts were self-evident absurdities. But why? The reluctance to accept an explanation of human activity in scientific terms comes from confusing the activity with the value of the achievement. It may perfectly well be that the activity of an artist can be accounted for in terms of his glands, environment, genius or what not. That does not devaluate his achievement. Yet there is always a tendency, when the mystery behind the creation of a great work is 'explained', to say – 'Is that all – fancy – just a matter of glands.' But in fact all one has done is to say, 'The Giaconda is the result of certain glandular activities in the constitution of Leonardo,' which is only another way of saying, 'The Giaconda is the result of the creative genius of Leonardo'; it says nothing at all about the Giaconda itself.

I can see no reason why every human activity should not eventually be perfectly well accounted for in precise terms of scientific measurement. But it won't make the slightest difference to the values of living.

5 March 1944   In the Jurassic layers of rock fossils have been found of an extinct species of oyster. The whole evolutionary history of the oyster can be traced. In its earliest stages it resembled the present oyster. It was the same size and shape, it lived in the same manner and clung to the bed of the sea; the chief difference being that the whole width of its shell was used for the purpose of securing itself to the ocean bed, security being its prime concern. In subsequent evolutionary stages the area of attachment decreases and the shell begins to curve, the spirals coiling back on themselves. As the introspective curvature becomes more pronounced the security of its hold lessens and the difficulty of opening, due to the curvature of the shell, increases. Finally the shell curves to such an extent that to open at all becomes impossible and its hold on the sea bed is abandoned. The species becomes extinct. All writers of introspective journals should bear this in mind.

Further geological note. Certain kinds of sandstone, found often in mountain regions, or even beneath the sea, exhibit under the microscope a rounded formation to their grains: proof that the sandstone was once a desert, and the grains rounded by the ceaseless erosion of the wind. The sand originally was rock, broken into boulders, worn down by the wind and water into grains, elevated into the sun and wind to be polished, resubmerged beneath further sedimentary accumulations, compressed once more into sandstone rock, re-elevated into hill and mountains ... the endless weary repetition of it all.

7 March 1944   In the army men live conscious all the time that their hearts, roots, origins lie elsewhere in some other life. They live as a planet lives revolving round its parent sun. They measure the hardships, privations, weariness here against the memory of a past that they hope to continue in the future. They may romanticize that past to counterbalance the present, but however far their fancies lead them they know there is a core of reality. All the while they live here an imposed life they know there is the other life still going on in which their absence is a dominant factor. The strength of this knowledge gives their present existences a limited and definite shape. Although it may contain the whole emotional range of their other lives they live the present with only a part of themselves. Since their hearts reside elsewhere they face the present with an armoured countenance. They are able to adopt the role that circumstances require without involving the whole of themselves and without destroying the intactness of their true lives. It is with this diminished version of themselves that they form all contacts, friendships, love affairs.

In my case the situation is rather different. I have no intact existence to which I belong other than the circumstances in which I find myself. The present circumstances are neither more nor less propitious to me than they are to anyone else but because I have no other existence to counterbalance them their limits are less clearly defined. Because no part of me is claimed elsewhere I can live here with the whole of myself. The curtains of the past and the future are drawn and cast no glow over the present. I live entirely in the present. And so I give the bewildering impression of being fully content and satisfied with this life. Leave is not with me the return to the security of a harbour, but a continuation of an uncertain present in a different location. Neither one nor the other is my real world but both are contiguous parts of a stream of existence. And so while at any moment I have the whole of myself to give, my companions have only a part of themselves.

It is in the nature of wartime friendships that they should be looked upon as temporary conveniences, destined to be short lived, subject to sudden change and disruption, and, because of the heightened tempo of life generally, that they should burn more brightly and intensely. Meetings and partings are quickly effected and to most people leave their essence undisturbed which is elsewhere and sensitive only to different fluctuations. But I respond to this brightness in depth. Sudden changes of surroundings are whole uprootings. The loss of a companion an intimate and complete loss. My demands naturally seem excessive because they are made to that part of people which is not here in currency.

I have one life, one track, one continuum of existence. Others have two lives and two tracks. When I tried to look upon leave as a thing separate from its enclosing periods of service it was infinitely disturbing and distressing. A shapeless ten days of distraction and lingering among the mournful relics of a meaningless past. When I look upon leave as a continuation of the present, a stretch of the rails through different scenery and a different gradient, it is possible to preserve some sort of continuity. In a sense I get more out of this life than the others because I can bring all my faculties to bear on it. I don't much like it but at the same time there is nothing else that I can say I should certainly like better. At the same time I have less stamina for the bad patches. The physical hardships of normal army existence crush and bruise my mind and force it to compensate by living in a hot house of sentimentality. I get lost in the minor miseries of cold, work, parades, and the sordid crushed discomfort of everything. I have not the sustaining knowledge of a separate existence somewhere else.

17 April 1944 It is a spring evening in England. The sun is still burning fiercely and the sky is a clear china blue. Outside the concrete hut where I am writing a long field stretches away to the line of hedges that separate it from the adjoining farmlands. The corner of the field nearest to me has been marked off with some coils of rusty barbed wire festooned between posts. The square is just big enough to contain two bell tents and the necessary space to walk between them. Empty food tins and various eating utensils lie stacked up in one corner. Articles of clothing have been crucified on the wire to dry. Pails and other sanitary equipment occupy another corner. An ablution bench is placed against the further bank of wire. In spite of the confined space and the barbed wire everything has the improvised look of gipsy life. Outside one of the tents an Italian is standing whistling to himself a tune which is unfamiliar: hands in pockets, his face emptied of all expression except a slightly sullen bitterness. But because of the clearness and youthfulness of the features the bitterness is attached to them lightly and not bitten in. There is nothing distinguished about him except perhaps that he is fair and his eyes are grey and his skin white which is unusual in an Italian. From a distance it would be more natural to take him for an Englishman were it not that his present precise location within the barbed wire makes such a thing impossible. Apart from him and myself there is nobody about at the moment; the guards have gone to tea and most other people I suppose are getting ready to go out. But it is unlikely that he is aware even of my existence because the sun is shining full on his face and the inside of the hut where I am sitting must be almost invisible. Nevertheless, there are only about five yards between us and it would be quite easy to draw his attention by speaking. Indeed in such a situation it might seem the most natural thing to do, something one could hardly avoid doing. But as it is, even if I wanted to, I could not speak to him, because apart from the regulations we have no language in common. Nevertheless, it could not be said that we are entirely strangers. There is quite a lot I know about him which years of ordinary acquaintance would never reveal. I know certain statistical facts such as one might find inscribed on a plaque below the cage of a wild animal. I know his name and the date of his birth and the place and date of his capture, and the name of his mother and father and his home town and occupation. Furthermore, I could, if I felt inclined, become acquainted with the state of his health, the nature of any past or present illnesses, the condition of various parts of his anatomy, his blood pressure, lung measurements, reflex responses, eyesight and ears, weight, urinary content, and the state of his teeth. The facts relate to things of unquestionable value and importance, but when I look at him I can only see an impenetrable human mystery.

18 April 1944 I want to set down all I can remember of what Graham Sutherland said last Sunday about painting. We were discussing the question of perfection in art. It started by S. telling us of someone who had bought a painting of his asking him some time afterwards whether he could do anything about a small area in the right-hand bottom corner which somehow the client found unsatisfactory. S. was much impressed by this and agreed to take the painting back and do what he could because he knew himself that this was the one point in the picture which was not quite resolved. That led on to the suggestion as a general principle that in all great paintings there was always one such point, a flaw if you like, which had not been completely resolved, and which was in fact essential to the strength and beauty of the whole work. The flaw could not be repaired without the whole painting being damaged. It was as if a painting were trying to approach a complete equilibrium but could never quite reach it; if it did it would disintegrate, the tension would snap. Whether or not a person was sensitive to this particular quality could be tested by asking him which he preferred: Bellini's 'Agony in the Garden', or Mantegna's. The Mantegna is obviously the more perfect. The articulation of the whole picture space is flawless; the transition from body to limb from limb to hand and hand to fingers is effortless and consummate. Bellini's is altogether different. There is a tremendous sense of strain in bringing the objects into relationship. A feeling of anxiety that it may at any moment not quite succeed, and the whole picture fail. This feeling permeates the whole picture, it gives a vibrant tension to every relationship. The Bellini is the greater picture. The Mantegna is the more perfect.

He mentioned Seurat's 'Bathers' as another example of a painting which was very nearly perfect, but was made into a great painting by the one or two places where it didn't quite come off. It is the recognition of these places that gives a scale for measuring the greatness of the achievement in the rest of the picture. He said in some of

Picasso's paintings one never seems to come to the end. One resolves form after form but still further forms are disclosed which need resolving. He would not like to have one of these pictures on his wall, he said.

I asked him if he thought it was still possible to paint the great myths; Prometheus, for instance, or a Crucifixion or an Agony in the Garden. I said I didn't see they had become any less valid for certain individuals merely because they had ceased to be generally accepted. He said there was no real reason why they should not be painted if one could feel strongly enough about them. The question of understanding the subject and not simply illustrating it was so important. It is essential that one can believe in the reality of the subject. For example, it is possible to paint a picture of a man being attacked by a dog because such a situation, though not necessarily experienced, is sufficiently near to experience for the imagination to be able to handle it truthfully. Whereas a man being attacked by a lion is incomprehensible to anyone who has not been so attacked, and so is not a legitimate subject for most painters. As for a Crucifixion he did not know whether there was anyone who could handle it. 'It is an embarrassing situation,' he said, 'to say the least of it, to contemplate a man nailed to a piece of wood in the presence of his friends.'

28 April 1944   Yesterday I went to Castle Howard. From the York road you can see the bone-coloured mausoleum riding in a trough of the wooden hills. The house lies invisibly tucked between two further folds of the hills. The day was gentle with spring and the sun hot with summer in the hollows that were sheltered from the wind. The green reborn earth tapped against the carcass of myself in which I walked alone with a silent fidgeting crowd of wishes. I walked down the lane to Welburn with the neat houses and old stone and ivy walls and then across fields skirting the edges of ploughland to the wood and over the stream and up the steep bank knee-deep in dry leaves and the furry fronds of bracken upstanding like a bishop's mace. At the top was the open sky and the elegant façade stood against trees in the distance. When I got to it everything seemed abandoned. There was no sound, I crossed over the broken wall and skirted the lake choked with weed and water lilies. The front lawn lay in neat symmetrical design, drawn out with box hedges and centred by a fountain of giant mermen with Atlas upholding a green earth. Everything about the fountain was hideous except the soft lichen-crusted stone which seemed falling apart from excessive absorption of light.

Lead copies from the antique stood here and there at carefully haphazard points. The lead too seemed to have grown soft through soaking in sunlight and the figures leaned grotesquely on terribly fractured limbs with abdomens and buttocks splitting open and bleeding; a green ooze of moss and black fungus. Everything lay in the still torpor of neglect and disintegration, as though at the bottom of the sea. The house throbbed with a honey coloured warmth as though the sun itself ran in its veins. Only a stone screen remained open to the sky and air on every side.

I walked back across the lawns and up the bank of daffodils and narcissi and lay down under one of the big trees. The air ticked with small insects, and a summerish haze added to the blurred outlines of the neglected gardens. How little of the life could be reconstructed from what remained. A hand covering a yawn behind closed windows; an expensive chair moved out of the rays of the encroaching sun. Bees and croquet in summer and long white dresses. Rosewood and velvet and leather-bound books unopened.

A small girl in a school dress came out unexpectedly from one of the far wings and began painting the pole of a tennis net. She seemed tiny and unimportant in the huge setting. Then from behind me appeared a youth in green corduroys who dropped me a glance and a greeting and swung down the bank with loose strides through the clusters of narcissi and out across the lawns to the stables gateway.

I walked along the wall of the orchard and through the half-ruined stables and the farm and out on to the road. The idiot obelisk rose monotonously in the distant line of trees. The road runs in a mathematically straight line from one obelisk to another with a rise in the middle topped by a sumptuous arch. Looking from the arch in either direction the tip of an obelisk lies like the pointer of a gyro-compass exactly in the centre. In a car one would be compelled to drive exactly down the centre of such a road. At the far exit was a notice saying: 'Out of Bounds to all Troops.'

16 June 1944 The tragedy today is that everyone has now come to accept the destruction in this war as a natural way of life. It has become too vast for them. Instead of being themselves enlarged by it they reduce its conception until it fits with routine habits. It is now just a question of small selfish griefs over personal losses. This is the ultimate betrayal of the dead.

I think we entered this war in a fairly adult frame of mind. In everyone's heart was the huge unspoken horror at the enormous massacre and destruction that was about to take place. People did not try to belittle this although they seldom spoke of it. They set themselves to a task which they felt was hideous and necessary. Dunkirk and the bombing of London were the first fruits of the crop they knew they had to reap. People achieved moments of real greatness during that time. They accepted the full weight of suffering without breaking, or taking it out on other people. Rather selfish people were suddenly able to be spontaneously generous.

By the time America joined in we were back again in our infancy playing at soldiers. Uniform was the smart new fashion for which all the girls fell. There were little squabbles over service medals and stripes. Heroes were fêted for their prowess at killing. Wounded soldiers, in spite of what had been seen beneath bombed buildings and in the gutters of burning London, were suddenly good looking young men in attractive head bandages. All the toys were brought out again, the big guns and battleships and charming nurses. The newspaper strategists began their exciting armchair yarns. This was the immensely exciting game for young and old; for anyone with a pencil and paper and map. Everyone not actually fighting settled down to enjoy the war. The purpose of it all was just to win. Peace aims were of only speculative interest like the fish and chips after the football match.

Now once again the towns and villages of France are being ground and battered to mud and dust. The wounds of 1941 are being cut open in bright red ribbons. People are being killed and maimed with absolute certainty and precision. But people prefer not to be reminded of such things. The thing is Victory, unqualified and unconditional. The human cost, as the financial, is entirely a matter of figures which can be extended indefinitely. Everything is organized, and smoothly running. Pity and compassion and all immeasurable emotions have no place at all. Men are broken, put together, reconditioned, and set in motion again. That is all there is to it.

Each part in the game is also interchangeable. German prisoners step off the boat at an English port smiling like tourists, waving to the camera men. From being hunted and slaughtered like vermin they are entertained as guests. They have simply moved from one section of the board to another where different things happen to be going on. The game needs an enemy and it needs prisoners. It is necessary only that everyone remembers to play the right part at the right time. A catastrophe would happen if someone smiled at an enemy or shot a prisoner, but apart from a slight uncertainty in the weather everything has been worked out and everyone knows his cue.

Attacking forces know they must move forward and hold strategic points. Bridgeheads know they must be held. Supplies know they must move up at the proper time. The enemy know they must go on fighting until they lose. Mines and booby traps must be laid and later moved, after blowing off a calculated number of arms and legs. The wounded know they must scream and wait to be picked up. The people who read the papers know they must buy flags to help the good looking young men with head bandages. France knows that she must supply marshalling yards to be bombed and wheat fields to be burned; also the map for pins to be stuck into. Churches and houses know they must collapse into rubble suitable for snipers and later on grandstands to view the liberators. A certain percentage of quite innocent people know they must get in the way of precision bombing.

So long as there is no cosmic catastrophe or gross mathematical error in calculation, and so long as the supply of living people and material resources holds out, there is no reason why the war should not go on indefinitely.

20 June 1944 Cinema tonight: an impressive display of the war material of the Allies. The accumulated wealth and skill from every part of the world. Orderly stacks of food, bombs, medical supplies, tanks, lorries, locomotives, guns, aircraft. A man checking the rows of boxes, a cranesman manoeuvring a heavy load on to the quayside. The aircraftsman putting the finishing touches to his machine. And on every face the same bright self-satisfied smile of people conscious that they are sharing together in an enormous undertaking.

Obviously there is no doubt about the achievement in concentrating into the British Isles the war potential of more than half the world. But each man sees only a fraction of the marvellous whole.

I know what it feels like to stack boxes all day as they come off a rolling belt. One thinks of the size and weight, the need to co-ordinate one's muscles to handling them with the minimum of exertion. Questions of smoothness and roughness are important, textures of wood and the nails at the corners. One is not concerned with the contents or its purpose but appreciates a box as an absolute thing in itself. The way the markings are placed, the raw smell of the wood, the way to avoid the corners catching in the rollers. One gains a tactile understanding of a wooden box, and beyond that is simply the framework of the working day. The time you knock off for lunch, or pause to light a cigarette. the soreness of hands and the sense of relaxation in the evenings. But all this has no connection with the contents of the wooden box or its relation to the war effort as a whole.

The only real thing seems to be the personal experience of the thing one is doing. The relation of that thing to other things is purely conjectural. The experience of loading packing cases remains the same irrespective of the contents or its destination.

By extension this covers the whole war. Each man is confined within the emotional field generated by his own particular activity. Driving a tank, loading shells into a gun, fixing pieces of plywood together, sweeping out a hut. And behind that pursuing his normal course of wondering, wishing, remembering, joking, and talking. One can appreciate the relationship of one's own activity to its immediate aim; the unloading of packing cases to the completed stack, the driving of a tank to the opposition of the enemy, the firing of a gun to the destruction of an objective. But is anyone capable of seeing his own part in relation to the true pattern of life today?

When a tank meets a tank both fire guns, objectives are hit, and men are burnt to death; but between the penultimate and ultimate stages there is no willed connection. The desired purpose is achieved when the objective is hit. Anyone meeting a tank and knowing it to be dangerous would fire at it in self protection, but few people would burn to death three total strangers in a steel coffin. And it is precisely in order to isolate the reality of this final phase, in order to depersonalise it and disguise it as something other than it is, that every ingenuity of language and psychological conditioning has to be constantly employed in order that human beings may be made into efficient soldiers. The whole problem of morale is how to bring what is essentially inhuman behaviour within the compass of ordinary human beings. Individual casualties such as certain war neuroses, and social casualties such as conscientious objectors happen when the immunization fails to take.

If the time ever came when it was no longer necessary to employ these techniques, if men could accept fully the ultimate consequences of their actions and affirm them as just and necessary and in accord with their human status, then one might be justified in saying our civilization was a failure. And just so long as this gulf is preserved and men are enabled to escape the full consequences of individual action, it can never be a success.

22 June 1944   At 4.30 one fine summer afternoon an aircraft dived out of the sky and sprayed a small village with machine gun fire. Such things happen every day, I know, but I want to consider this one particular instance. In two separate dives across the village, in the space of 38 seconds, 14 people were killed and 11 injured. The whole thing was photographed by one of the planes and we saw it in a newsreel.

I know perfectly well what a small country village is like. I know the general atmosphere of peace and fertility and the sense of a natural order of things. I know the hard and small sort of life the people live there. The tiny things they bicker about and the important things that they manage with an unconscious grace. I know what it feels like to be young and beginning life, and I can imagine something of what it will be like to be middle-aged and old. I know the complication of private things that go to make the life of one individual in that village. Then all at once 14 people are killed and 11 injured for no very obvious purpose. The dead are dead; it is the living that matter.

Let us increase the focal length and look closer. Those who are not physically hurt have suffered the loss of someone who was a mainstay of their lives. I know the immediate effect of such things. I can imagine as the years follow how their lives are changed and reformed to accommodate this unhealing wound. Some are strengthened, others incurably deformed by it. I can imagine the girl who was fond of music and played instruments and whose wrists are now shattered. Or the boy who did nothing in particular; but whose delight was in the sight of living things – and whose eyes are now blinded. I can imagine the elderly couple, with an only child, whose lives had failed to work out very happily, but who had come to find hope and justification for everything in this child. I can imagine the agony of the mother who holds the dead child in her lap in the unbelievable sunlight.

In ten years the whole incident will be forgotten. The aircraft will be forgotten, the pilot forgotten. The girl who might have been a musician will be the matron at the local school. The old couple will be dead. The boy who was blinded will be well cared for by an institution. In 38 seconds on a summer afternoon seeds of misery and grief were sown which grow for more than one generation. Something atrocious has been done, and someone must be responsible.

I can imagine the excitement of flying a plane. The sense of danger and responsibility. The moment when the fatherland relies on you. I understand the breathless thrill of the 500 mph dive, the tiny geo-metrical target, slowly growing closer, taking shape. The moment of satisfaction when the plane is pulled out of the dive and a soft pressure on the thumb-balls sends eight bursting scars of dust across the ground. Tiny figures scattering like chickens. The church tower grazing the bottom of the plane like a pencil. The timing, the nerve, the steady hands and eyes and beautiful synchronization, and the relaxed happy flight back to base through the fluffy clouds with the thought of stories and drinks in the mess.

I can understand the planners behind maps who deal in figures and codes and control an enormous mathematical equation with skill.

I understand the engineers and scientists who spend long nights with coffee and green eye-shades designing and perfecting the weapons of destruction.

I understand the statesmen caught in a web of precedent and honour who set the weapons in motion against their personal wishes for the sake of a clean page in the history books.

But something monstrous has been done and someone must be responsible. Who is responsible? Each in his own set of circumstances has only followed out the path allotted him. Each has displayed skill and courage and served a purpose beyond his own personal interests. Who is responsible?

24 June 1944 I see the average Nazi as a man driven to commit outrages partly by the pressure of circumstances, partly through belief in a set of ideas which are contrary to my own, partly through deliberate corruption of his judgments, and partly through the exercise of free choice. Behind every atrocity is a human being whose humanity has been skilfully twisted, whose hopes were fed on lies, whose natural longings were turned into depraved cravings. At what point does he cease to have the capacity to be human again? And at what point did he have the choice between being a Nazi and not being a Nazi and thereby incurring the guilt for his crimes? The magnitude of the crime itself cannot be the deciding factor. Many would have committed worse crimes than they did if opportunities had come their way. Many were driven beyond the satisfaction of any sadistic craving because they were caught up in something from which they could not break loose.

In this camp there was a prisoner who worked in the quartermaster's store. He was industrious, efficient, polite, and well behaved. I had many conversations with him about politics, his home, and France where he had been stationed some years before his capture. I did not like him much, he was too downright in his views which were those of a small and tidy mind, but there was nothing about him to suggest abnormal or criminal tendencies. Later it was discovered by chance that during his time in France he had been employed in a prison where it was his job to prepare, bind, and blindfold condemned prisoners for execution. The whole circumstances were discovered by his revealing in an unguarded moment of enthusiasm the fact that he had invented some gadget for hanging round the condemned man's neck which enabled the fire to be better concentrated. He had volunteered for his particular job.

' "Tout comprendre c'est tout pardonner" ,' says Koestler, 'is one of the woolliest phrases ever uttered', with which I agree in so far as the ethical judgment of an action is not invalidated by an understanding of its motivation. But an ethical judgment and its execution must hold out reasonable hope of effecting an improvement on the ethical level for it to be valid.

There was a small paragraph in the press at the time of the Kharkov trials when the deputy director of the Gestapo in Kharkov, aged twenty, on being sentenced to death besought the court through tears to let him live in order that he might try to undo some of the evil he had done. It could of course have been no more than a last minute effort to save his own skin. But it could have been otherwise. By ordinary ethical standards no man could more have deserved the sentence than he who had ordered the death and torture of innocent people. But his death will not redeem theirs or cancel out the crime. It simply adds to a crime which finally becomes anonymous. Sentiment and prejudice apart, it must be admitted that had he been given his life at Kharkov he might have had a zest for atonement which no one without his past possibly could have. Was not Paul regarded as the greatest of the apostles for precisely such a reason! By destroying the perpetrators of evil one does not destroy evil, but one may destroy a powerful potential for good. Of course, one could not hope to find much patience with such a suggestion just now.

If each case could be analysed in depth it might be possible to decide with reasonable certainty whether there was a potential source of danger or good for the future. Obviously this is not possible. One could perhaps make a distinction based on general psychological knowledge. It is more difficult for a person to be changed over a certain age than under. To the younger should be given the best treatment in rehabilitation that psychotherapy and human understanding can contrive, irrespective of the nature or extent of their crimes. To those over the age against whom crimes were proven one might say: 'The difficulties and risks of bringing you back into society are too great under the present circumstances. You are a liability we cannot and do not need to afford. Here is a cup of hemlock and the works of Goethe. The carbon monoxide will be turned on at midnight.'

6 September 1944 I am reading Fournier's *Le Grand Meaulnes*. Outside the rain has fallen ceaselessly for five days. Water stands about in wide shallows over the grass and paths. None of the prisoners can go out to work. As many as can have been given little jobs about the camp. Some, armed with brush and whitewash bucket, go round the huts painting everything within reach white. Some are chopping wood in a shed. Some are busily occupied simulating work in order to avoid being given it. Some are doing things for someone else to undo later. The air is damp and chill without life. Summer seems to be finished and autumn not yet begun. In this setting and mood, a mood which brings a seasonal nostalgia for firesides, quietly furnished rooms, the flicker of flames over a silver teapot, fine china, a smell of toast and withered roses, velvet curtains drawn across rain blurred windows, the descriptions of childhood in a small French town are peculiarly vivid. The old house with long dark corridors, the huge empty granaries overhead, frost and snow on the lawns and pavements. The stove in the gaunt bare classroom with a huddle of boys. The quietness and the sudden wild noises of games. The blacksmith's shop up the road, a brilliant rose of heat in the white winter cold. The long Sunday afternoon – 'tiède et pesante', grand-père, grand'mère. A sense of ennui without frustration. All this is as if I too had lived it, yet it is hard to find any correspondence in actual facts. Perhaps it is in the vivid sense of a primary security – the authority of family life and the school, an authority against which one may rebel, struggle, intrigue, which may at times appear sinister, suffocating, but which is always inviolable, beyond doubt, the hub of one's revolutions, that Fournier succeeds so well in recreating the spiritual environment of all childhood. In the simplest things there is a touch of magic. A world which is half real, half fantasy. Nothing is exactly predictable, no one knows in what degree a child's imagination will transform the most commonplace incident, yet nothing can shatter the primary bond of the child's security.

It is the season for feeling such thoughts. The world's pageant of summer is over. The stalls are empty. The marquees sag on their poles. The lawns become spongy with rain. The gay colour, the uniting warmth is gone. Life drains back into its roots, into the dark, into the womb, into dry and mossy holes scooped in secret places, stocked with food for the winter. It is the season when solitude is least burdensome. When a sense of security is not hard to achieve. The year's hunt is over, the prize has been won or lost. '*Wer jetzt kein Haus hat, baut sich keines mehr. Wer jetzt allein ist, wird es lange bleiben.*'

11 October 1944 The night they arrived was also the night of the gale. We heard it said afterwards that in the opinion of many it was the worst gale around these parts within living memory, but there was nothing to suggest its approach when the blurred ranks of field grey appeared at the entrance about five o'clock on a mild autumn afternoon. In the watery yellow light the only immediate difference between the straggling rows of men and the rows of kit that were stood alongside them was that the former could move of their own accord.

For weeks we had been sufficiently occupied with the details of administration to have no time to speculate on any personal aspects, but when the first words of German rang out on the still air a spell seemed to fall over the camp. One had the feeling of something sinister and dangerous being near. For a short moment when the guarded eyes of the British met the glazed stare of the lines of Germans, the well-rehearsed course of probability seemed to hesitate, and one felt it conceivable that anything could happen. Then organization took control and everything went as planned.

They were herded through the barbed wire and divided and sub-divided into groups and parties, and the NCOs with fluttering white papers went in and out of the slowing, shaping mass like sheepdogs. All was orderly and quiet. One was conscious of white faces and enormous staring eyes which followed one's every movement.

There was the search and documentation and medical inspection and allocation of huts and bedding. The search was first and took longest.

Three tables had been set up in the biggest hut with an officer or NCO at each and the prisoners formed up in three lines. Each in his turn emptied his kit bag on the floor and the contents of his pockets on to the table. We took their name and rank and regiment and age and religion and profession and gave in return a number of many figures. All this took time because of difficulties with the spelling and the fact that the interpreters had not yet arrived. A few knew some English and some of us a little German, the formal, excessively polite idioms of the phrase books, so the whole thing was conducted with the utmost decorum.

When they had first appeared all together it had seemed impossible ever to distinguish one from the other, but now that they came up singly to the tables quite important differences became apparent.

Some were hardly able to stand or speak, either from exhaustion or because they were hollowed right out with fear. They fumbled and dropped things, or they just stood trembling and inert. Some came up smiling and smothered the table instantly with worthless rubbish, shaking out their inverted pockets to convince us of their innocence, eager to supply a short history of each article and to disclose the identities of photographs. Some smiled cynically, saluted smartly, and were deliberately slow and casual. Others, a few older ones, cried quietly the whole time, letting the tears cut white channels down their grimed cheeks. They brought out their belongings like disgraced schoolboys showing their copybooks to the headmaster. Mostly, they were young. Some were just children.

Some had nothing but a few crumpled letters, a photograph, and a crust of bread rolled up in what might once have been a pair of socks. Others had many and various possessions. There was one who was short and fat with a bald head and thick glasses. He happened to be in my group and I had noticed him when he was still some way down the line because he was incessantly fidgeting and fussing and keeping a check on his things which he carried in two cases and two sacks. Everyone was amused at him because he was so like a flustered tourist who cannot find a porter. When his turn came he was sweating with anxiety and his hands trembled as he laid on the table one after another leather cases of shaving tackle, writing materials, books, fountain pen, a watch, a travelling ink bottle, and a long silver pencil. I felt his breath beating on the top of my head as I bent over and ran my hands quickly over his pockets. I picked up the silver pencil. It was the sort that is made to hold a short length of cedar pencil, not the modern propelling type. It was beautifully wrought and embossed with vine leaves and laurel and engraved with initials, not his own.

'What a lovely pencil.' I said.

His face lit up at once with pleasure. 'You like it – Yes.' I asked him his profession and he said he was an architect from Wetzlar. I told him to put his things away while I filled up the forms. He packed everything carefully away again into the two cases and sacks and moved off quickly and left the pencil in the middle of the table.

'You've forgotten something,' I called, and pointed to the pencil.

He stopped and looked confused and said nothing. I held it out to him.

'Your pencil,' I said. He took it uncertainly, not knowing what to do with his embarrassment.

'Thank you,' I said, 'It's not allowed.'

'Not allowed – ah – verboten – verboten – entschuldigen.' And he went off bewildered, submissive, fat, middle-aged, unhappy.

It took nearly two hours to get through. With so many people about it was the silence that was strangest. It was a positive silence like that of a cathedral, which made one want to lower one's voice. When the last man had left the air was rancid with the smell of dirt and sweat and exhaustion. A thick blanket of dust lay over everything – the soil of France. When we had finished and went outside it was dusk and the wind had started.

It began with a wild waving in the top branches of the elm trees beyond the compound. Doors banged suddenly and people walked as though they were climbing a steep gradient. Words were torn out of one's mouth before they could be uttered. As night closed in the wind bore down on the camp and fastened its million claws into every crevice. It tore screaming through the barbed wire and across the concrete and raced away howling into the dales. The two great marquees swayed and groaned like ships straining their moorings and searching for the rocks. The night was full of unidentifiable noises. Every inanimate thing found its own particular moan and note of protest until the darkness was crowded with furious torment. In the low howling huts the English lay and the Germans lay sleeping for the first time in safety. If anyone had called his words would not have been heard. All night the wind blew with fury, tearing at each standing thing, hollowing out all secret places, overturning the little tables of incomplete justice, impetuous, replenishing, cleansing.

16 October 1944   It was hardly light when I went over to breakfast. The air was a cold colourless grey. One of the prisoners who had arrived the day before was sitting on the low stone parapet outside the cookhouse. He had been sent to work there and was waiting for someone to tell him what to do. The ginger cat was crouched on his lap and he ran his fingers through the thick creamy fur, over and over as though he would absorb all the softness into them. The cat received this unusual attention with placid indifference.

When I came by half an hour later he was in the same position, his hands buried in the cat's softness. He head was sunk low on his chest and the wind blew on the top of his skull and caught locks of fair hair and flung them one after another across his forehead sharply like the leaves of a book. The morning flight of bombers was crossing the sky, low and invisible above the hanging cloud and filling the air with a throbbing blanket of sound. As I passed he raised his head and looked up. His face was white and smooth like a child's and his eyes, sunk in craters of darkness, were brimming with tears.

But the morning was cold with a sharp wind that brings tears easily to the eyes.

20 October 1944   There is a big fair chap who comes from Ashton-in-Makerfield – the road to Wigan Pier – one of England's debit columns. But he seems to have survived the degradation pretty well. He has a loose adolescent physique, smooth clear skin, big hands. There is a strain and uncoordination about his movements like a powerful machine that is not properly under control. He shouts and waves his arms at the Germans, gesticulating and urging them into position. His face is fretted with a perpetual frown and he is poised ready to pounce one way or another whenever things look like getting out of hand. But the prisoners have no intention of getting out of hand, nor of being hurried or disturbed by his excitement. They line up leisurely, chattering among themselves, slouching, grinning stupidly at passers-by. They take no special notice of him but carry out his orders with conspicuously less exertion than it takes him to give them. When all is in order and they are ready to move off, his face falls open into a vacant and slightly aggressive gaze.

Standing next to him at the head of the column is a German of about his same height and age. He wears cream coloured overalls over his grey tunic with brown circular patches. His greasy cap is pulled down on top of his ears and honey-coloured fronds of hair have sprouted out here and there. He carries a piece of white dry wood under his arm. Momentarily detached from the huddle of conversation going on behind, his face has also relaxed into the same animal vacancy. Both look out over the heads of the assembling squads and the lorries and the low shallow roofs of the barracks to the faintly reddening far off sky.

Behind each momentarily identical expression is a different personal history.

Behind one gaze is the grime and sweat of an ugly childhood where every small thing must be fought for and every advantage wrested from someone else. Rows of toy houses with blackened bricks. The Sunday streets washed by rain and boredom. The hundreds of beseeching grey-faced windows sickly looking like starved dogs. A small hard world closely confined, surrounded by the armed sentinels of the chimneys preventing escape.

Behind the other gaze is a past of excitement and violence. Marches, and rallies, and camp fires in the forests at night. Great emotions and little ideas. No responsibility and no loneliness. Leather shorts and small daggers and a complicated system of badges.

Now they stand side by side, each gaze filled with the same perplexity, a mirror and its reflection, each locked in the prison of his past, unaware of each other except as a cypher, a formula, a mass-produced caricature.

21 October 1944 He comes from the Gorbals. He is tall with red hair and the delicate looking skin that goes with red hair. He stoops a little forward, a habit induced perhaps by his tallness, and his neck curves forward and up from his shoulders in a clear sweep. Everything about his face has the appearance of curling slightly upwards like petals, his lips, eyelashes, and the lock of fine silky hair on his forehead. He talks with the soft liquid syllables of the lowland Scot and his vocabulary consists almost entirely of obscenities uttered with a caressing mildness.

The question arose of filling in the forms for the Army Education Scheme, showing the choice of subjects. I asked him what his civilian job had been and he said tiler and slate layer. I asked him what he wanted to do after the war and he said the same thing, of course. I said wasn't there something else perhaps that he was interested in and would like to take up and he said no, why, what was wrong with tiling and slate laying. I said there was nothing wrong with it but wouldn't he like perhaps to learn about something else.

'There's nothing anyone can teach me about my trade,' he said, 'I've been doing it for four years before the war. I know more about it than any of these buggers who get up and start spouting. And why should I want to know anything else? Where's it going to get me anyhow? I know my job and there always work for me to do. That's enough for me.'

'But is there no hobby or anything you'd be interested in developing?' I said.

'Hobby – what sort of stuff is that? When I'm working I'm working and after work I enjoy myself – have a good time. What's wrong with that?'

'Nothing – but aren't you interested in the world around you, what's happening, what other people are doing and trying to plan?' I asked rather sheepishly.

'Not from books or listening to guys spouting about it,' he said. 'If you live in Glasgow you see plenty going on. You don't need to sit on your bum all day reading about it. Where would it get me? – Just tell me that. . . .'

It would get him, if it got him anywhere at all, to a point of restless dissatisfaction with his present comfortable limitations; would leave him with doubts and uncertainties over what hitherto he had taken for granted but without giving him the intellectual capacity to rethink the problems all over again on a more complex level. But I didn't tell him this.

While we were talking his face was so clear and sensitive that it registered the weight of every word that was said to him. He came to this unit because a psychiatrist reported him as 'dull and backward at training and unlikely to make an efficient soldier'. He left here shortly afterwards on his twenty-third birthday.

22 October 1944 P. is nineteen and the youngest here. He has a fresh face and shy eyes and thick auburn hair. He sits huddled in the arm-chair by the stove with his enormous boots in the white ashes. He is careful to keep his eyes on the ground all the time, yet seems to be listening intently to everything going on around. If anyone speaks to him he looks up covered with shyness and smiles. The older men tease and pet him but he only smiles and says nothing.

At first he was given duties on the police, but when he was found one cold night curled up at the bottom of the sentry box fast asleep he was given twenty-eight days' detention and put on escort duties when he came back.

One day a letter came from his mother. It was written in the painstaking script of a child, the result of several fair copies. She had not heard from him and was anxious. The captain sent for him. He was pale and frightened when he went in and came out after some minutes blushing furiously and his smooth innocent face had a strange roughened look as though deep inside him something fierce had awoken and wanted to be expressed.

He is illiterate. It seems that somehow or other the question of teaching him to read and write was overlooked. At fourteen he went to work at a steel works where he had to catch metal sheets as they came off a machine and stack them. Later he cut up scrap metal into convenient sizes for remelting. His documents say 'very little schooling'. And his SP sheet 100A (Confidential) says: 'Lacks both intelligence and education. Cannot read or write. Has little ability.'

Officially his peacetime job is known as 'Scrap Boy'. What is to become of scrap boys in the new world? Can they too be melted down to make some useful ingredient for the *Wiederaufbau*?

27 October 1944 So Princess Beatrice has died in her sleep. At a time like this it is difficult to bring facts of this nature into any sort of emotional focus.

One old lady who married a German prince, who lost a son to German bullets. Who moved about her well-upholstered world with dignity and ease. Who cut tapes and opened bazaars and fulfilled patiently the empty conventions of a vanished world. Played croquet on the lawns of Granbridge and lived in a private suite at Carisbrooke where the windows look out on to giant yellowing chestnuts and still pines. Who collected the autographs of her cousins and nieces and children, the unhappy royal families of Europe, and had, so we are told, 'an exceptional talent for water colours'.

The elaborate machinery that isolates her world from ours is old and liable to break down yet still continues to work. In a world where the young die violently, unwillingly, out of time, she could succeed in dying her own special death in her own appropriate way. That is only as it should be. The matter becomes slightly vexing only when it is made out to be a public grief and loss. What scale can measure the timely death of one old royal lady and the murder of 10,000 young men in the unselective violence of battle.

4 December 1944   They were singing carols in the village as I walked through. It was cold and the wide sky was ablaze with stars. Under the lamp by the green they stood together in a little huddle and as I passed they were singing 'Once in Royal David's City'. They sang well. Not the raw piping of children, nor the throaty selfconscious mouthing of people who go carol singing for a social lark. They sang with trained voices simply, and the clear tones fell on the frosty air with the freshness that they once had when the words were spoken from the heart to celebrate a great story. At such a moment it was not hard to believe in the greatness of the Christian idea. There had never seemed to be quite so many stars as tonight. And the very immaculate peacefulness of the night – peace seemed so much a priceless unattainable and precious thing. And I remembered how the Germans sang 'Stille Nacht' the other night, and how impossible it is to stand out against that when it is sung by young voices in German. Something both in the singers and the hearers is transformed, as though it was a solemn rite commemorating something whose significance can no longer be clearly stated, but which must at all costs be carefully preserved.

9 December 1944   Otto was our mess waiter. He was small and thin and nineteen years old with golden hair and white skin and seven grey holes in his body from Russian bullets. He scrubbed the benches and the floor and kept the fires going. He set the tables for meals, brought us our food and cleared it away and washed up. In the afternoons, when he was finished, he would put a huge iron on the fire and bring in a bundle of our uniforms which he would sponge and press, sew on buttons and darn, or alter collars and necks to make them fit. He was a tailor's apprentice from Hamburg. He started work about six in the morning and was seldom finished before eight. The only time when he seemed anything but happy was when the wireless was blazing out the news. He did not understand the language, but I suppose the tone of voice told him all he needed to know. At such moments he would contrive if possible to be washing up so that he could bend his head over the bowl and listen intently to his own clatter. Sometimes in the early morning I would come in and find him examining minutely an English newspaper, as though it were something in code which close attention would eventually solve. The maps were the only things that helped at all. He would put a long white finger on the black spot of Hamburg and Cologne or Berlin and say 'vernichtet'. Feeling that the onesidedness needed some correction I would answer 'und Warsaw, Rotterdam, Coventry, London auch'. 'It is a great madness,' he would say solemnly.

Everyone in the mess was delighted to be waited on with punctilious German politeness. He moved with noiseless speed from table to table and no plate was left empty for a moment. When anyone spoke to him he sprang to attention and answered in clipped polite German. No one minded not understanding – it was intoxicating to be shown such respect. The men shouted ribald pleasantries for the pleasure of seeing him react, and roared with laughter. After a bit he laughed too and gave it up.

In the afternoons I would try to slip across when he was pressing trousers to practise some German on him. I would prepare some suitable opening sentence on the way over, getting the grammar and genders right, and deceived by my fluency he would answer with a torrent of words in which I quickly lost my depth. One day he told me about his friend Ulli with whom he had grown up and who had been killed beside him when he got wounded, but mostly he seemed to want to remember the wonderful leave he had when he left the hospital afterwards. Of his own country he thought only about getting back to his mother and sister 'when the Nazis had gone' and ski-ing in the winter. He always referred to the Nazis in the third person.

One day the order came through that under no circumstances were prisoners to work in the British lines. It was a week before Christmas. Everyone thought the order a great pity.

'So you must go away,' I said to him, 'have they told you?'

He shrugged his shoulders and open his arms with an extravagant gesture of despair and resignation.

'We heard this morning. It is an order. I know that with us too an order has to be obeyed. Man can do nothing.'

'It is a great pity – more for us I think than for you.' I meant it as a compliment, but probably I got the idiom wrong because he took no notice and went on – 'the Major had us in to thank us. Do you know –' he looked at me in sudden eagerness – 'he gave us each twenty cigarettes.'

'That was good.'

'It was very good – he need not have done it. And now we go out and work in the fields.'

'At any rate it won't be such long hours. You got no time off at this job.'

'But when you like the work it is not long. It was not hard to work here. It is everything when you work and people are pleased – people are friendly. Everyone has been so friendly. After everything we had been told and then you come and it is like this. It is unbelievable. I shall not forget what I've seen.'

The colour mounted to his thin face and he bent his head low over the bowl and stretched his arms into the grey water. He started speaking quickly almost as if to himself, and his voice grew louder and began to take on a rhythmic, hypnotic chanting, a voice that was naturally deep and seemed to come strangely from his small body.

'Everywhere people are taught to hate. Everyone must hate the English – but why – ? Hate, and kill, and what happens next? I remember when I was last on leave I went to see my uncle at Hamburg and he said to me "when the English get a foothold in Europe the war is finished" – and I told him he was an old fool and went out. But I knew he was right and I knew I was glad he was right. And I know too now who I hate, the most hated man in Germany.' He drew a greasy finger across the features of Himmler on the ABCA map on the wall and spat, childishly, without spittle – 'what have we reason to hate each other for? Tell me one reason. It only really matters that you meet people and know, doesn't it? The rest is all propaganda. Everywhere people read things and hear things; and when you are in the army you must obey orders, that is the same with you also, and then you meet and everything is different.'

He looked up and the beginnings of a smile lit his mouth, but it was an older smile than I had seen before. He finished the dishes and wiped the grease off his arms and dried his hands. 'It has been so wonderful here, and to think that this is what we were taught to dread more than anything.'

He had taken off his apron and put on his carefully pressed, chocolate coloured jacket. We stood for a moment not having anything more to say. The others were crowded round the billiards table watching a game of snooker. The wireless started to give out the nine o'clock news.

'Also, aufwiedersehen, Otto.' I held out my hand. He sprang to attention with a report that made everyone look up. 'Aufwiedersehen und danke, danke, viel danke.' His cheeks were fiery and his head blazed like a copper sun. He shook his whole body on the end of my arm. He sprung away abruptly down the room to where the others were clustered round the radio and seized each passive astonished arm in turn – 'Aufwiedersehen und danke sehr schön.'

'So long, Otto,' they called.

He raced out of the door with his face bursting.

2 May 1945 On the train coming back. From the window I saw two boys cycling together along a straight wide road which had just been washed by a shower of rain.

I saw an old man bending over a coop of chickens on a small wedge of grass and slowly dropping the grain between his fingers.

I saw two men striding forward across a sown field flinging out handfuls of white powder from a basket slung round their necks. The sky had gone a deep orange colour and we were running into fresh showers.

Each successive image was so vivid that I had the sensation of becoming entirely a part of the whole situation. I could smell the sharp tarry smell of the steaming road; feel the hardness of saddle and the slight ache in the limbs. I could feel the seeds trickling between my fingers, the slightly damp stillness, the smell of chicken dung. Then the spaciousness of the field and the striding forward into the wind and the need to keep the powder out of the eyes.

Each situation was unaware of the existence of the others; only through my observing them did they acquire a certain relationship. In painting one could try to express that relationship.

7 May 1945 Today I went to the river and the sun. Straight down opposite the farm the river bends in a steep curve and the bank is terraced in shelves of mossy turf. I sat under the shelter of the small earth cliff and took off my clothes. There was no one about and the sun was a steady stream of heat. There was no sound except the calling of birds and occasionally a shudder of wings as a large bird dropped down low over the water. I lay back and stretched myself into the brilliant warmth. Years have passed since I last did this.

Perhaps I am the last person in Europe who can still lie in the sun. The thought filled me with a depressing sense of uselessness. Silence lay over everything in a blue dome. The river swept soundlessly along, spinning the tiny clots of froth and combing out the dog-weeds. My closed eyes sunk beneath the burning ruby lake. My arms over my head drew the thin flesh tight over my stomach and the small cage of my ribs. I felt the searching light penetrating into all the dark corners. I knew the grey sponges in my lungs were awaking to the first ruby glow after the long darkness of winter. The air passed between my toes and over my groins. A deep sensual contentment descended over me. The tide rose all through the slow afternoon until everything was submerged in its reviving warmth.

7 May 1945. VE Day They had no wireless in the cottage where I had supper, so I didn't hear the nine o'clock News. Walking back to camp afterwards, the first sign of anything unusual that I noticed was a string of small triangular flags being hoisted up across the road by some workmen. The flags appeared quite suddenly out of the leaf-laden boughs of a chestnut, crossed a patch of sago-coloured sky, and disappeared into the dark foliage of another tree. They looked surprised to be there. They were not new flags. They had flapped for a jubilee and a coronation and numerous local festivals, and now they seemed to be getting a little tired of it all. They were faded and grubby and washed-out-looking. They hung languidly in the bluish evening air. The workmen tapped away at the trees and thrust ladders up into the ripe foliage, bringing down showers of leaves and a snow of pink and white blossom. Further on there was a cottage with two new Union Jacks thrust out from the window-sill. They hung down stiffly to attention. Against the mellow sun-bleached texture of the stone their strident colours looked ridiculous, and because they were there on purpose to disturb the quiet and familiar contours they gave a feeling of uneasiness. From there onwards all the little cottages were sprouting flags.

There was no one about to see them, and no very clear reason how they came to be there. Menacing each other across the lane with their shrill colours they were like a flock of rare and fabulous birds which had alighted suddenly and without warning, clinging to chimney-pots, window-sills and door posts. They were of many different sizes and shapes and attitudes corresponding partly to the income levels and patriotic fervour of their owners, and partly to a certain capriciousness which they seemed to acquire on their own. Some of them, having been unfurled, had hitched themselves up again shyly over the poles. Others had a narrow strip of wood fastened along the extreme edge, so that they were forced to suffer the maximum exposure. The large houses had older flags sewn together from pieces of silk with white painted poles and sometimes a gold tassel. The cottages all had new flags; little pieces of calico dyed with raw-looking colours. When it rained they would run.

Outside one cottage an old woman was standing in a black dress with folded arms. She stood there most evenings, and I had passed her a hundred times without either of us taking any special notice of the other. But tonight she seemed to be standing there for a special purpose, as though expecting something to happen. As I passed her she smiled broadly at me. It was an indescribable smile that lay right across the road blocking my way and demanding an answer. I acknowledged it and hurried past, feeling guilty and uncomfortable and afraid that I might suddenly be called to play some part I had not rehearsed.

On the dung-crusted door of a stable a V had been made with red, white and blue ribbon, and inside the V, hurriedly chalked as an afterthought, a red E. In the little window of the grocer's was a newspaper cutting of the Prime Minister. It was stuck on the window with four large pieces of brown tape like a police notice. In the window that has bird seed and bottles of sauce was a gold frame with a reproduced oil-painting of two exceedingly mild and dignified lions, and in the bottom left-hand corner the word 'PEARS'. In front there was a photograph of the Royal Family in sepia, with the word 'CORONATION' underneath and a round circle of rust from a drawing-pin. All the familiar and reliable things had suddenly disclosed a secret and unsuspected threat, though it would be impossible to say exactly what it was they threatened. But when the last house was passed and there were only fields and hedges and ditches frothing with tall white cow-parsley, there was a feeling of relief and reassurance.

Where the road swings sharply to the right before reaching the camp I crossed the little footbridge and sat down on the stile to smoke a cigarette. Between the layers of high lead-coloured cloud and the horizon a narrow margin had been left in which the sun burned an enormous liquid orange disc. The air was like a thin violet fluid. In the further field was the boy who drives the tractor every morning past the camp. He was shooing some geese under a fence and into the straw-strewn yard of the cowhouse. He walked slowly forward towards the geese and at each step brought both arms up simultaneously above his head as though he were lifting something large that had suddenly lost all weight. His skin and clothes were soaked with the orange liquid from the sun. When the geese had gone he went out of sight behind the barn.

The near field was full of sheep. The full, woolly forms with sharp accents of light against the dark grass, the alternation between light-coloured sheep and dark ones, small and large, had that air of carefully planned accident which one sometimes sees in paintings, but not often in nature. They glowed a deep gold colour like lumps of phosphorescent substance, and there were little pools of violet between their legs and in their ears. Two sheep had strayed down on to the steep bank of the ditch and were tearing ravenously at the thick, dark water-grass which met over their backs. They had pushed their way through gaps in the hedge and seemed to be expecting at any moment to be driven back. They were gulping as much as they could in the time, their eyes wide with anxiety. Standing almost vertically face downwards, they seemed to be in the most dis-advantageous position both for eating and for coping with any sudden emergency that might arise.

The grass in the field was lighter in colour and had already been grazed down to a short turf like the thick pile on a carpet. Each sheep was eating with a sort of desperate concentration as though it had not seen grass for some time. They just kept their heads down and moved slowly forward one foot at a time. But some, perhaps because their necks had got stiff, had bent their front legs and were kneeling on their little fluffy knees with their black hoofs tucked up off the ground so as not to soil them and their backsides sticking absurdly into the air. The rams had hardly any wool and their skins had that grey, flatulent look that dead sheep have. They seemed inflated with eating and walked about painfully and awkwardly as though they were pregnant. They seemed just able to eat and transport their cumbersome genitals and excrete the little shiny damp balls of dung from time to time. That was a complete existence. The only sound was the crisp tearing of grass and an occasional low grunt and from the nearer sheep the muffled reverberations of some digestive process and a blowing out of wind suddenly through the nostrils.

This, then, I thought, was the beginning of it all. This was perhaps the oldest thing on earth. Before cities and civilizations men had sat and watched sheep graze. In Canaan and Galilee and Salonika and Thrace, on the mountain slopes of Olympus and the Caucasus, on the plains of Hungary and the shores of the Black Sea, in Lombardy, Burgundy, Saxony, along all the routes where men had fought and followed, searching for a home and a pasture, sheep had grazed and men had watched them. Daphnis, Hyacinthus, Thyrsis, Corydon and the famous and anonymous shepherds of Galilee. And I tried to remember all that had gone on as an accompaniment to that watching, the immense architecture of hope that had been built up round sheep. The burnt offerings and symbols of love and innocence; the preyed-upon, the lost and the helplessly young. Sacrificed, worshipped, or just eaten, through mankind's long adolescence sheep went on being sheep, somewhere in the background of every picture, greedy and silly and perpetually anxious. And each year the same disappointing story of promise and unfulfilment. The tiny wet thing with enormous legs first learning to kneel in the winter grass, as awkward and dangerous looking as a child with a deck-chair. The insolent butting at the udders. The entirely beautiful and unnecessary prancing of lambs, movement purely for the sake of movement, only to be forgotten in a few months in a complacent and woolly middle-age.

Out of the north a flock of Fortresses came flying high. It was time for them to come and they crossed every night. The slowly-mounting noise focused the uneasiness in the air. Then I realized that tonight they would not be carrying bombs; the meaning of all the little flags suddenly became real. It was as if one had dreamt the noise; the approaching impersonal menace, the indiscriminate individual death and obliteration of cities, then at the climax of terror, waking, recognized the cause of the dream – after all, only aeroplanes flying. A sense of absolute security closed over everything.

The sun had gone and over the horizon was left a stain of dried blood. The air was the colour of watery ink. At the camp the German bugler was blowing lights out. The sheep had finished eating and sat with folded feet, looking without concern on the first night of peace.

11 May 1945 Paul – the German interpreter – came into the office this afternoon. I asked him what the general feeling was in the compound about Germany's surrender.

'It's hard to give a general opinion,' he said, 'everyone is very quiet about it. They crowd round the loud-speaker eagerly for every news bulletin and when it is over they disperse without saying anything. But I've talked with a quite a number of them. The Nazis for the most part are incredulous. They do not believe what is happening. They believe the facts of course but not what the facts signify. It is not possible for them to comprehend this idea of defeat. They have been brought up to identify defeat with their own personal destruction. They cannot reconcile defeat with their own continued existence. They cannot believe Nazism is finished as long as they are personally alive. And so they think the German surrender is just a sort of interval while the sides are reshuffled. "Why do you think we are being treated like this?" they ask, "all this food and comfortable barracks, hot water to wash in; of course there is only one reason, they want us to help them fight the Russians."

'You see, they find this idea much more natural than the idea of not fighting anyone. They cannot conceive an existence which is not directed eventually to a war with someone. They are not at all bitter about it. There was never any very deep hatred for the English. They feel hurt and humiliated that you always have to come blundering into European wars on the wrong side. But they do not bear you much grudge. They are prepared to overlook it if you will hurry up and come to your senses and help them drive the Russians out of their country.'

'What part does Hitler play now in their lives? What is the attitude over the reports of his death?' I asked him.

'All I can say is that some of the young ones cried when it was announced.'

13 May 1945 One sees a person daily, over a period of time, living in fairly close quarters such as here in camp, and then suddenly at a moment you become aware of them as a physical presence. The boy, for instance, on guard just now. He is one of the quiet ones who do not intrude themselves on life. They do not ask very much and they have not very much to give. They go on living quietly and suffering things without fuss. I have not spoken to him and do not know his name. I was standing drinking tea by the stove when he came in off guard. He cut two slices of bread, carefully, and spread them with margarine. He fitted some pieces of spam over the bread, pressing them into the margarine like mosaics. He placed the other piece of bread on top, making sure it was properly aligned, and pressed it down firmly with the palm of his large hand. Then he took a knife and cut it neatly down the middle.

When it was finished he picked up one half and held it out to me. 'Do you want some of this?' 'No I don't think so,' I said automatically – then at once regretted it. He sat down by the fire and fitted a corner of the sandwich slowly into his mouth. He looked down at the dog and stroked it with his heavily booted foot. I was not feeling hungry but I felt he had offered me more than food. Half a sandwich is better than no love.

1 August 1945 In front of me on the table are some flowers standing in a brown medicine bottle. Every two or three days they are renewed by the German gardener who cleans out the room in the morning. No one told him to put them there, no one has especially noticed it. They appeared after I had remarked, passing him one morning by the camp entrance, how nice the flowers were looking. As I look out of this window I see the other gardener coming across the allotment with his arms full of vegetable marrows. One of the marrows slips and he catches it neatly between his thighs. A guard passing at the time calls out something obscene and he doubles up with laughter, the marrows bouncing down all round him. They pick them up together.

Through the gates the last lorry loads of prisoners are coming in from the fields. The lorries swing in from the road and drive on to the wide concrete square straight into the horizontal rays of the setting sun. Before they come to a standstill the prisoners are springing off them from all sides, bronzed, bleached, gilded, shining; a year ago they were hollowed out shadows of men. Some carry now a fist full of wild flowers, a few apples, yellow and glossy, another a piece of wood which he will carve into something later in the evening. Later, too, there will be singing and music, not very good music, but there is always singing. Others will cluster together for talks, discussions, lectures, English classes. Everyone talks of the *Wiederaufbau* as a festival for which he must prepare. As the square slowly fills up with their ranks, hundreds upon hundreds, bronzed faces, clear eyes, talk, laughter, the atmosphere becomes charged with animal vitality. One is back again in the days of the *Wandervögel*. The open air life, the physical discipline, the stored energy. And again there is the sense of expectancy, of waiting for a lead, the spark that will detonate the energy. The grey lethargy of a year ago has quite vanished. There is a feeling everywhere of concord and happiness. It is not a mature happiness but the happiness of children for whom all the important problems, food, clothing, shelter are taken care of by someone else. The only ones who are not happy are those whose imaginations prevent them living wholly in the present, and these are not many. After living a year in this place it is impossible to go on talking about the German Problem, a problem of the German character. It is necessary only to secure a reasonably disciplined condition of life and the problem ceases to exist.

20 September 1945 Tonight I saw a street lamp. I suppose it must be five years since I saw the last. The odd thing was that I was not in the least surprised. It was several minutes after I passed it that I suddenly realized it was indeed a lighted street lamp that I had seen. I turned to look again to see if I could experience any surprise or amazement in the sight. But it was no more remarkable than any other street lamp had ever been. The gap of five years closed up and the habit of street lamps came back as automatically as the habit of the blackout has become.

The danger is that it will be only too easy to slip back into taking everything for granted, and everything we have learned in these years will be forgotten. It will be so easy to go on again just as if nothing had happened.

The lights go on and everyone mistakes them for light. But they are not light. There is no true illumination. There is just a garishness everywhere. The world is still dark. Once we knew this. Two years ago when the darkness was complete. There was no possibility of cheating anywhere. Even the smallest flashlamp of personal illusion had to be dimmed with two thicknesses of newspaper. And at that moment of complete unbroken darkness we could see the truth and had the chance to grow towards the light. In the true darkness, like the winter shoot in the ground, we sensed in ourselves where the light lay. But now there will be no more darkness and no more light. Only a feverish glare and a frenzied effort to cover up and forget.

4 December 1945 Reconciliation must be hoped for but not relied on. One must comprehend the complexity of things and recognize the possibility of solving one small part without pretending that the whole is solved. Success in life, as in art, lies perhaps in refusing to accept any achievement which one knows to be less than one's potential.

'Our boasted enlightenment is nothing more than the cool-headedness of people who don't happen to be in love. Our boasted tolerance is only a sort of indifference' – yes, but there is a slight odour of burning faggots about this. Open-mindedness was the thing Gill could neither understand nor endure. To him it was simply impotence, vagueness and confusion. 'If you get twenty different answers to a question then the only thing to do is answer the question yourself.' But you don't answer the question. You merely come to a private agreement with the problem which has no validity for anyone else. The best answers have seldom been made categorically, but with a certain elasticity and humility. Which is why, for me, Gide's doubts are more enlightening than Claudel's thundering affirmations.

'How can we know ourselves unless we suffer? Consciousness of ourselves is consciousness of our own limitations. When we enjoy ourselves we forget ourselves', Unamuno said. Why are the pessimistic philosophers regarded as defeatist when it is precisely they who are not defeated because they have gone on searching without the comforting protection of the drawn blinds of beliefs.

31 December 1945   And now it is all over. The cease fire has sounded and the world is at peace; or so we are told. All one sees is another outbreak of coloured flags over the stone cottages and people burning vast quantities of fuel which is urgently needed elsewhere. The war has divided us into two species between which there is hardly any means of communication; those who have been caught up in the destruction, and those who have escaped. Really to grasp the extent of the world's suffering no longer seems possible. One accepts it as a fact; but because no tremor of it comes to disturb the calm of this winter night one feels one has lost one's senses. There is absolutely no reason to believe the world is any different beyond the limits of one's vision. For centuries men lived like this and were none the poorer for it, but today we have reports of things which we cannot comprehend. All the time there is this gulf between incomprehensible facts and present realities. The plight of a million refugees in Poland cannot be understood in the Yorkshire dales.

The whole thing will no doubt be made clear in the history books. A turning point will be marked in the affairs of men. But there do not seem to be any turning points in life. The most one can say is that one was nearing the top of a hill and suddenly became aware that the gradient was downwards. Of course, one can invent a turning point much as mathematicians invent a certain measurement in order to make practical calculations from it. Theoretically the destruction has stopped and it is now possible to start building again. But in fact one will find that the destruction goes on of its own momentum like the light that comes to us from stars long extinct. People will continue to die from the war in scarcely diminished numbers, only they will not have the luxury of dying for great causes. They will die the rather unromantic deaths of starvation and disease. I don't know whether any means will be found to present this fact to them more attractively. There will certainly be less noise, fewer explosions and less falling masonry all over Europe. And finally as a garnish to the holocaust there will be the ceremonial deaths of a handful of War Criminals.

But we can no longer afford to sacrifice the present either to the past or the future. We must accept the fact that things have not worked out altogether as we hoped – though we certainly had no reason for thinking they would be otherwise. We have destroyed our world, doubtless with the best intentions, and it is no use hoping it will receive us back into its forgiving arms. The world we fought for was never further away than we have made it now. What was so efficiently destroyed in moments of bright courage must now be rebuilt in exhaustion and disillusionment. We have sown a legacy of evil for the future which will have to be reaped, and the harvest will not be improved by offering a handful of righteously executed thugs in exchange for a lost generation and a ruined continent. War is a reflection of the world's obsession with surgery, and the limitations of surgery have long been recognized in the consulting rooms. It was never really freedom we wanted, but the knowledge of how to live in freedom – the hardest of all disciplines.

Eight hundred of us live here together comprising three nationalities. It is an artificial military community lacking many of the necessities for a balanced life, neverthelesss there is no discord. What unhappiness there is we have brought with us from the past. There is nothing in the conditions to provoke strife or misunderstanding. It requires no special effort or machinery of adjustment for strangers to like each other and work together. The economic basis of our life, though meagre, is assured, people work not in order to get money for food or houses, which they will get anyhow, but because the work seems worth while in itself and contributes to the general good. The shoemakers, tailors, cooks, clerks do not have to compete in order to survive. They do not need to be continually seeking opportunities for self-promotion. They do the job which is theirs by choice and they do it well, because that seems the most natural way of doing it.

The world cannot improve, we are constantly being told, until people undergo a change of heart or rediscover a religious basis to life. These things may be necessary in the long run, but are they so immediate? It seems that when ordinary people find themselves living together in reasonable circumstances, with the basic economy of their lives secure, they behave quite simply in a reasonable way without any machinery for coercion. There does not seem anything very wrong with the human heart except that it so seldom has a chance to beat.

There are many people here whose natural and spontaneous reaction on meeting a stranger is to smile. They answer kindness with kindness, affection with affection and hostility with silence. But there are others who respond to kindness with mistrust, who approach strangers with suspicion, who pursue life with greed. Their true voice is no longer audible and they can act only as they've been conditioned to act. But they prove that humanity cannot be essentially evil because they are never happy.

It seems paradoxical that during the holocaust of destruction of the last six years I find myself coming more and more to the conviction that there is no such thing as original evil. I do not believe that man inherits ineradicable destructive instincts for the suppression of which laws, police forces and armies must always exist in society. There seems nothing in the natural world to testify to the existence of pure evil. Destruction and violence are the ultimate expression of the will to live when every creative outlet has been blocked. All human wickedness seems the result of mental sickness and misgrowth; through false values of a materialistic society and the inability to face the resulting distress. Evil is not a power in itself. It is a manifestation of distorted vitality. The unrecalcitrant Nazis here were always those with the most spirit. The real enemy is sloth and indifference.

I believe that the natural expression of man's spirit is in love, in the awareness of his own identity and uniqueness, and affirmation of the uniqueness and difference of those around him. Love is that state of delighted awareness of the existence of other things different from oneself; not the desire to possess or to be possessed by them, but to exist in association.

15 March 1946 The day before demobilization Rapid disintegration of personality. Integrity melting like ice in the sun. All poise, stature crumbling away. Increasing difficulty in maintaining the upright position. Automatic disposition to regain the pre-natal crouch. Anterior soft portions of the body seek protection. Storms of neurotic anger. Querulous hostility on every occasion that omits to pay me homage. Furious grappling to retrieve the fragments of lost personality. Despair as the roots are slowly drawn after five years in the warm earth. Over-appreciation of small benefits. The impassive grin currying favour. Laving of the wounds in continuous fantasies of self-esteem. Final dissolution in panic despair and self-pity. Womb-defence mechanism. Head under bed clothes. Childish oblivion. Have lost the scales of balancing gains with losses.

3

1948–1959

14 August 1948   Back from two weeks in France. Sentimental de-
bauch for the most part. Paris, Pigalle, new experiences on the dark
side. Regretted bitterly my inability to dance at the little *boîte de nuit*
where Karlo took me. Obsessed all the time by my baldness and
general unattractiveness (*angst* generators). Treasure nevertheless the
memory of K. – his debonair grace, his laughter, his easy availability.
His fantastic sordid little room in the roof of the Delrieu. Stairs,
naked lamps, labyrinth of corridors, pitch black, holding his hand
like Ariadne stumbling after Theseus. Bugs on the walls. The stu-
pefying heat of Paris which loosened my last hold on any sense of
reality. But the triumphant walk home to St Lazare at 4 am. Sense of
adventure sought and found. A pure experience. Then the *douceur
de Ré*. Benedictine-brewed sentimentality over R. Moments of real
joy. Much sun – much laughter – thanks to my companions – Patrick,
Colin, Tow. Blank misery starting at Newhaven.

Back now I become aware of this growing sense of doom which
has been going on for a year or more. Almost as though I were under
a sentence of death. Partly the sense of inevitably approaching war
again, partly the sense of my failure as an artist. Or rather the
realization of the flimsy premisses on which my career is based. But
again I am not sure. I compare favourably with my contemporaries.
But since I am unwilling to accept the small aims which assure them
a continued career, I think it possible that I may one day soon fade
out as quickly as I faded in. Then what?

Since I left the Army I have not grown stronger, though I may have
grown wiser. But is it a time when one can afford to be wise? Nobody
else I know of my age is still trying to *make* something of themselves,
they are all busy *being* themselves.

One of my big mistakes during the last two years has been trying
to model my behaviour on Johnny [Minton] – to emulate his debonair,
easy, irresponsibility. As though his success with people in this way
could somehow be passed on to me, like an infection. It was always
easier to tag along in his wake than strike out on my own. Now my
growing resistance to his way of life (of which I disapprove but also
envy) takes the form of making me peevish and morose, and thinking
less well of him than he deserves. Since it is impossible for me just to
live naturally in his ambience I should, of course, pack up and clear
out. But what exactly is my natural way of life? do the people I would
like to know simply not exist – or do they exist but not here – or do
they exist here and now and I, through some defect in myself, fail to
make contact with them?

18 September 1948   What to do about X? For some time now it has been evident that my relationship with him is entirely one-sided. He costs me anxiety, money, endless patience and loss of time, much heart-ache and uncomfortable boredom. Yet I feel tied to him. He has nothing to give except his helplessness and a sort of childish gratitude. He lies, cheats and deceives me. Yet his childishness somehow makes everything he does innocent. Certainly he is honest in the end – as honest as he knows how to be. How little people understand the *difficulty* sometimes of being honest. In his case it is the immensely complicated structure of fantasy, self-deception, self-justification which completely obscures the truth. What binds me to him is his helplessness and unhappiness. His complete dispossessedness – no parents, no home, no friends, no age, no proof of his existence at all. His pathetic visit to Somerset House to try to find out.

3 December 1948   '"Love the gold, the azure and the flame –" I detest that way of writing, that way of thinking. It would have exasperated both Stendhal and Flaubert. It smells of the tenor and the odalisque. It lacks both sinew and muscle. It is floating, vague and swelled with wind like a flag.' (Gide.)

How good that is. Where are the people here now in this country who think and feel with muscle and sinew in their hearts. Where should I look for them?

12 December 1948   Fearful days.

15 December 1948   Am very much aware of the necessity, at my age, for the purpose of forming human relationships, of possessing some degree of wisdom, authority and self repose. Yet I continue to try to win approval by displays of uncertainty, curiosity and a sort of wayward guile – qualities which, if they are attractive at all, belong exclusively to youth.

It is conceivable that simply by producing, like an actor, the characteristic behaviour required one may, in time, acquire the personality to go with it. Indeed it would not be surprising since it has been precisely by such methods that whatever qualifications I now possess have been acquired. It is far from reassuring, however.

25 December 1948   I thought last night – for my Christmas has been discoloured by such thoughts – that Johnny's use of life might be compared to a Thibetan's use of a prayer wheel. A circuit of activity is revolved with monotonous presistence in the simple belief that disaster can thereby be avoided and some lasting gain acquired. Almost every kind of experience can be tasted, but the revolutions are so quick that nothing can be grasped or savoured.

But this, and he, are only symptomatic of life today; and it is no use thinking one can defeat it by being ironical. This is the real enemy.

Every sort of shallowness is now expressed with consummate charm and skill. To be quick is to be successful. On the other side lies the danger of thinking that simply by being slow one is being more profound. Not at all.

One must not be surprised if in striving for what one believes to be the best one gets overlooked by contemporary life. Neither must one imagine that therein lies proof of any superiority. Silence can never shout down noise, but it can outlast it. And history is not pressed for time. Neither is it very consoling. If, at thirty-seven, it seems rather ridiculous still to be at one's beginnings, I pray only for strength to continue in the way I think I am going.

29 December 1948 What angers me about X is the impossible demand to reconcile that besotted wreck of a man with a painter whose work has power, control and sensibility. I am angered by all this wilful helplessness that seems to inflict everyone faced with personal difficulties. It seems an essentially post-Freudian disease, as though the insight gained into human motivation and complexity discredited such old-fashioned ideas as self-discipline and standards of personal behaviour, and one had no choice but be dragged along by the gut, deadening the senses as best one can with drugs and alcohol. Perhaps I'm just a prig. But I refuse to accept the contention that an artist is solely concerned with painting pictures. Being an artist implies having an insight and understanding above the average. It implies a certain attitude to life and a certain bearing and style as a man. It implies choosing a standard of values and accepting the obligation to try to live up to them. And I don't so much mean moral values as clarity of behaviour, a certain ésprit. Without this he is simply a knick-knacker.

5 January 1949 Demoralizing bouts of self-doubt and helplessness. Conviction that my whole position is a fraud and far from being the result of any innate gifts is simply the result of perfecting a technique of dissimulation, acting out the person I would like to be. However, there is no choice now but to go on until I'm found out. The exhaustion of doing nothing. Fears of being unable to work again, that I'm living on some sort of false credit which will run out. Feelings of guilt at watching all the people who go off to work in the morning past my studio window, and envy at seeing them come back in the evening to their simple pleasures earned – Ils sont dans le vrai – but it doesn't make it any less painful.

Avignon – September 1951   The backbone is the long boulevard, tree-lined and lit by bright shops and hotels, which leads from the station, outside the walls, up to the Place, mounting slowly all the way. The Place is the highest point and at the top of the Place is the Palais des Papes, highest of all. On either side the streets lead away, infected for a short distance with the chromium glitter of the boulevard, then gradually returning to the crumbling sun-baked stone. Finally everything piles up in shambles of dust, stone and litter against the turreted medieval walls which surround the city on all sides, holding it together. Beyond the walls is the Rhône, turbulent and green. Rats approach within twenty yards of the boulevard after midnight.

From the top of the Place where the descent is steepest the degradation is also quickest. Twenty yards beyond the Palais des Papes the windows and doorways of the houses are like the blackened eye-sockets of old skulls. Moorish children stand and stare in motionless groups like statuary. In the streets are tables with abandoned still-lifes of melon rind, half empty bottles of wine, dirty plates and the skins of figs. In the upper windows the older women sit moulded into the cornices staring and stitching. Just on the edge of the decline are one or two restaurants which have painfully dragged themselves up out of the mire to cling with nothing more than their chromium nails to the edge of the Place. The food in these is good and cheaper by about 30 per cent than in the restaurants of the Place. Slightly below these are one or two cafés which regardless of their hopeless situation have nevertheless decked themselves out with the tourist glitter but where the waitress is still uncertain, when you sit down, whether it is coffee or herself that you want.

I sat at one of these cafés yesterday afternoon during the simmering siesta heat and ordered coffee and cognac. There was a great domestic fracas going on inside when I arrived which, as soon as my presence was observed, subsided with a suddenness as though a chasm had opened up in the ground and everyone disappeared from sight. There were only two tables; I was the only customer. The silence persisted for some moments after I sat down. It was the stunned, rather ominous silence that results from a situation becoming totally changed by the introduction of an unforeseen event. A rapid and intense reassessment was necessary. Even the windows of the houses overlooking the square opened furtively one by one, but without disclosing the occupants, as though guns were being placed in readiness. Finally Madame approached cautiously and I gave my order. After several more minutes of hushed activity Madame and one waitress appeared again with the coffee and the other waitress brought the cognac. Then the patron appeared, ostensibly to tidy up the chairs and remove one or two quite arbitrary little pieces of rubbish which were in no way more obtrusive than the vast array of litter which lay all about. Then they too all sat down, at a discreet distance, to watch. As though it had been arranged, the door of one of the houses suddenly burst open and two little Moorish boys rushed across the square and stood in front of my table. They wore nothing but short woollen vests which, smiling shyly, they proceeded to lift above their tummies; then turned round to show me the back view. The gesture was quietly and deliberately obscene. A gasp of horror came from the group behind me. Madame rushed forwards, seized them by the arms and dragged them off screaming and protesting over the rubble and stones, pouring out torrents of threatening abuse. She returned, bearing an uncertain but reassuring smile, and sat down again, tense and watchful. To show how little the episode had disturbed me, and that I had no intention of hurrying from the haunt of vice, I asked for pen and paper. This unfortunately was less successful than I intended since one by one the whole family had to be called inside to help in the search. The children meanwhile, daunted but by no means subdued by the assault, lingered on the far side of the square and, suddenly free from supervision, renewed their obscene gestures from afar.

La Baignade   Opposite the city the Rhône divides and forms a large island in the middle. Nearer the city, the Grand Rhône is fierce and turbulent, but beyond the island the Petit Rhône is calm and gentle. Here is laid out the Baignade Municipal. A short stretch of the river bank has been dressed with pebbles and sand and stretching out into the water, marking the boundaries of the baignade, are duckboards attached to empty oil drums. There is a ramshackle wooden structure where, for the price of 40 frs, you can hire a changing room, but which in fact nobody but a few rather particular Frenchmen ever use. There is also a buvette with two long trestle tables beneath a sagging awning of bamboo poles where there is always a group of honey-coloured youths who never enter the water but stand about in unbelievably picturesque attitudes against a background of small dusty olive and fig trees, as though part of a fresco by Piero della Francesca. At the other end of the pebbly beach, as far away as possible from this Olympian scene, is a stretch of dried-mud dunes on which the Moorish boys roll each other until they attain the colour of volcanic ash.

Apart from the two floating moles which stretch out into the river there are also a number of others, either no longer serviceable or else ordered in excess of requirements, which lie about on the banks. Each of these, by accepted custom, is appropriated by a particular group of bathers and sunbathers and serves as a deposit for clothes, sandwiches and bicycles as well as a platform for deportment. We also have one to ourselves.

On Saturday afternoons the Moorish boys bring soap with them to the baignade. Several times they cover themselves all over with a froth of whiteness and then plunge screaming into the sienna-coloured water. Even the Petit Rhône is wide and, after rain, swiftly flowing. It is difficult to move up-stream from one mole to the next. But downstream one moves so quickly that it is difficult to avoid being swept beneath the rusty floating drums. The water is limpid and warm and very pleasant to swim in. On the opposite bank the baked and crumbling walls of Villeneuf-les-Avignon rise out of a bed of cypress and thorny scrub and the bleached pink roofs of the village cluster round. Beyond this a line of Cézanne-like mountains culminating in Mte Ventoux, which looks curiously like Ste Victoire.

A young cyclist with six gears to his bicycle, a member of the Cyclo-Club Avignonaise, told me at great length how one cycles up Mte Ventoux. He had the hard, wiry look of people who perpetually break records. He came over to ask me if I could lend him a *tourne-pic* (which I hadn't got). As soon as one Frenchman begins a conversation, a dozen others, who hitherto have completely ignored one's existence, immediately cluster round, eager to pick up any tail-end of conversation which may fall.

La Durance The Durance is wider than the Rhône, at least the bed is, but the river just now is reduced to one or two swift-flowing streams. It moves at the pace of a long-distance runner. Between the channels are wide open stretches of flat pebbles, dunes of sand, plateaux of hard cracked mud and, in the centre of the largest of these, quite thick vegetation of scrubby bushes, maize plants, and others which I can't identify. When you cross these parts it is hard to imagine you are in the middle of a river except that everything leans one way. And around the roots and stems of the growing things is a complicated tangle of débris of every description bleached to the same bone whiteness by the sun. It looks as though a typhoon had swept over it.

The river bed must be nearly half a mile wide in places and the only signs of life are bird footprints in parts of the mud which are still wet. The water is always shallow but so swift that it is impossible to swim. It is difficult even to stand upright once it reaches above your knees. When you sit down you are immediately swept away, bumping gently up and down over the pebbles and rotating like a paper boat. In the hollows of the pebble banks are lakes of still water the temperature of a hot bath. One can spend whole days walking about naked with no person in sight and only the white hot sky baking the skin and the grey dunes.

Each day the level of the Rhône falls a little. The water grows more sluggish and snail coloured. More mud-covered stones appear on the banks. The snow has all melted in the mountains now, I'm told, and there is no rain.

From Uzès to Avignon, after Remoulins – best *pays sauvage* to be seen. Estaurges, Rochford s. Gard. How the burnt bone landscape holds the light after the sun has set. Bronze and bone, scattered over with grey-green olive and black green cypress. Rock forms and silhouettes of villages are indistinguishable from a distance. The air a violet grey colour. No light comes from the sky but all the earth and stone is soaked in light. The moon rises over the ramparts of Avignon like a brass disc, hard and bright.

Palais des Papes   All the evil of this place, and most of its beauty, emanates from the Palais des Papes. The vast honey-coloured walls rear up into the night dwarfing and dominating the town by sheer size. A monument to pure power. The shattered conglomeration of houses, swept up against its bastions, are like the shells of beetles crushed and scattered by marching feet. The Palais today is no more than a vast empty vault for the sale of picture postcards and echoing with the insouciant voices of guides. It contains nothing and emits nothing. But its dominating sense of power remains. And when the flood-lighting is turned off at midnight the moon-coloured bulk remains, with its thin-lipped windows and high mean doorways sharply watchful and aware of the insect people who cross and recross the courtyard, the embodiment of sinister papal magnificence, power without beauty, glory without love.

Tonight a military band is playing on the balcony of the main doorway and all the living beauty of the city is assembled in the great courtyard. It is not at all like any English military band. Partly the black velvet sky, partly the French sense of drama give it an air of magic which is irresistible; the long thread of silver from a trumpet, a trio of liquid flutes floating on the air. But no one is entranced. No one is caught by the magic because their eyes and bodies burn with an equal beauty. It is only as though their presence had become audible. And their beauty is evil because it is without compassion. Everything can be bought; and so it is unpossessable. Flawless beauty is always evil. Perhaps that is why the greatest works of art always have a flaw, a point of weakness through which the heart can enter.

The beauty of the Palais des Papes has no such flaw. It is built on the rock and out of the rock and will endure as long as the rock endures. And the beauty of the Avignonais is gathered from the sun and the vine and the sharp olive; the perfect beauty of the mindless animal, strong and cunning.

Café des Arts 10 pm The mistral has blown now for five days, sweeping away all the languor of summer and leaving the sun bright and the air crisp as on a spring day in England. I left the hospital five days ago, feeling better but barely able to support the noise and maniacal bustle of this town. I ate my last dozen snails an hour ago, unwisely since my stomach is not really up to it. But I don't mind anything now as there is a Wagon-lit waiting for me on the 0.34 train direct to Calais, and tomorrow I shall be in London.

The cafés are empty now and the chairs are taken in where I sit in a blaze of chromium and neon and new plastic marble. Nearby two couples sit and sip and maintain the incessant raucous chatter that goes on and on like the cigalas. The two women, each time they laugh, regard themselves in some nearby reflective suface – presumably to check on the performance. It saddens me that the young seem neither to notice nor mind this self-infatuation. Svelte-footed youths pass up and down ceaselessly outside gazing through the glass windows, brown skinned, blue-trousered, hungry-eyed, empty-headed, quick-witted. But it is only 11.40 and there is still another hour to fill.

I sent off my bicycle for the sum of 2s 4d. Strange how simple and cheap some things are here. The enregistreur had just started to eat a large casse-croute when I brought it in. It took just the time to consume the sandwich for him to fill in all the necessary papers, munching slowly as he wrote and brushing the crumbs away every so often with his other hand. He kept nostalgically turning back the pages of his register referring to the details of previous bicycles which had been despatched. Only one dim, moth-stuccoed lamp was burning which gave everything a grey, ferrous look. Two other small soldiers were also eating sandwiches at the back of the little caisse, their bright eyes watching me keenly above their slowly munching jaws.

I drink a last coffee in the station café. The gnats begin to reconnoitre the night's prospects. A temporary animation flushes through the streets as the cinemas empty. Lights, voices strike up like sparks from the dark corners of the streets, and as quickly fade, leaving only the rats to rummage about amongst the day's garbage.

Five doors up from my hotel is a butcher's shop. The gutters, which normally run just a trickle of soapy water, suddenly, about nine o'clock each evening when the shop is closing, cascade with bright red blood. It is as though a revolution had started higher up in the Place de la République, only very quietly, without making a sound.

Paris 8.30 am, Train Bleu We creep quietly into the Gare de Lyon. The station is alive in a quiet way. Small groups of people stand about amongst piles of luggage. Young men heavily burdened with huge ruck-sacks move purposefully along the quay, bowed over, their boots ringing on the concrete. It is still too early for bustle or much noise. When I open the window of my red cabin the noise of Paris can be heard starting up. On the opposite platform the Simplon Orient Express crawls in, the flanks of the huge hot locomotive streaming with black sweat. The fireman rests his brown arms on the brass rail and gazes out with the vacant placid look of one who hasn't slept. Each shuttered grey carriage as it glides past is still filmed with the web of night. Blind looking windows, opaque as forgotten objects in a museum. An occasional dark gash of oil which has spurted from the racing bogies. Only the streaked white name-boards, high up, testify to its journey. ISTANBUL – LAUSANNE – PARIS. And between in wide spaced, dull gold letters – WAGON-LITS – CAROSSA LETTI. Further down the carriages bear name-boards of shorter, more complicated journeys. VENEZIA – MILANO – TRIESTE – PARIS, ROMA – MILANO – PARIS. All have been gathered together somewhere in the long European night. Presently the doors begin to slide open and ordinary looking, but expensively dressed, people climb out, their faces still folded in sleep and brushed over hastily with bright cosmetics. A huge open horse-box is drawn slowly along the platform and as each window is pulled down a pile of snowy white crumpled linen tumbles out. The uniformed *comptrolleurs* step down with their important brass bound leather bags of documents, and nimble-footed overalled men hop in with pails and cloths and long-handled brooms.

Last night I lay for a long time naked on the cool sheets and watched the lines of cypress trees swing past like the spokes of a slowly revolving wheel; the soft clapping of the rails, the steady gentle speed never faltering. I watched the wide warm Provençal plain under a fixed constellation of stars which swung now to the right, now to the left. The disturbingly sudden flash of light from the window of a house not yet sleeping. The wide mirror of the Rhône drawing closer, slipping beneath the wheels, and out again on the other side. Then back once more, like a sleeper turning restlessly in the hot night. A great pile of mountains suddenly are dragged back again into the plain, followed by a shower of little black cypresses against the horizon.

13 November 1951   Midnight: In the Army I used to sit up in bed like this in the glow of my candle with a sense of absolute security enfolding me. All my desires and their means of gratification within reach – coffee, cigarettes, notebook, ink and crayon. In complete possession of my inner world while all around me was the other, alien but not unlovely. One needed the alien barrack room to give edge to this cosiness, to threaten it, to demarcate its dimension in time with little walls of anxiety.

Now, when I can sit all night, every night, all day in bed the thing goes flat. I start this journal again simply in a desperate effort to break through this ring of lethargy which binds me day after day to frustrated inactivity. The very unreasonableness of it is so exasperating. I am not sick. I am not taking a rest. I am not on holiday. There are numerous tasks to be dealt with, but at the very thought of action a sort of dread sends me scuttling through every loophole of escape to pass time until I am exhausted with doing nothing. But why go on. It's all been said before.

December 1951   Looking back through the earlier entries in this note book (to January 1950) I see that each one repeats almost exactly the same refrain: frustration, creative lethargy, emptiness, inaction. Yet during this time I have had an exhibition of gouaches in August 1950, of paintings in October 1951, I have done the large Theseus painting for the Festival [of Britain] and designed and executed the fifty foot by eleven wall in the Dome [of Discovery]. Not to mention sundry designing jobs, book jackets, etc. Whatever their faults they are better than anything I could have done two years ago. So why not buck up – you poor old boy. Get up half an hour earlier than you need.

Do things out of routine. Ring people up whom you do not particularly want to see. Make an effort to be nice.

25 February 1952 'It is time we took a two-edged scythe and winnowed down these crustations of barnacles' – nice example of a mixed metaphor. It was spoken in the House of Commons some time and mentioned last night by William Plomer. Very enjoyable dinner party at John Lehmann's with Christopher Isherwood, W. P., John Morris, Johnny, and E. M. Forster. W. P. impressed me as being the most poised, most balanced intelligence, no axes to grind, no grudges, very kindly and likeable, immensely sharp witted. Forster inclined to allow himself to be old – to be humoured. A slightly sad and childish old man. Very likeable, but already a little apart from this age. Round like a robin, easily moved to laughter. A once natural zest for life appearing now rather as a habit. But with a wonderful economy and precision of language. 'Yes, we might take care of that in half a sentence' – in reply to someone's rather patronizing criticism of a passage in one of of his novels. One felt sure he would take a special pride in using only half a sentence where most people would use a whole one.

C. I. casual, rather rasping in speech, sentimental, looking like a dehydrated school-boy. Enormously interested in the superficialities of life.

Conversation was on Catholicism and the after life, brought to a halt rather firmly by J. L. 'We simply don't know, do we – pure supposition – no one has ever come back to tell us.' Everyone seemed to agree they were frightened of dying but not of death. Frightened above all of physical pain. I tried to contribute by offering rather tentatively Heard's theory of pain, but I didn't get across very well. Very nervous in such company – nervous of appearing stupid. Consequently I appear rather pompous. E. M. F. was the only one who noticed my remarks and appeared to think them worth hearing through to the end. Very nice manners.

But one could hardly say the conversation was at any point brilliant. It had the flat quality when people discuss ideas from polite interest rather than urgent necessity. Most animation was shown in telling anecdotes of a personal or scandalous nature. Very amusing the anonymous telegram received by Maritain (I think) shortly after Gide's death: 'L'enfer n'existe pas. Avertissez Claudel. Amusez-vous. Gide.'

An air of repleteness – of slight weariness. Here, one felt, were people famous in their age who no longer counted for anything really important. Who were unlikely to affect very much the future. Who incorporated, certainly, much of value from the past but were grown too comfortable. Quiet liberal values. Significant how often the name of Virginia Woolf was mentioned, rather as the disciples at Emmaus might have talked of the Virgin Mary. One felt a great light had gone out of their lives with her death, and they were all a little lost without her.

I still can find no mind today that is really in sympathy with mine. Not, at least, on the deeper levels. Only in the shallows can I splash around with others. It is probably my fault for expecting altogether too much. But I long sometimes, more than ever, for someone with whom to share the darkness – the great swells. I find echoes in Auden, Beethoven, Cézanne, but in no living person. I would like to know someone for whom one does not immediately have to start making allowances. Someone in whose presence I can be inspired, replenished, and from whom I take my leave carrying away more than I brought. Only in the company of very simple people, with whom I have little in common, yet through whom, because of their clarity, I seem to make contact for a few moments with the whole of humanity, do I sometimes get this sense of repletion. But this may be little more than a particularly obtuse form of conceit.

18 January 1953 Renoir: He indulged a purely personal delight which happened to be shared by others. He painted in the same way as one might outline in one's memory recollections and fantasies of pleasure. Because he was utterly unconcerned with any other aspect of painting beyond manufacturing mementoes, his mementoes acquire a compelling power, and he is rated a great painter. But it really is not very difficult to paint this way. No struggle or search is required, no reaching out, no surpassing. Just the caressing brush, over and over again – the same beloved, longed-for forms. And like Brahms, the same lushness, the same apparent profundity and richness which in the end leaves only a feeling of indigestion and smell of cigar smoke (the F minor piano quintet, but not the songs). It is not enough that he did it supremely well. There must be some quality measured in the ambition.

4 January 1954 The constant struggle against the idea of doomed failure. I tell myself this is nonsense in the light of facts. Outwardly I seem to succeed. The last show was better received, better sold. But all this is simply bitterness on the tongue. I delight in praise and instantly disbelieve it; despise it rather. 'Studio exercises rather than considered statements' – fair comment. But I confess myself absolutely at a loss. I can see only the possibility of fragmentary affirmations. Up till now my preoccupation has been with the technical means. Now I have my instrument, but what to play on it. Abstraction seems the way out for most other painters. But I cannot regard it as a solution. The language of 'pure' form is too subjective. I refuse to embark on anything as soon as the outcome can be foreseen; as soon as I know it lies within my grasp. Yet almost everything I do looks as though it has been done precisely because I knew how.

27 January 1955 Interesting account this morning from Dennis Williams of the time he lived and worked in a small room adjoining Francis Bacon's studio; idolizing Francis at the time, longing to be of service to him and ending by becoming so wholly enslaved to his personality that he was incapable of any independent action.

'There was nothing I could do. He would lie in bed in the morning, purple in the face, looking ill – terrible – unable to move until he had taken enough pills, but talking all the time about the paintings he had dreamed of. If I offered him a cup of tea he wouldn't drink it. He just didn't see me. I could have been anyone else and he wouldn't have noticed. I was in his studio one day and he came in with a suit which had just come from the cleaners. He laid it down on a large table in the middle of the room which was thick with paint, cotton wool, bits of dirty paper. He laid the suit down on top and said he had to go out for a moment. As the suit had just come from the cleaners I picked it up and put it on a hanger and hung it out of the way by the wall. My only reason for doing this was that I thought it would be helpful – a small thing – but something he was incapable of doing for himself. Directly he came back into the room, without saying a word, he went over to the wall, took the suit down and laid it again in the paint on the table. I felt absolutely shattered, as though my personality had been wiped out.'

It was moving to see how affected D. was by the recollection of this incident. I felt how easily I could occupy the same role in relation to him. His impressive dignity, his ardour and natural grace, his extraordinary physical beauty – supple – gentle – sensuous. 'He sees people as mountains of flesh,' Dennis said. 'He is obsessed by this extraordinary capacity for flesh to breathe, walk, talk.'

16 July 1955 Louvrier – Hôtel de la Poste. Douceur des rivières. Fine drive through the Normandy country south from Dieppe. Late lunch at the Arcades. Via Rouen – much bombed. Begin to get the smell of France again. Vosne Romanée for dinner. Discreet, pretentious hotel, but not disagreeable. Jardin d'Agréement. Dogs tied up. Trout streams (but no trout).

Chaumont – le château. Food. Chartres – glass. Illiers – Proust. Picnic. Pays douce. Le Loire. St Aignau for shopping. Scottish lowlands country. Treignac – scruffy – cats. All day virage driving, climbing beyond the Cère. Picnicked overlooking the Lot valley. Descent to Figeac, first southern-looking town – plane trees and heavy lorries. Détour to Conques – tourist Romanesque – very well done – first basilica church I had seen. Trésor unfortunately invisible owing to electric failure. Rodez – cold as March in Paris. Richness of France passing – always passing. People seen for the first time, once – never again. Odd moments of eyes meeting. A man looking back. A half smile, half wave sometimes. Then vanished for ever.

South opened suddenly on the descent into Lodève. Scream of cigalas from every tree. Good lunch in the large empty shuttered restaurant of the Hôtel du Nord. Fête on at Sète. Noise.

Collioure. Picturesque, lively, habitable. We decide to take minimum pension at the only hotel with rooms. Surfeited with looking. The photographer who prowls the beach all day in tiny shorts and a mane of fair hair down his nuque. Very self-conscious – very aware of the necessity of not catching glances. Cabana dancers at Banyuls – heavy slow moving thighs and springy ankles. Moon on the bone-coloured stone of the Citadel. The black sea, velvet night and the moon hanging like a melon in the darkness.

Vernet les Bains – despondent, damp, high altitude respectability of watering places.

25 January 1957   Much affected by the news of Johnny's [Minton's] death on Sunday night. Although long anticipated and felt to be inevitable the fact is profoundly shocking and hard to grasp. The one outstanding thing about him was that he was always so very much *alive*. He was never, as some people, half in love with death. But he was in love with destruction. And I can't help feeling that in destroying finally himself, this was meant to be just another unconsidered spontaneous act, a gesture which was not really intended to end in death. The funeral yesterday was in bright warm sunshine. A lot of flowers. (But who was the young man who sat in front terribly broken with grief who had to be supported out?)

Johnny will, I suppose, become a sort of legend now. After the rather dreary and desperate last three years of his life are forgotten, one will remember the scintillating creature one knew before. He was profligate in everything – with his affections, his money, his talents, and with all his warmth and charm, essentially destructive. He turned everything into a joke and a subject for laughter. People never stopped laughing in his presence. 'What does it all *mean*' he would repeat year after year, without really wanting to know the answer. But there comes a point in life when that question has to be answered or else one cannot go on. His influence was considerable on all who knew him, particularly the young, and not always I fear to their benefit. No one else could shine in his presence – his light was too strong – you were devoured and robbed of your identity – and he managed to persuade you that this did not really matter.

27 November 1957 Recommenced painting today after four days in bed. Worked on the second thirty by twenty-five canvas ('Landscape with Figure' 1957, Arts Council) in which I seem to be purposefully trying to make a composition of mutual contradictions. Figures which aren't figures, landscape space which is something else, shapes which are neither abstract nor figurative. A little of this sort of thing makes me very tired and I try to reason the thing out. What am I doing and why? But that line of enquiry leads nowhere. Certainly I am following a scent, but it is very buried and extremely irrational.

23 December 1957 On the whole human beings seem to have behaved best when at sea; apart from the galleys and pirates (and even in the galleys conditions were worse when in port).

7 January 1958 Agreeable sense of poise, purpose and drive continues. I note this simply in the hope that, by being given mention, the mood will be persuaded to remain. The sense of purpose, of course, is confined entirely to my work. It can hardly be said to apply to the rest of my life after the interminable fiasco of my relationship with J. W. all last year, and the year before. But as long as the painting holds ... No spectacular results, but a sense that I know where I'm going. One can't hope for more than that.

17 January 1958 It is a sad but true fact that ultimately my happiest moments are spent not in the presence of another but alone. Short lived perhaps, but of an intense satisfaction when one is in harmony with oneself and through that with a rather generalised idea of the world. Nevertheless ... Yesterday painting there suddenly came to me with a clarity as though someone were speaking them in the room, the words from Luther's Bible which I had memorized years ago when I was learning German: 'So hat Gott das Welt geliebt dass Er sein eingebornene Sohn gab auf dass jeder der am Ihm glaubte nicht verlorenen gehe, sondern ewiges Leben habe.' Not that one has to believe it – but the sheer beauty of the language – the idea – is enough to surround you with a sort of immaculate stillness. Or last night hearing unexpectedly someone on the radio sing 'Anachreon's Grab'. One can be almost terrified at such moments if another is present in case one is forced to share his lesser enjoyment.

14 July 1958 Why are people always talking about 'defending the truth'? The truth needs no defence. It is the one thing which is absolutely indestructible and unsinkable. It is half truths like 'Freedom' and 'Democracy' which need defending. These fill with water and sink before a single lifeboat can be launched. All truth needs is to be seen and heard. It will look after itself after that.

30 August 1958 Madrid: Feel like a wine that does not travel. Acid, turbulent, but not as bad as earlier on. Could not really look out of the plane (my first) until we were over Spain. You sit on an upright padded coffin and boiled sweets are brought round on a large platter like a last sacrament before take-off. But after about two hours I lost the tight sensation that it was going to blow up or fall down. Everyone else, of course, seemed completely relaxed reading the morning's papers. England and France covered with a thick quilt of cloud through which appeared at intervals patches of mournful landscapes in a half light. Impossible to believe that people lived there. But over Spain this changed to a basking ochre panorama of incredible subtlety of detail, everything conforming to the hard geological formation.

25 December 1958 Depression continues: Cancer morning. All the symptoms. Decide that I must be thoroughly medically examined before I leave for the US (a perfectly practicable course), but my mind leaves go of that, since it appears lacking in morbid nourishment, and very soon I am drafting the letter from Iowa Hospital to my doctor, while I await the operation which will certainly prove fatal, accusing him of gross neglect of duty.

The cloud lifts periodically, just long enough to let me write in this ironical vein. But the situation is a real and distressing one. I cannot hold it at bay.

'Oh come all ye faithful, joyful and triumphant' sing the Salvation Army outside my studio window. I cannot think of three adjectives less applicable to the general situation at this time. We are neither faithful, joyful nor triumphant. We could of course be courageous (I say, without any meaning, just to encourage myself). Resist the temptation to take my temperature again today. I feel in the rôle of one whose duty it is faithfully to write up the log-book of a vessel doomed beyond any hope of rescue. Phrases and ideas occur to me all day long, which I do not bother to write down. Finally even writing becomes preferable to the strain of inaction.

A pleasant-looking youth comes up the road with two romping boxer dogs. My spirits lift a little at the sight. But as he approaches nearer my window, and I strain my eyes to absorb as much of the vision as possible, so my anxiety increases, almost to the point of panic, that he will suddenly look up and see the hideous Scrooge-like face staring at him. The image of myself seen in his eyes so obscures my vision of him that I move away quickly in disgust. I try to recall similar situations in the past and how I dealt with them then. Self-alienation it is called (I think). Weak ego-identification. Many have it.

29 December 1958   Complete return to normality today. Mood of confident euphoria. Manic breezes fill all my sails. No need to write about it.

24 January 1959   We are lying out in the middle of the Cobh estuary. The sky is a pale eggshell blue and cloudless and the sun sparkles off the water and the white deck. Almost windless, it is as warm as a spring morning. Tongues and promontories of land surround us like an enemy fleet and the town of Cobh lies ahead as flat and artificial as a stage set. The air is salt and fresh with an underlying breath of hot oil, detectable everywhere on the ship, like the smell of a foreign country. Gulls float slowly up and down, level with the deck, wary and hopeful, and letting out a shriek of disappointment when I merely look back. There is a low rushing noise, like an escalator, coming from the ventilators and a continuous high-pitched squeak from a winch.

While dressing this morning I was surprised to see my porthole slowly obscured by a tall cylindrical object passing a few feet away. I opened it and discovered the *Blarney* was drawing alongside, its funnel level with my cabin. The decks were white with frost and a small group of people were huddled by their suitcases which were labelled 'New York'. At intervals over the side hung lorry tyres; not just single ones but four at a time, one on top of the other. As the ship touched these slowly spread out, like a fantastic chocolate sandwich, and squealed like pigs. This was repeated several times until the ships were made fast and settled down together.

I have been allotted a place at the chief engineer's table in the restaurant, but the chief engineer has not yet appeared. There are two other people at the table, a mild elderly businessman who crosses the Atlantic constantly, and to whom the whole thing is a matter of routine, and a young bearded Canadian who is crossing for the first time to Montreal. I did not ask him why because I suspected the answer would be a dull one. He knows I am going to the University of Iowa and would like to know why, but I am postponing as long as possible the moment of disclosing my profession from dread of the inevitable questions which must follow once he knows I am a painter.

The menu is enormously extensive and pretentious – there are, for instance, six different kinds of bread – but the range narrows itself somewhat when the food is actually served. There is also a 're-commended' table d'hôte for those who lose themselves in the full one. The dining room is only one-third full so that one is overwhelmed with service which does not make for a very relaxed meal.

We left the *Blarney* in Cobh estuary in brilliant cloudless sunshine after tearful farewells to the Irish emigrants, and the land has faded from sight. The sea is growing inky dark with a slow rolling swell, the first real indication that we are on water, although we are already 250 miles from Liverpool.

The bearded Canadian isn't a Canadian at all but comes from Blackpool and is going to Montreal as a travelling salesman for his father's firm who makes children's clothing. In his cabin he has a large trunk filled with samples. He had difficulty in explaining these to the Customs since his passport states that he is unmarried. We had drinks together before lunch. He has a gold watch and bracelet, gold cigarette case and gold lighter. Nevertheless, he is very insecure and keeps worrying about the possible problems he may meet and whether he will come back with any orders. I adopt a reassuring rôle, rather half-heartedly. He finally asked me what I was going to teach in Iowa and when I told him I was going to teach painting said, much to my surprise, 'I thought you probably were' and happily left it at that.

Sunday There is quite a big sea now, running with us but slightly across our course. The sky is grey and spatters rain now and then but it is extraordinarily mild. Standing in the stern, which seems no wider than a channel steamer, I watch the sea gather into a dark copper-coloured peak, draw near and tuck itself under the keel, then gradually lift us up to what seems an incredible height above the water, until the whole ship begins to tremble with annoyance, then slowly put us down again; the whole thing done very gently and playfully. Inside you have to pause now and take aim before going through a doorway, otherwise you're liable to hit the jamb. It has all the unpleasantness of being drunk without the sense of irresponsibility.

The Canadian has taken to his berth and the engineer is still with his engines, so the businessman and I have dinner together. In fact he is also an engineer with a house in Nassau, whither he is bound at the moment. His manner is curiously shy and diffident and his hand trembles when he lights a cigarette. He is also immensely bored and looks at me incredulously whenever I remark on anything with enthusiasm. The only affirmation he would allow himself was to agree that the weather is good in Nassau. He also has a compulsion for buying sweaters and confessed with a bewildered air that he had bought five from the Irish merchants who came aboard from the *Blarney* yesterday. I remarked on what nice presents they would make – since they were clearly not the sort of garments he would wear himself – but he said they were not intended especially as presents; in fact in the back of his Jaguar were dozens of sweaters which he had bought at various times and didn't know what to do with. But when I suggested, for want of something better to say, that this must show some interesting psychological compensation, he looked at me with alarm and said nothing. He is not an easy person to talk to, but at least he is not hearty like most of the others. At dinner last night two of the Canadian officers wore spurs.

Monday The wind has switched to the NW and is too strong to stand against unsupported. The sea is coppery black and combed out in white plumes like a circus horse. It no longer lifts the ship playfully but assaults it rudely, galloping in against the side. The ship creaks and whinnies and it is foolish even to attempt to steer a straight course across the lounge without support from the backs of chairs. Everyone looks as if he's been struck with Parkinson's disease. There is a nasty feeling that one's brain is coming loose from the sides of one's skull.

The chief engineer finally appeared at lunch yesterday. Each of us was formally introduced by the head waiter and we shook hands all round. He is a pleasant man, a Scot, easily amused, very relaxed and informal. The businessman and he, both engineers, naturally made most of the conversation; technical points to do with turbines. At the end of the meal he casually asked us to his cabin at seven.

I went up about ten past and was conducted with some ceremony through the door marked 'Officers Only'. It was an extremely formal affair. We all shook hands and sat down in three huge armchairs. A steward came and asked us what would we like to drink (every possible sort of drink could be procured). By the side of each chair was a small table holding dishes of salted almonds, smoked salmon, olives, potato crisps, a packet of cigarettes, matches, and an ash tray. It was like the preliminaries to a summit meeting of the big three. An hour passed thus and then we went down to dinner.

Just before lunchtime we ran into a small snowstorm. The sea went a sickly grey and you could watch the screen of reddish black cloud moving towards you across the water. On each side of it was brilliant sunshine. You could see exactly its shape and size and the moment when it would arrive. For ten minutes everything was obscured in a wild flurry of feathers and foam. Then the sky went yellow, then white, then brilliant sunshine again, with the tail end of the snow streaming across the blueness like a plague of locusts. But the wind, far from being mild and balmy, was now suddenly icy cold and impossible to stand in.

At lunch the conversation fell to icebergs. Someone wondered whether we would be likely to see any, but the engineer said no. But you might in September. How, we asked, were they detected at night – by radar? Radar was no good, said the engineer, as often no more than an ice-cream cone was projecting above the water. You detect them by smell; you smell the seaweed. But what happens, I asked (anxious to play a part) if the man on watch has a cold? But although everyone else seemed to think this quite amusing, the engineer looked rather annoyed and said nothing. Later on he said that if you smell ice at night the best thing is to shut off the engines, then you just drift with the icebergs and when you wake up in the morning there they are all around you.

We are now riding a full swell. It is like standing on the rump of a slow-moving horse. One moment you are weightless, the next your ankles feel as though they are going to give way.

Tuesday   All decks are out of bounds this morning. We are doing about five knots against a full gale. The seas are mountainous and terrifyingly splendid to watch. It started just before dinner last night to get really rough (although no member of the crew will admit it's rough). Nevertheless, sipping my martini in the lounge, all the little dishes of nuts, olives and canapes suddenly moved swiftly to the side of the tables and reversed themselves on the floor. Instantly stewards appeared and in seconds all was ship-shape; fresh supplies were put out. At dinner it was the same. I took a mouthful of food, my plate moved sharply off to the left, and the engineer's plate appeared in place of mine. It got worse during the night and it was impossible to sleep. Every ten minutes the entire contents of the dressing table slid off on to my head, until I got up and packed everything away into a drawer. For about five hours they shut off the engines and we bobbed like a cork. I lay on my back (to stop rolling out) and listened to the suitcases in the cabins sliding across the floor and bumping one side and then the other. The sea was up over my porthole which two days ago had seemed miles above the water.

It turns out that the chief engineer is an amateur painter and sent in two pictures to the John Moores exhibition a year ago which were rejected. I knew this would happen sooner or later. He said it all started when he saw someone painting in Greenwich Village and thought it looked quite simple so he asked what he needed to buy. He bought what he was told and back on board settled down to a series of seascapes. They were an immediate success. He sold them to members of the crew for £2 each (two guineas to the officers because they think in guineas). So great was the demand that he had them photographed and sold the photographs for 50 cents. He did the skies first, then the boats, then put the sea in round the boats. He did five or six a day.

Of all the trivial distractions designed to persuade first-class passengers that they are not really at sea, the most irritating is the Sylvania light quartet which plays insipid palm court music in the lounge at tea time. And to an audience of never more than six, since tea time coincides with film time, and often only to myself. I don't know when I have seen four men engaged in a sadder occupation, one can scarcely bear to watch them. But no, they are, after all, making music of a kind. Sadder really are the listeners.

Wednesday The gala dinner last night, which I had been quietly dreading, turned out in an unexpected way – a discussion on Art. It started with the menu cards. Every card has a full colour reproduction of some painting, specially commissioned, I suppose, by the Cunard Line. The one on our table was of a woodland scene with bluebells, winding paths, etc., and had been painted, so a footnote told us, by a woman painter who had lost both arms and legs in an accident and had learnt to paint with her mouth. This piece of information only made the banality of the result all the more embarrassing, as it would have been no better had she had the full use of her limbs. After donning our carnival hats we found ourselves engrossed in a discussion on the Meaning of Art. By now we knew each other well enough not to have to pull punches, so the argument became lively and heated. The engineer, as one might expect, while disliking modern art kept a tolerant and open mind on the subject. But the businessman was militantly opposed. Nothing which cannot be reduced to figures has any meaning or value for him. Art he regards as positively hostile, and modern art the work of criminal lunatics. When I tell him I am precisely such a person he clearly does not believe me. No modern artist would be travelling first-class to begin with. He obviously doesn't know what to make of me and suspects that I am pulling his leg. He has the resigned look of someone whose leg is pulled often, because he is not at all aggressive and quickly gets lost in argument. He never reads, except what he calls 'trash', nor listens to music; nor goes to the theatre nor looks at pictures. He has no hobbies – 'work is my hobby' – and is only happy working. Since he is near retiring age this situation obviously causes him moments of anxiety. The Canadian kept a safe distance from the argument and ready to join the winning side. And it continued long after the other diners had left and the stewards were hovering in the background to clear the tables without anyone getting their point across to anyone else; the three of us wearing our paper hats, rather flushed from a bottle of burgundy and looking like a scene from a René Clair film.

Friday We reached Halifax this morning at seven. Everything white with snow and real lumberjacks swarming about unloading the cargo. With the sight of land again the reality of the ship seems to diminish, and I am impatient now to get on to New York.

2 March 1959 Am the possessor of $2250 – stupendous. I could buy a Ford Thunderbird and a pair of two-toned shoes, or a rain-coat from the smart University shop in 'London Fog'. It was Byron who suggested it last night after I had taken them out to dine and was admiring a Thunderbird outside. 'I would just love to see you go back to London in one to impress your friends.' 'But I haven't got the personality to go with it.' 'You don't need the personality if you've got the Thunderbird,' said Kay, 'that's why people get Thunderbirds.'

20 March 1959 Greyhound bus: Chicago – Los Angeles – Thru. Flat rich countryside. Space and sun. Red oxide barns with silver pinnacles. White timbered houses like Essex. Black and white cattle. Black purple soil layered with streaks of pale blue snow. Ochre sticks of corn stubble. China blue sky with hawks. Pink pigs burst out of the black earth like truffles. Hinky-Dinky super-stores. Nothing over 100 years old.

> Amerika du hast es besser
> Als unser continent das alte
> Hast keine verfallenen Schlösser
> Und keine Bassalt.

Approaching Omaha. The fascination of waiting rooms where people are organized for doing nothing – for waiting. The air of expectation; of probing contacts. Curious notice in Atlantic – FOR SALE – NIGHT CRAWLERS. And small blue signs everywhere which say 'EVACUATION ZONE' (from Indians or H-bombs?), and the extraordinary prevalence of mortuaries, neon-lit and glittering like cinemas.

June 1959 – Mexico   By far the most interesting thing about this city for me is the beauty of the people. Walking north this morning from the Zocalo into the old parts face after face passed which transfixed me. Perhaps some racial purity, unmixed blood, gives them that clear passionless sensual remote calm. You see it in the old sculpture, nothing has changed. These boys lived centuries ago. The gentle shelving back from the chin to forehead with the eyebrows folded like small wings. Disdainful lips, steady gaze, a warm sudden smile like a lotus flower opening. I can think of no city in which I have seen such continual beauty.

The extraordinary calm of the young Mexican selling rugs outside the hotel to two paunchy middle-class travellers who haggled and bargained and beat him down inexorably. At no point did he lose dignity, or a sad, patient remoteness. Of course, they got the better of him. It was raining and he had to carry home what he did not sell.

Life in the Grand Hotel: a page boy enters asking for Miss Sanders. He is in fact no longer a boy but shows the lines of premature maturity in his face. He passes slowly through the room. Suddenly his face is galvanized into a brilliant smile which is almost as quickly extinguished. I turn to search for the recipient and see an elderly lady with grey hair in tight curls, blushing furiously and sipping her tea. Probably this is the moment of the day she waits for.

You cannot move five paces without small sad-faced children coming up to sell you Chicklets – they must be a sort of chewing-gum. Nobody buys any. Whoever thought up the idea they would be required in such vast quantities?

The great piles of green and red melons beneath the sagging awnings of the market. Rows of pomegranates neatly opened like flowers showing their crimson glass-like flesh. Piles of dark green courgettes on darker sacking. Different coloured beans like seeds in a corn market. Tortillas being cooked at every corner – sacks of dead skin filled with terrifying contents. Flat cactus leaves threaded on string (to eat?). Avocados of every size and shape. Piles of ox horns by which one passes quickly. Narrow alleys covered right over with awnings so that the light is pearly and there is only room to pass, one at a time, between the stalls. The old couple behind their stall with just a few courgettes carefully grouped and graded for size. Both grey. Both asleep and reclining upright against each other for support like old trees.

A humming bird poised outside my window this morning while I was dressing: at least I suppose that is what it was. About the size of a large moth with a long and narrow beak. It seemed able to move backwards or forwards with equal ease like a small helicopter. But the black raven is so heavy and clumsy that every time he alights on the tree two or three mangoes fall to the ground with a dull thud.

During the storm which breaks every afternoon between four and six (it used to be between four and five, but since the atom bomb it is no longer so punctual) all the birds fly screaming into the Indian laurels in the Plaza like fighter planes returning from an engagement. The noise is deafening. The rain falls in solid sheets and within minutes the roads are rushing with ochre-coloured water. Everything has to stop. It seems ridiculous that so much water can fall in so short a time. Dogs squeeze apologetically behind your chair to go to sleep; but quite ready to be kicked away without protest if necessary. At each flash of lightning all the lights dim, as though the town were connected to some celestial circuit. It goes on like this for about forty minutes and then stops. In five minutes the streets are dry and virginally fresh like the sands after the sea has retreated. And the ceaseless passage of large American cars starts once again, though it is Mexicans and not Americans inside them. Americans come here in the winter when the temperature is exactly the same but it does not rain. You can select your own temperature by altitude. Mexico City is coldest, Acapulco hottest. Cuernavaca, in between, is just right – about 75°. Also one can eat a proper meal at night and still sleep (apart from the bull-frogs) whereas in Mexico City this was impossible. Something to do with the altitude. I never believed this but it is true.

As I was drinking an aperitif and writing outside the Bella Vista this evening I became aware of a youth leaning against a car on the other side of the road and watching me intently. Each time I looked up he tried to catch my eye. Finally I let him and we smiled at each other. He came across rather uncertainly and I indicated the empty chair by my table. He sat down. He asked if I was American. When I said I was English he immediately took hold of my hand under the table and laid it on his knee. He was wearing a pink shirt and blue jeans and was obviously out to kill. He looked about sixteen but he could have been fourteen or eighteen. He said his name was Miguel. Conversation was not easy as he spoke no English, but it was soon apparent that his Spanish vocabulary was not much larger than mine. We got across with infinitives and hieroglyphs. He had ten brothers and two sisters, all of whose names he told me, all of whom were farmers, and he, the youngest, worked as a sandal-maker in the town. Did I like sandals? Yes, but I had some. Would I like another pair? No. But he would make them for me for nothing. Why? *Porque te quero.* I look up *querer* in the dictionary and see it means to like or love. (Maddening ambiguity of foreign languages, as if it made no difference.) Had I been to Tepostlan – very beautiful – he would come with me – he was on holiday. I hadn't, so we have arranged to meet tomorrow morning and take the bus.

Saturday Caught the morning bus with my 'guide' for Tepostlan. A rattling drive through fine wild country to this village set in a circle of high savage peaks. His name is not Miguel but Raul. And the reason he gave me a false name was because '*Yo decia qui no me ibras a entender*'. Impossible to decipher. But it seemed not to matter as our relationship is not exactly an intellectual one. He had with him a folder of about fifty sheets of used carbon and a new comic, which he was in the act of buying when I met him at the bus stop. He could not explain why he had the carbons. '*Los compre*'. The bus we went in had little painted curtains with tassels round the windscreen and a little plaster Madonna inside lit from beneath with a red rear lamp. There were also bouquets of lilies in the corners. During the journey we either held hands or he linked his arm through mine and pulled gently at the hairs on my fore-arm. His own skin is a smoked velvet colour and as soft as chamois. Hairy arms must strike him as very exotic. About every twenty minutes he would ask '*Que pensas?*' – difficult enough to reply to in any language, and if I stopped smiling for a moment, just to relax the muscles – '*Es triste.*'

We had lunch at a rather grand posada run by Americans. He was somewhat overawed by the situation, apart from the waiters he was the only other Mexican, but he behaved with that natural quiet dignity which very simple people seem to have. There was no easy conversation to help out, but he gave me constant reassuring glances and deft, Oriental-like touches. Impossible to tell exactly what these mean or what he is thinking. His expression one moment is childish. The next it is filled with a sad compassionate understanding which is ageless and timeless. I can understand almost nothing of what he says, though he understands my stumbling Spanish, which occasionally makes him laugh. So as with the deaf and dumb our communication is almost entirely visual and tactile. It was obvious we were a source of interest to several tables during lunch but not, I thought, disapprovingly. Their amused curiosity was what might be shown to someone who had brought in a large and picturesque poodle. I felt at any moment someone would get up and stroke him. Also the waiters, I was pleased to note, treated him with the same diffidence and concern that they showed the other guests. He refused the offer of some money when we got back for his services as guide – he earns the equivalent of three shillings a day at Beltran, the sandal-maker – but thanked me gravely for a happy day. Then, looking round quickly to see that no one was following, he backed into the shadow of a doorway and took my hand and kissed it and ran off quickly without looking back and clutching his carbon papers and comic. Tomorrow we have arranged to go to the Vista Hermosa.

Sunday Mañana. I waited thirty minutes at the bus stop but he did not turn up. I felt ridiculously put out and jilted. Serve me right. Spent the morning swimming and romping with the N. Orleans children in the hotel pool. But the boisterous friendliness of the Americans has suddenly become unendurable. Walking through the square after lunch I come upon Raul sitting on one of the white benches and almost in tears. What had happened? He had missed the bus in from Amacuzac and had to wait for the next one. But I thought he lived in the town. No, he lived in Amacuzac. I look it up on my map. It is about 35 kms away. He had asked for me at the hotel but old Penario, the patron, had told him I had left. All this took half an hour or more to discover with the aid of dictionaries, pencil and paper, three-dimensional diagrams of match boxes, twigs, pebbles, and the usual deaf and dumb gestures. At the end of it he seemed more cheerful. We had a coffee at the Bella Vista. Something to eat?

No thank you. He had a stomach ache. He pulls up his T-shirt to show me the place. Just there. He takes my hand and puts it against the spot. I take it away. I am not used to stroking a smooth brown belly in public. '*No te enoyas?*' he asks suddenly. More work with dictionary and pencil and paper – 'Am I annoying you?' No Raul, no. But it's impossible to explain. We have to settle it with smiles and a gentle touching of fingers. I notice he has on nail varnish and am shocked. Could he be. . . . But it is necessary in the factory he explains. Otherwise the nails crack and splinter with the dyes. I half believe this only. I notice a patch of plaster on his neck just beneath the collar of his shirt. What's that? *Langusta.* Lobster – impossible. More research. He finds it for me in the dictionary. Locust. The insects in the trees which make the hideous noise all night. I take him back with me to the hotel, making sure that old Penario sees us. He does, and quickly busies himself with papers on his desk. The hotel is short of tourists at this time of year. I give him some anti-vioformo tablets for his stomach. He gives me a quick hug and a kiss. We arrange to meet next day if his stomach is better.

Monday   Apart from the bored rich Americans who stay there and spend the day sipping Rye Collins in the shade, the Vista Hermosa is as good a place of its kind as I have seen. Splendidly set in wild mountainous country it is an old monastery, partly restored into a restaurant and guest rooms, the rest of the ruins left as they were, but excavated and filled with water, fed from a high aqueduct, to form a series of azure blue swimming pools flowing in and out of dark grottoes and bright sunlight, lined with fountains and tall crumbling walls and sprinkled over with the crimson petals of bougainvillea. Raul was as enchanted as I was, for in fact he had never been there either. He had only been told about it. And he warned me constantly on the way that it was very expensive. But to make sure I wasn't cheated he insisted on getting the tickets when we went in (20 pesos – about 11s which also included lunch).

At first we were the only people swimming and we chased each other through the fabulous blue water and tumbling fountains; a breathless Zeus pursuing fleet-footed Ganymede. Then he performed for my benefit a series of ambitious, but not altogether successful dives off the board. At the end of each one he would swim back to where I sat, shoot out of the water like a seal, embrace me and ask if I would like him to do it again. I became aware of the cameras of the more indefatigable record hunters clicking away in the shadows. I hoped they were not blackmailers. But beyond that I was past caring about appearances and gave myself up to the enchantment of the situation and my beautiful and charming little Mexican friend. And as though in approval of this, while we were waiting after lunch for the bus to take us back, the sky all round the horizon was black with storms and teeming rain. But where we stood by the side of the road watching the long lines of peasants and donkeys coming in from the fields was a pool of green sunlight suitable for an apotheosis. It was he who pointed this out. It seemed for once the gods were not angry.

Tuesday   For me the whole of Mexico now became focused in Raul and our strange silent relationship. There was no point in visiting stones and monuments from the past when I had the companionship of the living present. So I cancelled my plans and each morning except Sunday, which was for God and his family, I would meet the bus from Amacuzac and we would set off somewhere of his choosing. If it was fine we would take a picnic and bathing things and go to some place where we could swim. When it was cloudy we would swim in the hotel pool, have lunch and take a siesta afterwards. With effort we might exchange ten sentences of conversation in the course of a day. For hours on end we would say nothing and neither was bored. Each day he brought with him some books, usually a simple English primer or school grammar and would sit entranced while I read to him the banal English phrases which he did not understand. Then he would read to me the parts in Spanish. He would sleep a little cradled in my arms. And then always there came a moment towards the time of parting when his laughter and gaiety would suddenly die out and he would take my hand carefully in his two hands, as though I were a child, and gaze long and silently into my eyes while his own filled with tears until he could see no more and crushed his face against my shoulder.

Painfully and at length I had already questioned him about his family. Was he happy at home? Yes. Did he get on well with his father and mother? Yes. Did he get on well with his ten brothers? Yes. Had he got friends of his own age? Yes, but they were only *compañieros*, and he pronounced the word with contempt. But in answer to my questions at such moments he could say nothing but would kiss me over and over again on the eyes, forehead, cheeks, ears, like a mother soothing a fretful and inquisitive child.

The last afternoon before I left, while we were dressing in the hotel after a bathe, I slipped a 100 peso note into his shirt pocket and begged him to keep it. *Quisiera te dar esto*, a phrase I had carefully rehearsed for the occasion. He had accepted no money from me all the week and refused even to allow me to pay his fare home each evening. He said nothing, nodded acceptance as though in shame, then slipped slowly to the floor and abandoned himself to sobbing at the foot of the bed. The obvious extravagance of the situation was no longer sufficient to preserve my detachent and I became involved in his grief. Not normally given to crying, I was surprised how painful it is to produce tears. Tears not of grief at parting but of defeat and bewilderment at the pain I had caused. It was as though I had beaten him to the ground and thrown him away. And as soon as he saw my distress he forgot his own and was concerned only with comforting and drying my swollen eyes. We stood together in the bright afternoon light and the buzzing of insects for what seemed an eternity of meaningless grief. When it was over and I had finished packing he said quite simply, as though it had been obvious all along: 'When you go I shall have nothing.'

29 June 1959 – New York Ninety-eight degrees in New York today. 'Good for nothing but the expansion of metals.' How do people live in such a place. I sit in the Astor Bar, sipping a Rye Collins and barricaded behind my notebook (the public always keeps a respectful distance from a writer) simply because it is the minimum walking distance from my cool room at the Woodstock. It is obviously the dullest bar in New York and no one could believe why I should sit here. But I am as helpless as a gaffed fish in large cities in the heat. There are dozens of places which would suit me better, but I do not know them.

Raul in Amacuzac. Three or four times a day his memory returns with such force that it shatters the present reality. I stand stock still in the middle of the sidewalk. People must think I'm mad, but they don't show it. New Yorkers are accustomed to madmen, particularly around Times Square. The ridiculous pricking of tears behind the eyes. But it is like trying to keep in sight a toy kite which has drifted away in the wind. Its isolation and loneliness increases, but at the same time it becomes more and more difficult to identify until in the end its very existence is in doubt.

What will become of you? Trapped in your huge family of farmers you escaped as far as the nearest city and met me. I offered the promise of something fabulous beyond the horizon and then forsook you. You accepted without complaint. You shook hands quietly outside the cathedral, said goodby in English in a voice which was scarcely audible above the noise of traffic then turned away quickly before the tears broke and walked up the hill without looking back.

Beneath your smooth cheeks are the lines of someone already old who knows his fate. *No te olvidare nunca.*

I romanticise as usual. But there was something about you which despite the vast distance of background, race, language and age brought us together in compassionate understanding. Your hands, like the petals of a flower warmed by the sun, seemed to give life to everything they touched; never searching or grasping but touching in confidence and trust.

Amerika du hast es besser? – No. You are grown old too young. A flashy veneer conceals your lack of feathers. You have become airborne before you have learnt to fly, space-conscious without understanding the earth beneath you. You cannot create with the hands but fabricate with elaborate machines. You could not have laid the topaz and vermilion paving outside the Bella Vista. You would not have thought to place more than enough seats. Your country is too large and fertile – too rich. I prefer a country built on basalt and lava rocks. I learnt more of life from the palm of Raul's hand than from all the complicated network of your glittering highways and supermarkets.

25 July 1959 [Alan] Bowness, on the Documenta Exhibition, Kassel, while finding most of the painting bad, nevertheless can say 'there does indeed seem very little that this new language will not eventually be able to express'. Surely one of the most remarkable statements a critic can make. Here is someone who, while looking at pictures which 'make considerable demands on those trying to familiarise themselves with it', is suddenly struck (the word 'indeed' seeming to imply something in the nature of a revelation) not by the qualities of the pictures he is looking at, but by the pictures which will, or may, be painted in the future. How is this done?

Presumably because he sees present all the visual vocabulary necessary to the painter – light – colour – shape – movement – even 'visual imagery'. And yet he denies the possibility of a 'representational art' today. In fact, of course, he may be right, and I do not know why I set out to try to attack him. Obviously a way through must be found and not a way back. What is chiefly irritating about this painting is not the work, but the extravagant claims that it supersedes all previous work and gives the artist 'freedom' which he is supposed hitherto to have lacked.

Also interesting in the *New Statesman* is [John] Berger on the Romantics. 'The Massacre at Scio' fails because it is an 'art dream' and not a true interpretation either of death or slavery – i.e. it does nothing to encourage men to 'know and claim their social rights' (surely one of the least helpful definitions of artistic values ever invented). How many crucifixions, flagellations, etc, fail in exactly the same way. They give neither a true interpretation of what it is like to be nailed to a piece of wood, nor what it means to murder a god. What it does offer, as always, is a personal emotional experience engendered by the sight or thought of these things and transposed into plastic symbols, offering the spectator empathic identification with suffering in a heightened aesthetic context. The results *can* be utilized for social reform, religious education, or private aesthetic pleasure, as the case may be. If Berger's contention were true, then the paintings which have made men *most* conscious of their 'social rights' must be the best paintings. The results of such a selection would make an interesting exhibition, but one unlikely to include many paintings generally regarded as masterpieces.

4 October 1959   'Into this setting he placed a figure. He was happiest with only one, because in this way he avoided dramatic tension.' (K. C. on Vermeer).

But looked at less complacently the relationship of a figure to its environment can have plenty of dramatic tension. One need think only of the struggle of a Cézanne bather to remain in harmony with, yet separate from, its surroundings. Admittedly a single figure avoids psychological drama, which arises when two or more are present, when inter-personal as well as formal relationships have to be solved. A favourite device of Vermeer (and myself) is to turn the second figure back to the viewer, thus presenting the viewer in relation to the first figure.

4

1960–1965

January 1960 'Do not be afraid of the past. If people tell you it is irrevocable, do not believe them. The past, the present and the future are but one moment in the sight of God, in whose spirit we should try to live. Time and space, succession and extension are merely accidental conditions of thought. The imagination can transcend them and move in a free sphere of ideal conditions. Things also are in their essence what we choose to make them. A thing is according to the mode in which one looks at it. "Where others," says Blake, "see but the dawn coming over the hill, I see the Sons of God shouting for joy."' (Oscar Wilde to the stinker, Bosey [Lord Alfred Douglas].)

The heady confidence of the Romantic, so beguiling, but spinning to his doom. Like a pilot trying to land without elevators whose absence, provided he looks straight ahead, he is unaware of.

The past is irrevocable in the sense that it cannot be altered or erased, though it may be susceptible to different interpretations. But one reaps what one has sown, or had sown in one. But there is a difference between other people's past and one's own. The past of other people is the compost in which one grows one's own present. It can be broken down into nourishment, or it can strangle, depending on the success of one's root formation. One's own past one carries with one, some of it fruit, some of it dead wood. But it cannot be broken down and it cannot be discarded. Those who attempt this end on the analyst's couch, or elsewhere.

Supreme example of the ironical mind: Evelyn Waugh's remark – 'The total destruction of the human world does not appal me provided it is done, as seems likely, inadvertently.'

27 April 1960 Wisdom is acquired through keeping still. At least the sort of wisdom which is most fruitful and nourishing. I do not see the sense in rushing around all the time in search of 'experience'. A few quite ordinary things seen over and over again during the years can acquire a sort of richness. They can also acquire a suffocating dullness, depending perhaps on the wisdom of their choice in the first place. Depending in fact on whether they *were* chosen or chosen for you – dumped on you. Many people think they have chosen what in fact they have merely accreted, like barnacles, and so have to keep rushing off to get a breath of air.

Sensations on becoming a success – nil.

Extraordinary how success, like cancer, settles and develops in one person and not another.

Uselessness of the nostalgic backward glance – wasting the present. The only use of the past (memory) is to illuminate the present and point to the future. Americans are all forward looking, though they long for a past, and make the most of what little they have.

13 May 1960   The Home Secretary told Mr Abse (L., Pontypool) in the Commons yesterday that he regretted to say that two youths, aged seventeen and nineteen, sentenced to Borstal training, were sexually assaulted in Cardiff prison by two cell-mates aged twenty. A third boy aged seventeen was also assaulted by one of the assailants in an attempt to commit an indecency.

And I am supposed, like any 'decent' member of society, to throw up my hands in outraged horror. Well I don't. I can think of nothing less shocking or harmful to anyone than five boys in a prison cell passing the time in a little vigorous and enjoyable sexual combat. Is one to believe that a boy of nineteen 'sentenced to Borstal' (i.e. not exactly a milk-fed calf) could not, if he wished, defend himself against the advances of a boy one year older? What do people imagine by the term 'sexual assault' in such cases?

No doubt a middle-aged MP (man or woman) picturing himself being sexually assaulted, or picturing more likely his beloved son who no doubt he still thinks of as an innocent babe, would suffer, in his imagination, a severe trauma. In reality, however (which is scarcely conceivable but certainly not impossible), he might feel quite differently. I have yet to meet a man who was sexually assaulted as a youth, and is honest enough to admit it, who does not recall the occasion with pleasure and gratitude.

When will adults get a sense of reality about these things. Do they not know that boys 'sexually assault' each other all the time – just for kicks. And does it not occur to them that there may be some who would like to, but are too shy and inhibited to go about it, who, on reading such accounts as this, may actually come to look upon prison as an exciting and desirable place to be, and take the necessary steps to get there. What seems to dismay their dim puritanical souls whenever the question of teenage sex comes up is that people should enjoy themselves without incurring all the responsibilities of marriage and children which they have had to.

19 June 1960   Anniversary of my meeting with Raul. His memory hangs close over the days. His letters arrive about once a fortnight. Each airmail stamp costs him half a day's pay. Each letter says almost exactly the same thing. He tells me nothing about himself, what he is doing, but fills the page in his elegant script with a long unpunctuated mis-spelt lament in Spanish which takes me hours to decipher, though now I am beginning to know the phrases by heart. I have to reply at once, otherwise another expressed letter will arrive a few days later demanding to know what has happened to me. And I have to reply in the same vein with the same phrases since the only Spanish I learnt was with him. Thus the unreality of the relationship is assured. I might be writing to Ariadne on Naxos.

20 June 1960   Unreality? –

In the Nietzsche–Wagner correspondence (which I have just been reading) did either side really know what the other was about. 'It is impossible for me to recognize greatness which is not united with candour and sincerity towards one's self. The moment I make a discovery of this sort, a man's achievements count for absolutely nothing with me, as I feel that he is only playing a part and everything he does is based upon insincerity.' Nietzsche comments on W's conversion to 'religion' in *Parsival*, which he suspects to have been motivated by reasons connected with promoting the success of Bayreuth.

But the factors of self-search and self-awareness are found only in some creative people and not necessarily the greatest. The blindness, duplicity and self-will which marked Wagner as a man, also allowed him to create the extraordinary Ring. Nietzsche misunderstood the significance of each; or rather he could not reconcile the truth of the work with his idealistic requirements of the man.

The moving thing is Nietzsche's silence. 'For wherein lies true greatness of character if not in the ability to take sides even against one's self, if truth demands this?' Which of course he did, to his ultimate destruction. To the artist truth can only be partial. The whole truth is outside the cognizance of man.

Nietzsche and Wagner at Sorrento – one might do a painting of that one day.

28 June 1960   Travelling companions who incessantly draw your attention, with enthusiasm, to things which they are sure must interest you (as a painter) and which in fact do, but which you have already seen and digested in your own way without saying anything. But that won't do. Everything must be seen and appreciated all over again from their point of view.

'A flower is to be watched as it grows, in its association with the earth, the air, and the dew; its leaves are to be seen as they expand in the sunshine. Dissect or magnify things and all you discover is that oaks, roses and daisies are all made of fibres and bubbles ... but for all their peeping and probing nobody knows how.'

Many artists today claim that their abstract paintings in fact derive from the microscopic world of cell shapes, nuclei, etc., to which they turn for inspiration. But this cannot be felt knowledge or real experience, which is limited to the capacity of the human senses. Or perhaps I'm out of date.

Some large charcoal drawings lately, of no importance. Impossible to get, to keep things in focus. To hold a steady course. The balance of my mind is not very strong. Perhaps everyone is the same. The never ending struggle to get the best out of oneself. It is not simply a question of knowing yourself, but of accepting what you find out, and coming to terms with it.

2 August 1960 Much like these two quotations illustrating the fundamentally different attitudes to life of the Greeks and the Hebrews:

'As is the life of the leaves, so is that of man. The wind scatters the leaves to the ground, the vigorous forest puts forth others, and they grow in the spring season. Soon one generation of men comes and another ceases.'

'As for man, his days are as grass. As a flower of the field, so he flourisheth. For the wind passes over it and it is gone, and the place thereof shall know it no more.'

For the Greeks a passionate delight in life with an acceptance of mortality. For the Hebrews despair and resignation from the start and transference of all interest to a hypothetical life to come. What bad luck to have been brought up a Christian. Is not the 'problem' of life, the eternal conflict between the spirit and the senses, an invention of the Christian Church (or maybe of Christ himself who was certainly a moody man)? Did the Greeks have a 'problem' of life?

'The most striking distinction between the erotic life of antiquity and our own no doubt lies in the fact that the ancients laid stress upon the instinct itself, whereas we emphasize its object. The ancients glorified the instinct and were prepared on its account to honour even an inferior object; while we despise the instinctual activity in itself, and find excuses for it only in the merits of the objects.' (Freud in 1910.)

There's no doubt which side I'm on.

1 September 1960 Impressions of Venice: Meaningless beauty and squalor. Meaningless? – because I see, but do not partake. Beauty of the past. Beauty of the present people. The way the Vaporetti conductors moor and un-moor the boats at each stop with deft, gentle movements of the hands. No fuss. The way they remove a foreign hand which happens to be in the way (they just pick it up and put it out of the way). The boy unloading a barge in a side canal. He wore only a straw hat and jeans so low on his lean hips that a rim of black pubic hair was visible on his nut-brown skin. Yet he was totally unselfconscious. None of the narcissistic posing one sees so often in England – a road-side striptease for the passing girls. All his movements were strong, vigorous, purposeful and skilful. He seemed totally happy and absorbed in what he was doing. Yet the barge was carrying stinking wooden piles which had been pulled up from the bottom of the canal.

Italians seem to be wonderfully free from motiveless neurotic behaviour. Watch two friends meeting unexpectedly in the street. No guards go up. No covering up of suppressed hostility with false hysterical enthusiasm. But a warm, relaxed physical greeting. Hand on neck, arm round waist, shoulder. Yet not a meeting between 'close' friends, because after a minute or two they casually part. But, of course, the English always romanticized Italy. We are marvellous in crises, when every odd is against us. But give us the problem of just living together as a community and we tear ourselves and each other to shreds.

4 September 1960 Interesting the way the Venetians totally ignored the realities of the Christian myths they were called upon to illustrate. Not a trace of agony or suffering in the Crucifixions or martyrdoms. They were simply an excuse to celebrate their enthusiasm for life and art. For instance, the only thing in the magnificent Crucifixion in the Scuola which is contrived and unreal is the crucified Christ, which absolutely anyone could have painted (and possibly did). And the 1000 martyrs of Carpaccio, each writhing in ecstasy as they try out new poses and positions and juxtapose ever more inventive and unexpected portions of their anatomy.

Scuola del Carmine A young man reclines languidly naked on a stone pilaster with his ankles secured by chains. Leaning towards him, legs astride, vigorous as a young stallion, a dark-haired youth is trying to draw his attention to a sharp-pronged instrument which he holds in his hand and is about to use with evident relish on his body.

Behind the wan youth another man grips his shoulder apparently to get him into a better position for cutting off his head with the sword he holds in his other hand. At the foot of the pilaster is an assortment of severed hands and heads looking like stale charcuterie. Attendant horsemen and armoured soldiers fill out the composition. The painting is not good. But what is interesting is the extraordinary passion and conviction with which the dark-haired executioner is painted.

5 September 1960 I seem to resemble some primitive form of life, an amoeba perhaps, which lives almost entirely off its own inner resources, hermaphroditic, unstable, able to take in only minute amounts of nourishment from outside, and that with difficulty. So it is no good my trying to 'see' Italy. The barge full of boiling tar which suddenly appeared down a small canal this morning, black, with a plume of blue smoke drifting past the half-naked brown bodies of the workmen shovelling grey cement out of another barge was more life enhancing for me than all the rhetoric of the high baroque. But the paranoic ceiling in S. Pantaloni was worth a try I suppose. It might have worked; for children perhaps. But going to length of fixing cut-out figures over the actual arches – but you could argue either way – the arches are not so good anyway. And certainly the whole thing, space and illusion of space, adds up to something. But it was good to get out into the little oasis of the courtyard of the Archivo di Stato.

6 September 1960 SS *Mediterranean*   Ships suit me. All anxieties of travel vanish once aboard. I like the small limited world. At dinner I sat next to a widow from Dusseldorf. She had all those qualities one remembers in Germans before the war. Warm and motherly. With a childlike enthusiasm and excitement for everything going on. A happy face, and hands always at the ready for applause, but round her eyes a network of tiny lines gouged by sorrows. A woman who would weep easily and rather prettily and has wept much. Her husband was killed by Hitler. Tears sprout again as she tells you this with a shy apologetic smile. Now she travels alone, whenever and wherever she can. Anxious to learn, anxious to meet people. Not really expecting very much but enjoying everything with gratitude.

The ship is simply a large tramp steamer masquerading as a liner. Music in the lounge and elaborate menus. But this afternoon, when it rained, water poured through the deck into the first class corridors. First class is given to everything. There are no class divisions in the ship, no directions, no times of meals. The general purpose of the ship is to be enjoyed. You can wander anywhere, play with the compass, climb into the lifeboats, fiddle with the ropes. If this makes things a bit more difficult for the crew, by having to clamber over piles of deck chairs to get up to the bridge for instance, this is accepted quite without protest. No one seems to give anyone orders. There is not a single notice anywhere telling you what to do in case of emergency. The band is charming. Five young Greeks all with the famous long black lashes over half-closed eyes.

Towards the end of dinner the ship was rolling quite considerably. Then, just as everyone was leaving, three jets of water shot into the saloon through the open portholes. The stewards jumped neatly out of the way, but no one shut them.

Reaction of the crew when the water poured through the deck during the storm: one caught sight of the inundation, stopped abruptly in his tracks, looked at it with his hands on his hips, made a loud hissing noise, cleared his throat and went to the side to spit. He goes off to find someone else who performs exactly the same ritual. Meanwhile, the water continues to pour through. There was nothing to be done about it except lament. In half an hour the sun was out again and everything dry.

Brindisi: 8.30 am Sun already hot and everything shimmering in white light. A small dark Italian boy walks along the quay level with the deck. He carries a tray of food from the canteen and looks along the line of faces on the boat. He has a sharp slinky look with a polite smile which would ignite swiftly if occasion warranted. He slops the coffee out of the cups through not looking where he's going. An eye for the main chance perhaps, but too lazy to make anything of it should it come his way.

Aegean Passed Ithaca in bright moonlight last night. Stood in the prow with two German boys watching a huge fire burning somewhere on the mainland (could it have been Troy?). Then up at six to watch the passage through the Corinth canal; very tight fit. Now sailing through Greek waters in the pearly coloured morning air. Might be off the coast of Scotland or Ireland. Steep-rising islands all round, wooded and soft contoured.

Athens, Saturday Wonderful ride out to Sunion yesterday. Honey-coloured and ochre landscape, dry, brush scattered. Paddy Leigh Fermor, Alan [Ross], Jennifer, Jonathan, Victoria and her Hussar,

Bumble. A large part of the day is spent in organizing the movements of this group. It is only when you get out of Athens that you get any conception of what Greece is like, past or present.

Aegina Not sure of the day but it doesn't matter. All days the same. Stillness and heat and the sea like distilled water. Bathing at Moni. Gleam of amphorae deep among rocks, but be careful of urchins when you put your feet down. Ouzo at the harbour in the evenings. Brown boys and pink boats loaded with dark green melons. Fish suppers on the terrace overlooking the grey pistachio trees. Barrels of retsina, pine branches stuffed in the bung holes. Bill Sansom here with magnesia round his lips.

Last week we sailed, under the usual conditions of chaos, to Mykonos. Everything white and windy – bora blowing. Exhilarating crossing to Delos. All day wandering amongst foundations. Only things standing: the lions, long limbed with weather-worn features. Sea Homeric coloured and rough. Woollies needed all day.

On Sunday Alan and I set off for a tour of the Peloponnesus by CHAT. Corinth – Nauplia – Epidaurus – Mycenae – Tiryns. Splendid setting of Corinth, and the clear layers of Greek, Roman and Byzantine building. The setting of Mycenae – very proud – grand without pretension. The gate whence Agamemnon set forth to conquer Troy. His bathroom floor – a single slab of black granite crossed diagonally by a grooved drain. The calm and majesty of the panoramic sweep over the Argive plain to Argos on its small and shapely hill. Difficult to imagine the neurotic misery of Elektra in such an open air setting. Two vast sweeps of mountain rise to the north and south and Mycenae crouches on the web of rock between.

Tiryns – earlier than Mycenae – praised by Homer for its beautiful walls, which are French polished to a shining ebony by the oily fleeces of passing sheep. Birthplace of Hercules. At Nemea, where he slew the lion and we stopped with brake trouble on the way back, they sell bottles of red wine called Lion's Blood which makes you potent and strong.

Friday, 23 September 1960 Last day, hot and windy with small clouds racing. Yesterday to Poros and Hydra, both impressively picturesque, but I prefer Aegina with its scruffiness and ordinary activities. Alan and Bill saw me off – gently. Shall I come again?

6 August 1961 Sandford St Martin   A month of fairly intensive work, ending in the usual baffled defeat and utter perplexity. Seeing some of my earlier things here I wonder if I haven't entirely lost the thread. Yet there is not one thing which, at the time of its completion, I could have said with certainty was worth keeping.

23 September 1961   Think that the thirty-six by forty figure of 4 August one of the best I have done. Yet it was done with the sole aim of painting myself out of my clichés; to avoid doing what I knew (with a little trouble) I could. Negative intent. Yet the result looks positive and purposeful. Perhaps at last I have tapped a strata which lies beneath consciousness. The trouble has always been that I insist on being in control all the time. I have a fear of spontaneity and mistrust what probably I wrongly regard as 'accidents'.

8 October 1961   Seething with anger and suppressed aggression. Great loathing for all known human beings (the unknown, of course, are always exempt). Cannot see how life can go on without it becoming more and more impossible. All efforts to improve the human condition in whatever sphere have about them the futility of a man trying to fit a hundred matches into a box designed for fifty. *There are too many people.*

Life, as biological existence, is grossly over-valued. We cling to the ethics of an underpopulated world. Life as a means to an end, human fulfilment, is all that matters. And only a limited number of people can live on the earth's surface at any one time. No one is the worse for not being born. But being born, everyone has the right to a condition for self-fulfilment. People are adaptable, but there are limits to what you can adapt to, without reverting to the status of a bivalve. Perhaps that's the idea. It would be typical of God with his passion for symmetry. A full circle. What could be more perfect.

The aged, crippled and insane are forbidden to die, even if it means lying for years flat on your back in a metal box. They are not even asked. Only the young and vigorous may die and kill each other (under State orders, of course). Even the unborn must live once they've popped out of the egg. Though it's apparently all right to throw the eggs away. But nobody likes this line of argument – it smells of the gas chambers.

I would advocate voluntary extermination camps (Eternal Rest Hostels) for those who felt they'd had enough. Free alcohol and crunchy, sugar-coated narcotics. There should be as much rejoicing and family congratulations over an elderly suicide as there is over a new born birth – (good old So-and-so, I hear he's *made room*).

It's no good expecting Nature to keep the balance. No doubt she will continue to look after biological existence, but she was never very interested in human life. We have deprived her of her classical bacteriological weapons (reserving them for our own possible use) but lack the nerve to put anything in their place. We cling to the primitive existence-at-all-costs. But having usurped command, it seems that sooner or later we must employ the strategy and ethics of a commander, before the natural order re-establishes itself in a way which may not at all be to our liking.

12 October 1961 Am very well aware (from time to time) that I am living at the extreme end of my adolescent tether, which is getting very frayed and threadbare from constant holding. In order to live into middle age one must stop asking certain questions and behave as though one knew the answers. One must mature. This means, I suppose, living by some set of spiritual values which you regard as more important than the gratification of the senses. I find these difficult to discover. Life without sex or alcohol, for instance, should be worth living, though the idea fills me with gloom. If one is forcibly deprived of these things one adjusts, no doubt. But to deprive oneself wilfully, for the sake of higher things – there is something distasteful about the idea of abstention. On the whole I do not think I like abstainers. What is more it leads to spiritual pride (I discover with glee). I like self-mortification when it leads to a heightened sensual awareness, like starving before a good meal or going without sex for a week. But I doubt if I understand what spiritual values are. The most profound sensuality, as in the best music and painting, seems to me to achieve a spiritual quality, but not by mortifying the senses.

W. T., who also keeps a journal, tells me that he writes up at the end of each day interesting or remarkable things that *other people* have done or said. That seems to me mature. But nobody need expect much of that sort of thing from me. For one thing I never remember what people say, or if I do the words seem to exist on their own, separate from the speaker. For another, I am always too involved with my reactions to them and what they're saying to see the thing clearly. Mature people know instinctively in any given situation what is appropriate to reveal, what conceal. They don't give everything all at once, or else nothing at all.

Which is why I do not think I'm a good tutor. Because I can't tute. The young should be confronted with firm, uncompromising, but passionately held points of view, which they can accept or reject;

preferably reject. Whereas I see, or try to, everything from their point of view, and go frolicking around in the wake of the Big Questions, with which I am just as concerned, though less urgently so, having managed to get by quite well without finding the answers. When I do take a 'firm line', usually from exhaustion, it is often slightly phoney, which they at once detect. What is so marvellous about the young is their (apparent) patience with the fumblings and hesitations of the middle-aged. Either we should answer or be shot dead. Sometimes perhaps, with our expensive life-jackets and more buoyant tissue, we can save them from actually drowning, but we can never teach them to swim.

December 1961 Thoughts on Painting: Space is very much in the air these days with painters; particularly 'pure' space. It is said to be the ultimate raison d'être of a great deal of painting and sculpture – the experience of pure space.

If I lie on my back on top of a hill and look upwards I get a sensation not of pure space, but of a blue dome enclosing the hard ground beneath my back. I get a sensation of space when something crosses the dome, a bird for instance. But it is still not an experience of pure space, but of bird-in-space, because if a moment later another different bird follows the same arc the sensation is not the same. And if two birds cross the sky at the same time in different directions the sensation of space is even better.

So as far as I am concerned space is simply the element which separates one object from another. I cannot appreciate one piece of space against another.

In painting we are told that old-fashioned space, perspective, is illusionistic (and therefore out) whereas cubist space and, even better, non-objective space is 'real tangible space'. But as far as I can see all space in painting is an illusion, whether it comes forward or goes back. What is real is the flat surface of the picture and the important thing is what has been painted there.

I sometimes think that space is being used as a more respectable word for nothingness, and that what many artists are doing is demonstrating the fact that they have nothing any more to paint. They manoeuvre the pigments on the canvas as they might if they had some end in view, but in fact they are accompanying rather than expressing their inner states of mind. I have nothing against this. It may be the only appropriate painting for an age such as this. Much more tiresome is the stuff that is written about it.

Kandinsky 'The object is a fiction situated outside reality.' But that represents a *discovery*, valuable and significant only to Kandinsky. It is not a truth, valid for all artists. Another could say with equal justification 'the object is the whole of reality'. Each artist must make his own discovery. But too often these utterances are taken as standards by which to measure the value of other artists' work. Those who inherit Kandinsky's abstractions must look elsewhere for their material. Art is abstracted from life and not from art.

Abstract Expressionism 'We faced the canvas with the self, whatever that was, and we painted. We faced it unarmed, so to speak. The only control was that of truth, intuitively felt. If it wasn't true to our feelings, according to protocol it had to be rubbed out.' Remarkable the romantic, narcissistic self-delusion implied in a statement like this. And it has the sadness of a rather lonely child dressing up to play a secret game the rules of which he has to make up as he goes along. And in fact the situation was essentially the same for painters in the past, only they didn't dramatize it. Nor did they think that truth, or their own identity, could be found by staring into a mirror. Nothing worth while could possibly result from such an attitude (and in fact nothing has, for it was written by a very minor member of the group).

It is altogether more alarming when a critic of international status (Michel Seuphor) can write as follows: 'Thus it has been only logical to take cubism to its natural conclusions, and to cut out the traditional subject and give final expression, in a clear style and in absolute liberty, to the values of pure art as they appear to the artist.'

The very style makes one cringe with its absolutism and finality. There were no 'natural conclusions' to which cubism had to be taken, any more than cubism was the 'natural conclusion' to the work of Cézanne. Artists conclude their own work, and in so doing hand on certain technical equipment for subsequent artists to use if they wish. Cubism was, and is, a method of depicting volume on a flat surface. As with impressionist colour or Renaissance perspective there were historical reasons why the discovery was made at the time it was. But once made it becomes part of the inherited equipment of all subsequent painters.

But this won't do for the art historian with his mania for discipline. Artists must march in straight lines, and keep step. And if one of them thinks to do a little pirouette on the way, because he feels that way, he will soon discover that his 'absolute liberty' is a good deal less absolute than he might suppose. 'Nudes, still-lifes, landscapes, have all lost their substance,' M. Seuphor tells us, 'and have nothing essential to offer man today ... the real subject is painting in itself and for itself.' In fact the artist has 'absolute liberty' to follow the party line or else ... And so that there shall be no doubt what is required of us, he goes on: 'Art freed from subject implies and enforces the absolute necessity for creativeness ... the object of art is now more than ever to find a personal and inexhaustible mode of expression, the image of our profound inner being.' What, one wonders, does M. Seuphor think Giotto, Michelangelo or Piero were trying to do? Keeping in line and illustrating bible stories? But if one tries to see some sense in the idea that 'creativeness' is a variable necessity in art (which is not at all easy) then one might think that is of greater importance in figurative painting, when there is the constant danger and temptation to relapse into narrative illustration, than in the case of abstract painting where every mark the artist makes cannot help but be 'creative' in the sense that it represents nothing but itself.

But all this would matter little enough were it not for the fact that it forms a perpetual barrier between the artist and the ordinary sensitive intelligent spectator to whom he would like to communicate. It does nothing to help him respond to the qualities which distinguish good painting from bad, of whatever kind, but merely to recognize styles, with a totally false set of values for judging one style against another.

Totally unprofitable is any consideration of the right *style* of painting today. The painting which can now be seen to matter from the beginning of the century is that of Picasso, Braque, Matisse – not Picasso, Gleizes, Metzinger, or Matisse and the minor Fauves.

Shapes which result from a war with reality. Shapes which follow an a priori conception. (Cf de Kooning before and after 1952.)

What finally seems to happen to the 'absolute liberty' of the artist today is that he gets trapped in his own personal mannerisms. Hartung's endless primary school exercises in penmanship. Kline's compulsive imitations of his own signature.

The technique of Abstract Expressionism is of use only to those who can experience the apocalyptic. (Did I say that, or did I read it somewhere?)

The vitality (and hence the importance) of painting generally stems from its lack of deference – its rootlessness. No cultural impedimenta in the eyes of the artists. 'Closes all gaps between thought and action – gaps which are produced by a sense of history.' (Tillim.)

Its main sources were anarchy and a sense of decoration. Its achievement was to show how much could be done with so little. Its failure was that it brought no disciplines, no restrictions which would enable growth. It offered the artist perfect freedom, the kiss of death. It tried to express directly the prime values of painting which, like happiness, are the by-product of a search for something else. Since it had no aesthetic it had to substitute historical or dramatic values – the painting as record of an event, the artist as hero unarmed before his canvas. Such fantasies can appeal only to a society deeply frustrated by having had its spiritual problems transposed into economic ones.

It is claimed that Abstract Expressionism showed for the first time that a painting, instead of being a depiction or arrangement of images (real or abstract), was itself an image. But this is unremarkable since it had already been demonstrated by Mondrian or Malevitch (among others), and in a sense could apply to good painting of any style in which the total effect is more than the sum of the parts.

It depicted on a magnified scale the simpler human emotions to a society which had lost touch with such things. The tranquil mysterious warmth of a Rothko, the brassy crash of a Kline, the squashy sensuous drip of a Guston come across with the impact and immediacy of a well-designed poster. Thereafter, it has nothing more to say. Like a drug it operated on the law of diminishing returns. But since nothing has been required from the spectator in the first place, he cannot complain if he gets little in return.

The futility of the search for the Absolute – symptom of an age without religion which cannot tolerate the anxieties and insecurities of relative and purely human values.

'The impact of an acute triangle on a sphere generates as much emotional impact as the meeting of the figures of God and Adam in Michelangelo's "Creation".' (Kandinsky.) Not to me, boy.

12 March 1962 'Variation 15,' writes a critic reviewing a piano recital, 'demanded an immediate round of applause.' Really? – I would have thought that Variation 15 and all the other variations demanded to be listened to, not clapped at. Nothing to me is more senseless and distressing than the hideous noise of hundreds of moist palms being banged together which immediately follows, and is often superimposed on, the closing bars of great music. It is inconceivable to me why people should feel an urge to do this. The only possible follow on to great music is silence. Anything else is an anticlimax and shatters the effect. It is painful enough anyway to have to climb down again to 'reality' without being slapped down by hundreds of little hands all round you. But it doesn't seem that many people share this view. (Clapping is, however, quite useful after a bad performance to help to clean the sounds out of one's ears.) It exemplifies, of course, the role which art is required to play in society now – to stimulate comment. It is the same with painting. It has been said that art *speaks for itself*, but is it allowed to? Never. A host of middle-men rush in between explaining, interpreting, commenting, unscrewing and feeding the thing to the viewer bit by bit. Even the artist himself is expected to join in. Nobody should be allowed to have any work of art explained to them, whether music, painting or literature, until they have first of all learnt it by heart. By then it would probably be unnecessary.

19 March 1962   The feature of the Jazz pub where I sometimes go, is the noise. It has the quality of a physical substance like hot water. It surpasses all auditory levels and you feel it in the diaphragm, solar plexus, walls of the stomach and spine. Once the pain threshold has been breached it is soothing and almost sleep-inducing. Orpheus perhaps affected animals by similar means.

I read somewhere that when someone is speaking to you under conditions of noise one attends automatically to the messages reaching one ear while disregarding the din which bombards the other. There is, however, an MI5 in the brain which is keeping watch on the stream of anonymous noise to make sure that nothing really important is disregarded, such as a mention of one's own name. The same thing happens in sleep. The loaded word is not consciously heard but it causes a galvanic skin reaction. The same thing happens with the printed word. If one skims through a book the eye will instantly pick out loaded words, and the skin reaction in such cases is even stronger.

5 June 1962 – Clarbeston Road – 9 am   A boy walks slowly down the length of the platform touching the cardboard boxes warming in the morning sun, flicking the string on a parcel, looking down the wide empty rail and waiting for the train to Fishguard, which is puffing quietly and blowing out steam further down the line and getting ready to come in – rather like an elderly actress once famous who knows her best days are over and that it is only a small country theatre half full but determined all the same to do her best. Ugly and uncomfortable, there is a sense of security about railway stations which the luxury and comfort of an airport lounge can never provide.

April 1963 – Rome   Up early to S. Pietro in Montoni. Wonderful position overlooking the city. Quiet. No one about. Spent much time in front of del Piombo's 'Flagellation'. The sensuous fullness of Michelangelo – a sort of dreamy *volupté* – but more refined, more aristocratic (I think Michael A. did the cartoon – should know these things). Same flow and blending in the modelling of the limbs, but less stringent, less passionate. Almost something of the detachment of Piero. The colour cool and sonorous. What a time they had – flagellations, crucifixion upside down, every device of physical torture. Perfect masochistic co-operation of all the victims. Never a hint of any real suffering as in Flemish painting where people seem to be tormented even by the everyday clothes they wear.

Could one do a flagellation today – with a small f? The sport has not exactly died out. (P. says he often has to treat three or four patients a week with deep wounds voluntarily incurred this way.) But since it is now regarded as a sexual perversion it would presumably be classified as pornographic.

Neither S. Peter's nor Bramante's famous 'Temple in Montorio' is 'beautifully proportioned' as the book says. The one is elephantine, the other irritatingly miniscule, as though designed for dwarfs. Both lack respect for the physical presence of man. So also the earlier Roman building, which is much improved by being in a tumbled-down state. New it must have looked very like the Vittorio Emmanuele monument. Intended to impress. What is perfect, and for me the most beautiful thing in Rome, is the Campidoglio – size, texture, colour, proportion. It is grand, dignified, but never overbearing and radiates a sense of well-being. Marvellous at night looking out across the Forum and then up at the rows of marble genitals hanging from the black velvet sky.

Everyone should see Rome first at night by floodlight, starting at the Colosseum and walking north. The spirit is then present but the shattering scramble of modern life held back. The light reveals what matters and leaves the rest in darkness. Everywhere one is impressed by the Italians' skill for presentation. They may not be great creators but they have a perfect sense of style. One sees it in their dress, cars, and the intricate and skilful gladiatorial combat which goes on all day between pedestrians and traffic. All is designed to test one's nerve: and pity the poor traveller who loses it. They do not treat kindly the timid and shy. It is the same in shops. One is rewarded for one's skill in bargaining. You get nothing for being virtuous or simple.

5 May 1963 Very good evening with P. W. last night. Am impressed by the way in which he accepts people's mad, eccentric and destructive patterns of behaviour without himself becoming involved more than is necessary. Very good story of one of his patients who *needs* to have an incompetent doctor. More and more I get the feeling that people who have been through analysis form a new race. They are the only really 'free' people.

Someone said recently of a psychiatrist (he meant a psycho-analyst): 'He receives only what a man rejects; nothing live ever falls into his hands.' Few statements could be more defensively untrue on so many different levels. Of course it was said by a catholic; to whom, having made his pact with the nursery Daddy, objective truth must for ever remain invisible. In fact of course the analyst, when he receives anything, receives what is most alive. It is the persistent vitality of the disturbing subconscious element which makes the man attempt to reject it, or come to terms with it. The whole meaning of analysis rests on the truth that man is not master of himself, though the majority can get by with acting as though they were. Typical of the catholic arrogance is the assumption that the act of rejection implies the lifelessness of the thing rejected.

If a man can make a private treaty with himself, projecting God, and settling for some reasonably comfortable form of self-deception, good for him perhaps. But he should not pretend that he is thereby making any useful contribution to human knowledge and understanding. Nothing blocks the growth of the human spirit today more effectively than the power of the Church.

'The austerities of faith against the clatter and despair of the senses.' But one could change the adjectives round with equal truth and say: the clatter and despair of faith against the austerity of the senses.

The catholic (or the religious man) assumes out of hand that the sensual man is the self-indulgent man. It never seems to occur to him that the appetites of the senses can be governed and controlled at least as well as the appetite for faith and belief. And how many more abominations throughout history have been done by the man of faith, than by the sensual man.

One might almost say that Catholicism is an ethical perversion in the same way as masturbation is a sexual perversion. Both are private and personal ways of avoiding the issue – the difficult issue of living for a time on this earth with others.

26 May 1963 – King's Cross Station Would you claim that you loved mankind? –

No I would not. They are a nasty selfish ugly stupid species. Speaking generally. Speaking about the mass. Christ was a fool. Love mankind indeed. As soon love a nest of ants.

But individually – one at a time – take the man opposite?

Fortyish, balding, pasty yellow complexion, clear eyes, clean mouthed. Doesn't drink much. Plays games. Thirty-six perhaps. Properly dressed – dark suit, white shirt, silver grey tie. Obviously travelling on business.

And undressed? –

Neck suggests a lean body, long thighs. Keeps in training. Lawn mower on Sunday. Perhaps squash. Long boney fingers. Clean, but not manicured nails. Not self-conscious. Totally unaware he is being observed and documented. Buried in the *Daily Telegraph*. Not stupid. Engineer perhaps. Looks as though he would be patient and crafty.

So you might perhaps love mankind one at a time?

If they were rarer. If one came across another one now and again. But there are so many of them. Nothing can be loved in such quantities. As well try to love bacteria.

He would have been a quiet boy at sixteen. Top of his class. A swot. Not particularly attractive but loyal. Always looked older than he is. Eyes have that delicate bluish baby skin round the lids which reddens easily when he cries. Which he doesn't. Too reserved. Not given to demonstrations.

Probably not more than thirty-five. Nicely spoken. Is in the wrong part of the train for Leeds. A Leeds man? Possibly. But no – he would have known the right coach.

Factories. Coal. Smoke-streaked chimneys. Rows of pill-box houses with washing. Large empty purposeless green fields with posts at the far end. Breakfast time. Packets of cereals in each little box. Potters Bar. Mock Tudor further up the hill. Coffee instead of tea. Might well have a good figure, but only visible in the bathroom. Not likely to be caught walking about naked. Flat bellied. Big knees. Size 9 shoes. If the train crashed and we were crushed together he would behave well – thinking of others.

Wears buttoned cuffs and not links, braces and not a belt. Two points of a Persil-white handkerchief. Married with children. Ring? No. How odd. Doesn't approve of rings on men perhaps. Or could he not be married? Impossible. Nothing of the bachelor about him and too old to be still with Mum.

Am certain he has not thrown one glance in my direction. Totally incurious. Which page of the *Telegraph* is he reading?

Or is he being very cunning. Does he know exactly what I'm doing? Sized me up completely the first moment. Knows all about my type. In that case he is not married. Married men in trains are always disapprovingly curious of non-conforming strangers.

Interesting new landscape. Naphtha Reforming Gas. Different shapes and colours of objects. Gangs of hot stripped workmen with shining stomachs. Mostly coloured. Might be going through the Punjab. Marvellous long supple torso like a Comice pear. Train too quick. Pang of loss when something passes too quickly to be fully seen.

Back to the green fields and little black tarred railway boxes, one window and a door, built always of such unnecessarily heavy timber. Old sleepers perhaps. Snug, basic security boxes.

Seats for morning coffee. Train much too fast now, swaying hysterically like a toy. Cups jingling.

First-class Jew opposite. Man of substance. Grey and yellow expensive spectacles. Heavy signet ring. Thinks a lot. Has the two short deep brow-furrows of thinkers.

Not a bad looking lot all round. Solid, reliable. No talking. No women or children. Businessmen. Several take saccharin out of pocket phials. Watching the waist line. Might love about 5 per cent. But not the one with a tight lipless slit for a mouth like a badly sewn-up wound.

Cow parsley. Bicycles in hedges. Wide empty river. No one in the fields. All sown and growing. Small houses with prominent drainage systems. Cars parked in station yards. Linesmen in blue overalls leaning on picks. Train watching. Sun gone in. Kneeling women weeding. Five miles to Peterborough.

Man, woman and dog standing in a field like a Millet. White horse with a long black glistening penis like a flat-ended hose. Not like a Millet. Price Shand. Young trucks moving by themselves on sidings practising how to run. Tennis courts with lifted nets. Unused. Work time. Peterborough North. Big black pipes peering over into open tanks like something waiting to be sick. Peterborough types with lips peeling back off their small front teeth showing the gums.

Wakefield. Victorian brickwork. Solid, graceless, but very fine. Design conscious. Colour and shape of each brick carefully considered. Expressive and human. Feeling of the North. Sense of a different country. Crude and dirty but warm-blooded. More bios than anti-bios.

7 April 1964   The New Generation exhibition at Whitechapel. After all one's thought and search and effort to make some sort of image which would embody the life of our time, it turns out that all that was really significant were toffee wrappers, liquorice allsorts and ton-up motor bikes. So one could have saved oneself the trouble. I understand how the stranded dinosaurs felt when the hard terrain, which for centuries had demanded from them greater weight and effort, suddenly started to get swampy beneath their feet. Over-armoured and slow-witted they could only subside in frightened bewilderment. One hoped, I suppose, in the end to hand on to someone who saw further, had more talent, more youth, energy, more time before him, to complete what one had started, or relayed from the past. But not this. Perhaps it is the iron curtain between the generations, which one had always heard of but thought to apply only to the past, across which no comparisons are valid.

Compared to their work my own, and that of many of my generation, must appear indecisive, uncommitted, full of contradictions and unresolved. This may indicate some degree of awareness but also, and consequently, an inability to make decisions. Such a combination in many spheres of life, politics say, would be disastrous. Fortunately art is an end product and not a means to an end. It is not required to find the answers. It is enough if it examines the problems and states the conflicting nature of experience in positive forms. What is disappointing in the work of so many of the more talented young painters is not so much the nature of the experiences they appear to find interesting but the bland, positive, hard-edged assurance which leaves out of account the one thing which seems to me most characteristic of this age, namely its basic contradictions and dialectical quality. To find a form for this is difficult. The difficulty for the young is so great that they borrow the form of someone else's experience and embroider on to it minor variations of their own. This is natural enough and there is no harm when the borrowed form is rich enough to sustain their own growing sense of life. But today the form borrowed is simply that of another artist's escape solution. A form so thin and pared down that it is no more than a mannerism and of no value except as the statement of the artist who first made it.

'People endowed with the ability to make decisions necessarily see situations as being simpler than they are.'

Some notes on painting – August 1964   The strange thing about a retrospective exhibition of some twenty years' work – at least for the artist – is the appearance of orderly planned progression, as though the whole thing had been foreseen from the start. Whereas at the time each painting was just another attempt to solve the same problem. The result in each case defined the limits of one's ability, not the measure of one's intentions. The fact that these limits can just be seen to be slowly extending is the most reassuring evidence that one is still alive.

Afterwards the difficulty is to persuade oneself that it was not a posthumous exhibition. As with any exhibition, the best way to escape that trap of finality is to keep some work back and go on working while the show is still on.

The problem – my problem – is to find an image which renders the tactile physical presence of a human being without resorting to the classical techniques of anatomical paraphrase. To create a figure without any special identity (either of number or gender) which is unmistakably human: imaginative without being imaginary. Since it is impossible to conceive a human form apart from its environment, an image must be found which contains the simultaneous presence and interpenetration of each. Hence the closer and closer interlocking bombardment of all the parts, like electrons in an accelerator, until the chance collision, felt rather than seen, when a new image is born.

A critic once wrote that I seem to be obsessed with what it feels like to have a body. He was right. Maybe other people take the fact for granted, after a short period of tactile investigation in childhood. But I find it a constant baffling mystery – the duality of I and myself. *Je est un autre.* When we hit it off for a time the going is good. At other times it is a constant bickering warfare. It is a commonplace that one's body belongs more to the environment, to nature, than to oneself. Hence the need so many people have for rigorous disciplines and self-mortifications.

In art, as in life, one aims at achieving reconciliation – equilibrium. The mistake is to imagine this can be done by eliminating the hostile forces. Equilibrium is the balancing of antagonistic forces and is always a precarious state of tension, as in a pair of scales correctly measuring weight. One can imagine that a stupid pan might long for the weights to get off the other end so that it could settle down in peace and quiet beneath its pound of sugar, like the painter who claims that the act of painting is enough because it offers the illusion of perfect and untrammelled freedom of expression.

Expression of emotion is different from discharge of emotion. A man in a violent temper is not himself expressing rage – he is just raging. Expression is the purposeful control of an emotion for a determined end. Expression utilizes and incorporates into itself the medium of expression. Both are changed in the process of creating the staple expressive image. Discharge of emotion, although it occurs through some channel, does not incorporate the medium and issues in an unstable state. It vanishes like a cry. I would like to be able to paint a crowd – that abstract entity referred to by sociologists as the masses. An amorphous compressed lump of impermanent shape reacting as a mass to environmental stimuli yet composed of isolated human egos retaining their own separate incommunicable identities. In the past artists have usually dealt with the problem of crowds by turning them into assemblies. Assemblies are orderly rhythmic groups of individuals which act and are acted upon by mutual consent. The behaviour of an assembly is at least compatible with that of any member composing it and often surpasses him in achievement. The behaviour of a crowd follows its own laws and generates its own energy. It is inferior, humanly speaking, to any one member composing it and usually acts contrary to his interests, and can even accomplish his destruction.

The idea behind the Laocoön myth, at any rate to me, is that it represents in supremely dramatic form man's conflict with his environment and with himself, his own body. Serpents, for some reason, have always been the chosen representatives of evil, temptation, and the enemy of the spiritual; possibly because of their extreme plasticity and appearance of having a slippery surface (in fact they are dry and warm). Their continuous vertebral construction gives them the power of unpredictable movement and ungaugeable strength, and their uniformly armoured surface without the vulnerable articulation points offered by subsidiary limbs gives them the appearance of being invincible. The encounter was distinguished by extremely stylised violence – the motionless tension of the strong man bending the iron bar. And maximum physical contact was assured with the enemy whose pliable surface could be moulded to every part of one's body. The fact that Laocoön and his sons were not condemned to death by strangulation in the normal inescapable way but given a sporting chance to conquer by their own strength or cunning is unusual in classical myth. Who won is not really known, since the contest is still undecided.

19 September 1964 Driving back from Worthing, where I had deposited M., I realized shortly before I got to Horsham that I should pass the turning which said to Christ's Hospital. With mixed feelings I decided to go back. I had not been for about twenty years. I thought the term would not yet have started, but after passing Barnes Green I came upon a bunch of them on the Barnes Green run, one of the longest and most dreaded ordeals. They were going in the same direction as I, so I came upon the stragglers first. They were mostly new boys wearing the stiff hard colours of their new house-jerseys. I passed them slowly and reverently on the far side of the road. I could hear their desperate gasping breath, their sweating heads rolling in pain on their shoulders and the lifeless slap of plimsolls on the hard tarmac. And I knew how they would glance up with the dazed longing of convicts at my free and effortless passage. I felt ashamed of my privileged position and the mad thought occurred to me to stop and offer the last two or three a lift.

The afternoon was warm and sunny. Everything looked the same, yet in a strange way different – mellower and smaller. I parked the car outside Coleridge and walked away from it quickly, feeling absurdly guilty. I half expected a voice to shout *Vaughan, what on earth do you think you're doing here with a car.* The organ was thundering out in the chapel and I went in. A tiny boy, no bigger than a black-beetle, was slithering about on the high wooden bench of the console producing a glorious and splendid noise. It gave me the same tingling sensation of gratitude and excitement of years ago. I looked again at the Brangwyns. It was like looking at my own face – at something so familiar that it was part of me. Nothing surprised. I had carried away no false illusions. They were exactly the same. In each one were the same details which particularly pleased or displeased me, and the same secret thoughts and fantasies which I had left there years ago when I had stared at them day after day for eight years.

But the presence of the boys was different. They all looked healthy, angelic and slightly unreal in their fancy dress. It was no longer possible to see this costume as normal attire. And one or two whom I passed in the avenue, and looked at with a detached and automatic interest, smiled, and said good afternoon. This astonished me. I cannot remember such greetings being given to strangers from the outer world. Or did they perhaps think I was a new master with whom they should get on to good terms?

Partly it was like a dream – so much instantly familiar as though one's identity still belonged there, but also unreal, as though neither the place nor I really existed. Some things were different; pop-art paintings visible through the glass doors of the art school, the circle of fir trees round the school bog. That more than anything made me feel old. Whole new trees where before there had been none.

But there was no sense of the past, and this is what I found it difficult to understand. There are things one comes upon unexpectedly and one remembers – ah yes – that was then. They revive momentarily a forgotten experience which one has outgrown. But there were things at Housey like the Brangwyns in the chapel, the sound of the organ, the table in the dining-hall opposite the pulpit at which I had eaten so many dreary meals, the smell of Prewitt's wholemeal flour, gravy, wet mops, which evoked not the past but a sort of timeless present. They did not seem remote or sealed off. They seemed to be part of me. It was not the widening recognition of Time Regained, but an awareness that I was still carrying around with me these unassimilated trappings from childhood which I could neither outgrow nor discard.

7 October 1964   The show looked attractive – colourful – appetizing; I'll say that. Individual pictures rather better than in the studio. But for some reason I felt extremely remote from the whole thing, as though it had been done years ago, or even by someone else. Consequently I was free from that embarrassed feeling of 'exposing' myself, which always afflicted me in the past. This may be due to a more remote and objective style of painting. Or it may be due to the fact that one no longer cares so much about what sort of impression one makes.

[Eric] Newton – the old lizard – compared me shrewdly with Watts. We both have the *grand manner* – whatever that is. In fact I have secretly admired Watts for many years, while deploring his paintings. But his ideas, his conceptions.

It has always seemed to me that *truth* is something one recognizes rather than something which can be proved. The most infallible systems of argument cannot force you to accept the truth of something unless you *feel* it is true. It would seem that the only truths you can accept are those you already know but have forgotten, or were never conscious of. The *moment* of truth is always a moment of recognition.

10 October 1964 'If anyone should attempt to express a hasty condemnation of my reticence, I would advise him to make the experiment of being franker than I am.' (Freud: 1914. Traumdeutung.) Wonderful dry, ironical dignity of the old man. The stoical patience of his agonizing death at 20 Maresfield Gardens (outside which I now park my car each time I go down to the bank in Finchley Road). 'What a man of eighty feels is not a topic for conversation,' he replies in answer to birthday greetings from Einstein. But what gives someone this tenacious hold on life that he prefers living in agony to dying in peaceful oblivion? I admire its dignity, but it seems to serve no purpose. He could have hastened his end. He had no religious scruples to impede him.

Three measures (according to Freud) for dealing with the miseries of the human condition: *powerful deflections*, which cause us to make light of our misery (a sense of humour, I suppose, would be a deflector). *Substitute satisfactions*, which diminish it, and *intoxicating substances* which make us insensitive to it. (Wer Sorgen hat, hat auch Likör.)

Freud's objections to universal love: (a) love which does not discriminate forfeits part of its own value by doing an injustice to the loved object. (b) Not all men are worthy of love.

19 October 1964 An indication that I am more ambitious than I like to think I am is my strong resentment that I was not one of the six painters chosen to represent England in the Premio Marzotto, one of the two selectors being someone who has always claimed to think highly of my work.

'Joue avec les cartes qu'on a.' But how in heaven do you identify them? Middle-aged, myopic, through filmy tears of self-regret and angst, it is impossible even to read the numbers.

13 December 1964 Much moved by 'Generation X' – a series of tape-recorded interviews with teenagers. One admires again their honesty, lack of pretension, refusal to be bluffed. One sympathized (a little uneasily perhaps) with their total rejection of the false and hypocritical values on which society operates. But sentimental self-identification with the young is the worst thing you can offer them. They are not interested in the tattered remains of your own youth which you treasure so highly. It is necessary to appear to have beliefs. But what can one set against their desperate plea and paranoid destructiveness?

1 January 1965 From midnight to 2 am, I mingled with Generation X, about a quarter of a million of them, between Piccadilly Circus and Trafalgar Square. I did not notice one ugly or uncomely person. Fleet-footed, warm-hearted , tender, perplexed, they were good to look at and good to be with. Conspicuously unpleasant, as is usual on such occasions, were the police, looking and behaving as though there was imminent civil war. I dare say it is not their fault. The fountains were full of wet boys instead of water. The roads were blocked with stationary traffic. But in two hours I saw not one clumsy, brutal or vicious gesture. All was in good sport and good heart. Yet the few members of my generation who were still out of bed (whom the police were presumably protecting) acted as though they were dealing with an invasion of rats. No one was doing any harm, yet all the time one was 'moved on' in that suspect friendly manner the police are taught to use. Areas of the square were put arbitrarily out of bounds, challenging the young, quite naturally, to try to cross them. As soon as one did, shoals of police would chase after him, looking ridiculous and undignified. What was the point. There was no violence. But people must not be out in the streets of their own city enjoying themselves at 2 am. 'Come along now – let's all get home to bed, shall we.'

Groups of youths went along the lines of stranded expensive cars shaking hands with the irritable occupants. It was interesting to notice their hesitation in approaching a car with only one occupant. The most daring did. The rest passed on to the next. It was a totally charming gesture with just the right amount of ironical insult. The rich were stranded and helpless, the poor were mobile.

12 January 1965 'For life means being born into a community and fulfilling its duties. Once these are called into question, once their infallibility is called in doubt, once they have to be romanticized to be found beautiful so that one may live by them, then decadence has set in.' (Lukács: reviewing Thomas Mann in 1909.) Weirdly remote point of view which seems to advocate nothing more than the life of an ant. (Was he a Catholic?)

19 January 1965 Maclaren-Ross's account of the Painters of the Forties in the *London Magazine*. Completely perverse, absurd and untrue. He simply did not know them. We thought him a fop and an arrogant talkative bore. We pulled his leg, but he was too conceited to realize this. How can he claim to write of such people and such a time. But since he too is now dead there is no point in challenging him. But that is how history is written perhaps. That will survive as the story of those days.

But they were not like that. For a time there was real life and gaiety. Real things were happening and being done. People were alive. Nothing seemed impossible or too vast to attempt. With today's young it is different. It was expressed very clearly by Ian H. (one of my students): 'What I admire,' he said, 'is a painter who has really committed himself; who has got himself into a position where only very few things are possible.' Morris Louis affects him in the same total, almost physical way that Cézanne affected me.

25 January 1965 Ronald Laing (Tavistock Clinic) talking on human relationships: unless we can understand each other there is no hope for the future, he says. Understand perhaps, but not pardon. At any rate it is better than 'we must love one another or die' which was always a hopeless prescription. How could we? From the very beginning the human race has distinguished itself by killing, torturing and preying on its own kind, not for food or survival, but for pleasure – from inner necessity. There seems a need to make others suffer and see they are suffering. Other societies have accepted this fact and made provision for it. Cruelty was organized into ritual. We reject this as primitive savagery and so our crime figures increase with the general level of vitality.

The ten boys who drew knives and stabbed the pianist and his friend in a Brewer Street club last night – what does one make of this? Was it a sort of necessity relationship on both sides?

29 January 1965 It astonished me how great was the reaction to Churchill's death this week. One thought he had been dead for years. But this universal acclaim, this response which goes beyond all political and national bounds, must mean that the world sees him as something very important which they have lost. A man who acts without inhibition or self-doubt. The last of the Pre-Freudians.

Not a great man by my standards because he lacked sensibility and the faculty of judgment. He did not need to understand because he had the power to delude. Outside the simple context of war he was mistrusted, and rightly, because he had nothing to contribute to the more sophisticated and unheroic problems of living in peace. But it is interesting to see revealed the extent to which the world still looks for a father figure who will simplify the issues and permit heroic solutions. Churchill enabled everyone to live the childish fantasy of his finest hour. How reluctantly we inhabit our century.

In order to arrive at what you do not know
You must go by a way which is the way of ignorance.
In order to possess what you do not possess
You must go by the way of dispossession.

Both Eliot and Churchill died within weeks of each other in the same winter. Eliot sought the truth, regardless of the consequences. Churchill the heroic fantasy, regardless of the truth. The one understood. The other lived. To understand does not require the death of young men.

13 February 1965   *Les Biches* at Covent Garden. Exquisitely danced with a mocking and stylish irony. One of the best things seen for a long time. Decor as fresh as a spring flower. Any young painter who still thinks 'space' was something discovered in the 'fifties should go and see it. Suddenly one sensed again what ballet once was, and achieved. It gave me the same tingling, almost anxious excitement that I felt in the first room of the Guggenheim collection at the the Tate. Once felt it just couldn't *go on* being so good. What an age to have been working in, everything in flower with creativeness, shrewd, ironical, and full of zestful experiment and hope.

And later strumming through the score which I must have bought about 1935 I remembered those desperate years at Unilever. Coming home in the evening and plunging straight into the piano, which I play badly, to try to kill the hateful frustrated day and hold off for an hour or so the stifling domestic evening. Never having the skill to create my own world effectively, but struggling with a sort of hopeless despair to escape reality. To create that magic world which ballet, then unseen, seemed to symbolize.

Unhappiness in childhood is bearable at the time because one knows no difference. The unfulfilment and constant frustration is taken for granted as being 'life'. It is only later on looking back one sees how different it might have been – should have been. And the sense of waste and lost opportunity is unbearable. There is so little to remember with pleasure. And so one goes on ridiculously trying to have the things now which one should have had then, and which now are truly impossible because one is too old, but were possible then if only one had known it. Nevertheless, one was luckier than some. I come upon these remarkable words written by a young schizophrenic patient during her period of recovery (quoted by D. Laing):

'Everyone should be able to look back in their memory and be sure he had a mother who loved him, all of him, even his piss and shit. He should be sure his mother loved him just for being himself; not for what he could do. Otherwise he feels he has no right to exist. He feels he should never have been born. No matter what happens to this person in life, no matter how much he gets hurt, he can always look back to this and feel that he is lovable. He can love himself and he cannot be broken. If he can't fall back on this he can be broken. You can only be broken if you are already in pieces.'

'Reality is too difficult to bear. We cannot do without auxiliary constructions.'

The problem remains whether to act within what appear to be the limits of one's potential, and thus assure a measurable success, or to accept the challenge to surpass oneself, and risk disaster. The answer is simple in youth. But now – how does one know one's limits?

10 April 1965 – Casablanca Continue to read with mounting irritation (but there is nothing else to hand) Julian Green's Diary. What is tiresome about so many of that group (even Gide at times) is that with all their protesting to love the truth they are basically dishonest. They tell only what can be beautifully expressed and does them credit. He goes on over and over again about his 'temptations' – struggles against the 'sins of the flesh', 'weaknesses', 'giving way to pleasure'. What's he talking about? Masturbation probably. Then why not say so if truth is the object? But that would be *indiscret*, mortal sin to a Frenchman of letters. I do not mean that journal writers are under an obligation to disclose their private acts – they are not often interesting – but it is pointless to refer to something vaguely and obliquely which they seem to consider of prime importance. Either say nothing at all about them, as with Pepys and Kilvert, or tell the truth. The truth is not always beautiful or flattering, but it is often of value to others.

And all these meaningless religious ecstasies he describes at compulsive length. They convey nothing of the true inner calm of the mystic to which he pretends. He half senses the truth about himself (he reads and re-reads Stekel on Anxiety with an almost morbid fascination) but refuses to face it. His behaviour, in fact, is typical of the neurotic defending his neurosis by every possible means against the threat of truth.

'I keenly feel the hypocrisy there would be in attempting to reconcile a life of pleasure with religious practices.' For heaven's sake. Who is likely to succeed in living a 'life of pleasure'. And of what point are religious practices unless they increase one's capacity for pleasure. Oh yes, I know he means spiritual joys as against carnal pleasures – the old meaningless Pauline distinction.

But if one does try to live a life of pleasure, and accepts opportunities which promise pleasure in all its forms, one soon discovers that pleasure resides in giving pleasure, carnal or otherwise. And pleasures of the body are also pleasures of the spirit and mind. And the pleasure of being alive on this earth is having a body and mind to develop and fulful which is difficult enough anyway, never mind what comes after. Of what possible interest is a human being today who firmly believes, or incessantly protests, that the real life is after death. Why doesn't he make room, and get started.

11 April 1965 – Marrakesh Arab world. Bazaars. Everything in fantastic over-production. Nothing seems to be sold from the piled stalls. No more than perfunctory efforts are made to get your attention except in the stalls which sell tourist goods. Nobody cares. Crowds gentle and smiling. Hot spicey African smell. Cummin. We wandered through with Omar, our 'guide'. If you do not go with a guide, or someone who looks like one, you cannot move for swarms of children fighting to offer their services. In the afternoon visited the required palaces and tombs. All very beautifully done, but Moorish architecture quite without meaning for me. Too spiritual perhaps, too symmetrical, covered with minute manic filigree decoration, which is as tiring to look at as it must have been to do. Dark gloomy discomfort of the concubines' rooms in the sultan's palace. Hard wooden bed, hard couch, carpets on the walls instead of the floor. No feeling of voluptuousness. Perhaps the upholstery was provided by bodily fat.

Snake charmers, boy dancers dressed as girls, colourful water carriers selling a poisonous liquid in brass cups out of a blackened skin. All a bit shoddy-looking like a run-down theatrical troupe. Continuous, tireless, undirected movement of the crowds.

Sheep being gathered everywhere for the great slaughter on Tuesday. *Gorge du Mouton.* Men carry them round their shoulders like furs, tie them to carts, to donkeys, stuff them into the boots of cars. At first you assume the animals must be dead, but on closer looking they are not. They are dazed and uncomplaining and do not appear to be at all alarmed. Everywhere the feeling of lazy, hopeless amiability. Whatever happens is the will of Allah and so there is no point in striving or worrying.

13 April 1965 – Taroudannt Drove over the Atlas yesterday morning. Endless virages. Roads unpaved, dangerous, but no traffic. Tremendous mountainous landscape rising to snow-capped peaks. Absolute silence each time we stopped. Voices and small sounds carry over vast distances. Alpine-type spring flowers in abundance. Flat-roofed mud villages slotted into the hillsides like fungi. Thought of Tibet. All green vanishes on the south side. Red, ochre and olive. Camels instead of horses. Deafness on descending.

Taroudannt is one-storied and built of mud and straw surrounded by twelve foot thick walls. Foreign Legion was here and left one run-down French colonial hotel. Marhaba. Gloomy but comfortable. Dining room like a Naafi. Garden full of cacti in man-sized jars. Nothing to do but walk the mud streets and sit in the garden of the hotel. Arabs vary in colour from blue-black negroid to café-au-lait. One small boy had red hair. They look less diseased here. Their movements are always graceful and gentle (except the young ones on bicycles or scooters). When they are not moving they sleep away the day crouched in their hooded djellabas. Heat and white light surround you on all sides as though in a clay oven, but it is never oppressive. Cool breezes come in from the sea and night falls swiftly from a green and orange sky.

19 April 1965 Driving north from Agadir by the coastal road. Marvellous dry luminous landscape, scrubby foothills, cinnamon-pink and ochre-white earth dotted with dark olives and patches of glowing saturated colours from the peasants working in the fields. Camels, oxen or donkeys harnessed to the ploughs. Flocks of black, brown and white goats. Shepherd boys in bluish white djellabas. When we stopped for a moment by the side of the road to smoke a cigarette one left his herd and came running towards us. One's instinct was to think he must want something; but we were wrong. We had stopped on his territory and he came to greet us. He shook us gravely by the hand and stood smiling. He did not understand French and so it was impossible to communicate. We stood silently smiling at each other in the white stillness while storks flew overhead. He indicated his flock and the landscape and his gestures seemed to imply that everything was at our service. When we got up to go he touched his head and his heart and then kissed us gently on the back of the hand and stood quietly to watch our departure. The incident was absurdly moving, hardly believable today. It was like living in the Old Testament.

The cotton djellabas start a deep indigo blue and bleach in the sun through every tone of the colour until they reach a bluish white. The same dye must be used in the paint on all the shutters in Essaouira, which are indigo inside and pale cobalt outside. Other colours – an intense saffron yellow often seen with a cool faded maroon which is almost the colour of the soil.

At the market at Agadir a boy in the virginal bloom of adolescence swathed in blue with the hood low over his dark eyes sat patiently before a tiny group of vegetables spread out on the ground which he had brought in from his garden. He was so beautiful to look at that it took one's breath away. And to justify staring we bought all his four pounds of waxy yellow potatoes. Since he could not tell us the price in French we handed him a note and waited for the change. He was too shy to look at us and counted out the change slowly and with difficulty, passing the coins from one large hand into the other as though it were a lesson in arithmetic. As we walked away he called us back in confusion. He had given us 5 frs too little. His cheeks were flowing with soft velvet down. His big supple hands had perfectly kept nails. But at no point could he raise his head to look at us. He sat quietly looking down in a strange humble dignity.

Later at B.'s we were introduced to one or two other youths of the town. One in particular impressed me by his beautiful manners, his clean and well-kept appearance. One would take him for a French student from a good family. Yet he lives in the filthy shanty town, with no water or sanitation, which was put up by the authorities years ago for the earthquake victims, in one small mud-floored room which he shares with his mother. His father and brothers were all killed in the earthquake. That was the environment in which this graceful and elegant young man grew up. B. I think is paying for his training at an agricultural college. B., who years ago lived in expensive elegance in London and is now retired, also lives in one bare room in the town and devotes all his time and much money to giving a reasonable chance to such people, who have obvious talents, to escape from the intolerable poverty of their circumstances. In Agadir there are thousands of such boys who were small children at the time of the earthquake. So far as one could discover the government does nothing about them. Huge hotels and office buildings are going up in the new town, but the shanty town remains. There is nothing unusual in this of course. What is strange is that so many seem to survive without becoming corrupt, vicious or delinquent.

A number of them appear to make a reasonable living by prostituting themselves to tourists who walk along the sand dunes which go for hundreds of miles along the coast. It is not often they have the luck to come upon a single woman walking alone, but they act on the assumption that all European males are passive homosexuals unless they look French. And they importune with such whole-hearted enthusiasm and persistence that even this appears quite innocent and uncorrupt.

I was sitting reading one morning at the place where we usually bathed when a youth suddenly appeared seemingly from nowhere and sat down quietly beside me. You never seem to hear an Arab approach, they just materialize. We exchanged greetings and he asked me what I was doing. I pointed out that I was reading. He sat quietly for some moments watching me and waiting for me to get to the end of the page. Then he asked me if I would like to go into the bushes with him and *faire du pi-pi*. He looked at me with a broad smile and steady brown eyes. He was about fifteen or sixteen. I thanked him very much but declined. Why not – he asked in tones of astonishment. Because I was reading, I said. Clearly he did not accept this as a valid alternative and suggested he went off and found me someone younger, asking what age I preferred. I implored him not to bother, explaining that I was quite happy reading and would shortly be going for a swim. He remained quite quiet for some minutes, looking at me with a puzzled, almost offended expression. Then, thinking perhaps that I hadn't properly understood him, he unzipped his trousers and invited me to inspect his equipment (which, as with many Arabs, is somehow maintained in a state of permanent erection) and began to explain and demonstrate its method of operation. I expressed my admiration and suggested, rather hurriedly, that he might like to smoke an English cigarette. This he accepted. We sat and smoked and talked about the weather and where I had come from and where I was going to. Then when I took up my book again, feeling rather ill-mannered and ungracious in doing so, he got up and drew his tattered djellaba around him. '*Et bien – plus tard peut-être.*' He bowed gravely and shook me by the hand and glided silently back into the dunes.

15 June 1965 Numerous letters congratulating me on my CBE. Extraordinary how many people notice such things. It would never occur to me to read through all the columns of small print in the Honours List. Obviously I don't know how to behave.

Life is really a great cheat. One is brought up to pursue success. To reach the top. But the higher you go the more you leave behind.

The more difficult it becomes to maintain contact with the simple things and people who are knowable and lovable. Top people are effigies. No one thinks they have any problems. Or if they do they are certainly not interested in hearing about them. I remember John L.'s remark the other day when I gave him a lift in my old Morris back to the Slade hostel: 'I never thought you'd have a car like this. I thought you'd have an E Jaguar.' Symbol of having made it. Of being beyond the pale. An untouchable.

So now when I do not telephone people I would like to see (from the same basic inhibition of imposing myself and making the first move) they naturally think it is because I am too grand. They are not good enough. I have more important things to do. They cannot realize one is still a lost child wandering through a wilderness of confusion. And why should they? The immature should remain inconspicuous, otherwise they store up more trouble for themselves.

9 August 1965 Symptoms of being in love; a slight feeling of inflation on the left side of the thorax, as though something were lodged there – some winged creature. Appearance of having lost weight (P. remarked on this last night, though the scales show the same). Zest, and lightness of step, followed by a sudden ache of longing – for the presence of the loved one. The ache makes itself felt not in the region of the heart (as poets suppose) but along all the moist surfaces of the skin; hands, arms, thighs, belly. A feeling of negative contact. The indescribable sweetness of knowing there is someone you care about and who cares about you. The small brochure of physical memories which one goes through again and again, the memories getting brighter (and further from reality) the more they are caressed. Unusual marks on various parts of the body like small stigmata.

But the conjunction of love is needed only so long to replenish the reservoirs of memory. Already one hastens the departure of the exhausting demanding presence so that loving may be undertaken in absence and the inner world of fantasy restored to its normal order.

17 August 1965 One's hold on life these days is tenuous. People die in the streets of Los Angeles, Vietnam, Chicago, London. People who a moment before had been wholly involved with living. Then they are lying in a stream of their own blood which flows down a familiar gutter. Only a chalk mark on the side-walk separates life from death. I am amazed that I wake up each morning alive enough to read about other people's death. But I cannot hope to perpetuate this. One morning other people will read about mine, while sipping their coffee, like Mme Verdurin, on their balconies. One must arrange things so that death will not create too much disorder. So that what is unfinished can remain unfinished without confounding what has already been achieved. This is difficult when one is accustomed to living on the natural assumption that there will be a future.

5

1967–1977

1 January 1967 Usual mild expectant anxieties. How many more diaries will one need to buy? Will even this one be finished? One takes yet one more step up the ladder, feeling it sway ever more dangerously, the drop even deeper. Will one reach the top?

An extraordinarily warm and totally unexpected letter from McWilliam about the *Journal and Drawings* which for some reason I find more reassuring and encouraging than anything anyone else has written – possibly because he's the only heterosexual to have written 'in gratitude'.

Also an extraordinary New Year Eve with Bryan. He had asked me to dinner 'and then maybe we might go on to a party if we feel like it'. Rings at 6.00 to confirm I am coming – mentions, jokingly the Quiche Lorraine & Daube de Boeuf – asks me for 8.00. No idea what to expect. Will others be there? Rings about 7.30 to ask me to make it 8.30, 'You'll see why when you arrive.' Arrive 8.40. Bryan, tired, dressed in rags, smell of paint, all windows open and piercingly cold. Keep my coat on. Explains he has had a terrific day with painters, decorators etc working in the kitchen, which is in total disorder. But the table in the dining room is immaculately laid for two. He is dying for a drink and starts the process of making a martini. We sit at opposite ends of the laid table drinking. I have put on a suit, thinking it might be a dinner party, and feel rather tricked. Admiration invited for the painted ceilings, pictures (idiotic Lee Krasner fills the whole of one wall – dull Ceri Richards on the other – remember with irritation the small oil he 'bought' from me and never paid for and which is now for sale at the Redfern, with the gouache he did buy – so much for his admiration for my work). Suggest, as he's had such a tiring day he might like to come out, but don't press this, since the table is obviously laid for a proper dinner. About 10.00 he starts to prepare the first course – yoghurt with cucumber, pimento, herbs, etc. Sit down finally to eat this ravenously about 10.45. He then announces that he has some delicious veal, vegetables etc with which he intended making a marvellous stew but it would take about four hours.

Agree that it would hardly be worth starting now. Insist am not really hungry – which I was. Consume cheese and biscuits and wine, all of which is delicious. Suddenly notice it is midnight. We can go to Craxton's party or Neurath's. Choose Craxton's. Rings and says will be along in half hour or so. Then wonders if it's worth it. Instead we go upstairs with a glass of brandy and he plays on the gramophone the whole second Symp. of Sibelius by Karajan – loud and impressive which brings tears to his eyes. I sit rather soporifically and just let the thing go. About 1.30 I refuse drinks and leave.

The sort of social evening which I could never dare inflict on anyone, but which B. can do and almost make it seem agreeable, until one looks back afterwards. Arrive home ravenous and make myself two turkey sandwiches.

The small room in my mother's flat which was 'mine' from the age of about fifteen until I moved into the larger front room at twenty-two or twenty-three and where I had my first terrifying and unexpected orgasm as a result of tying up my genitals with my pyjama cord; where I experimented guiltily with the whole repertoire of masturbation techniques from electrical stimulation (very crude and unsatisfying then) to threading cotton through my foreskin in pursuit of God knows what fantasy: where I also painted the four large panels for Christ's Hospital and all my other early works; is now occupied by a young boy of nineteen called Stephen, a friend of the student who rents the larger room. He moved in some weeks ago with five suitcases of books, cooking equipment, electric heaters, clothes, and other belongings which are now stacked from floor to ceiling. He has no job but spends the day 'writing' – without saying what, rather wisely, to M's ceaseless inquisitiveness. I passed him on the stairs once going up. A tall lean youth, fleet-footed, shy looking, lynx-like, attractive. I hear endless anecdotes about him from M. – the huge stew he cooks for himself on the one evening he is allowed to use the kitchen and then warms up night after night for himself, alone. He is supposed to have a girl friend, but on the wall over his table is a photograph of a good-looking young man slightly older who is not his brother. The more I hear about him the more curious I become to know what goes on in that little room. Does he too do the same things as I did at that age? Are the walls and salmon-pink paint work (a surprise from my mother on leaving school – she had had it decorated in a style she thought I would like, being artistic, and not as she herself would have chosen, with the inevitable result that it was one of the most disastrous decorative effects ever achieved; sickly and hideous beyond description. I had to pretend it was exactly what I liked – since it had cost a lot of money – and live with ever after) saturated with the guilty anxieties and secrets to which they were witness through so many years? One may safely assume that he masturbates there sometimes, but how. I would dearly like to be one of those walls one night. I feel a curious affinity, almost tenderness for him simply because we shared that room, lived there through one of the most intense periods of our lives very much alone.

14 January 1967 Self-indulgent? – Yes – I have always been so, when opportunity allowed. Drink and sensual pleasure are a sort of compensation for the empty misery and loneliness of my early years. At least I held out longer than most of my generation. And a certain inherent orderliness prevents me from going too quickly to excess. Most of the others are dead now or wrecks.

But it is only with people who profess to love me that I am really at my worst. I cannot be even normally civil, the cramping emotional demands suffocate me. But with my friends, who make no demands, I am reasonably considerate and loyal – or am I? Why am I always making scandalous remarks behind their backs? I think I do it jokingly – or rather to make what I imagine will be amusing conversation and thus appear in a good light. Privately perhaps each of them thinks of me as wholly untrustworthy.

11 February 1967 I may be able to say in the end, like Gide's Thesée, 'J'ai fait mon oeuvre'. But I shall not be able to add, alas, 'J'ai vécu'.

17 March 1967 Returned late last night after dull dinner with Griffin (Kinross and young camp) to find J.W. (to whom I had given my key that morning so that he could come in and have a quiet night preparatory to going to H.H. [Harrow Hill] today) drunk and asleep in my bed and a tough looking layabout thug (I thought) asleep in the spare room – where J. should have been. Haul him out of my bed into his friend's and lock all doors, valuables etc. Retire to bed with two Tuinal, seething with anger and timidity.

Wake early and plan aggressive tactics to displace them without losing face or dignity. Had told J. the night before to be out of the house by 8.00. But since he was stupid with drink and half asleep, assumed he would have forgotten. Decide, after rehearsing many alternatives, that I will get up at 8.00, wash, shave and make myself look respectable; then go into their room, order them to get up instantly and get dressed, and, in order to appear reasonable, say they may come into the kitchen for a cup of tea before they leave. Plan witty and sarcastic remarks to make over tea.

At 7.45 a knock on my door, which of course was locked, and J.W. stands there, dressed, looking apologetic, with a cup of coffee for me. 'Come in and meet Jimmy', he says. Thus he always manages to turn the tables and avoid aggression.

25 March 1967 Easter Saturday: H.H. there with M. and R. Came up on Wednesday. From the previous Wed. until the Tuesday night the longest and most perfect Karezza ever. Extraordinary buoyancy and zest throughout the day followed by four to five hour sessions (electric) each evening. 3 grs Tuinol – perfect sleep – fresh next day. No ill effects after a mild ache in the groin which passed off after 48 hours. I note this simply to record that there is something unique and supremely satisfying in this process as has been repeatedly claimed. Mostly it lies in the sense of self mastery and superbly controlled pleasure. There is also something in one's initial orientation, of course, since it does not always work out this way.

27 March 1967 Small lead wheel from a toy dug up yesterday. Spokes missing, broken away, leaving small stumps – perfect corona collar. Memories of childhood – similar flywheel put to masochistic use. Had this one? Another boy – here? The thought is strangely moving and disturbing. I would like to think it has been so used. And why should I assume I am the only one? Possibly commoner than one thinks. J.W.'s urethral fetish. Had I not read about a case in Psy. J. I would certainly have thought – as he did – that he was unique.

24 August 1967 I took my leave from Johnny this evening without ceremony or dispute but with mutual awareness. He was fresh out of Pentonville, as often before, but without the debonnaire poise which before has guaranteed his acceptance – without the groomed considered appearance – testimony of respect – auto et allo –. He was drunk, boring, dully loquacious, insensitive. I saw him for what he now represents (not perhaps what he is), the recidivist; with all the trite deceptive falsity. Sheer dullness. I watched his death. Or the death of an illusion. And while watching, R. rang from Essex, confirming his remoteness – complete non-understanding.

This has been the cruellest year I can remember – so slow in its torment. Empty – not harsh. I feel nearer to death than life on my 55th birthday.

2 January 1968 The relationship between Vaslav Nijinsky and Diaghilev. If one could understand that, there would be no more doubt. Nijinsky was the incarnation of beauty unequalled. Diaghilev a man of rare insight and sensibility.

7 January 1968 A good poem by Larkin in the *S. Times* excellently analysed by Ricks – momentarily transforms my day and raises a corner in the blanket of depression and boredom wherein I now live constantly (hence almost nothing in this Journal for over a year). What is the point of endless repetition of the same theme.

Saw my second 'blue' film last night at X's. Two girls – unattractive tarts – strip a good-looking teenager, nail and lay him out on a table. One girl masturbates him slowly while he plays with the breasts and nipples of the other who stands behind his head. The attractiveness was the taut stretched length of his body, arms above his head, helpless, accepting passive stimulation while actively stimulating someone else. Thereafter the film deteriorates into the usual boring and slightly disgusting close-ups of female genitalia and copulation. Also good when he was made to copulate lying on his back with the girls taking turns to impale themselves on his cock and withdrawing before he could achieve orgasm. Remarkable that he could retain an erection during twenty minutes of this sort of treatment. He finally masturbates vigorously himself so that the audience can see the ejaculation over one of the girl's legs. Although sexually stimulating to watch at the time, it is the memory that makes a satisfactory masturbation fantasy afterwards (I used it this morning) whereas the memory of a still photograph, or actual sexual experience would be less so.

24 October 1968 Reading at intervals, with great enjoyment, the memoirs of René Gimpel.
On Forain: 'He keeps his colours in a special piece of furniture, heavy and foursquare. This man who puts so little colour on his grey canvases, has a terrifying array of tubes, like a pile-up of cartridge cases after a battle.'
On Berenson: 'His small face, like that of an anaemic lion cub.'
Monet at 80: 'My eyes are getting worse. I have to wear glasses for reading, and most of all for eating fish.'
(What was Monet's yellow dining room like? Does it exist still? Also the two sideboards which he painted in tones of yellow.)

The fantastic creative energy of the old painters, never flagging, never doubting, brought finally to a halt only by physical paralysis or death. How one envies them. Yet it was not absence of doubt which enabled me to produce what I did in the past but more stamina to endure the strain. Now there seems no longer the moral obligation to struggle on. Perusal of pornography – by far the most important thing to me at the moment – is so much more enjoyable and beguiling.

As a result of this all too obvious loss of moral tone and softening debauchery, what work I do should be clearly inferior to what I did before. Maybe it is – but it's not obvious. Perhaps I am saved from total collapse by my lack of natural facility. It would not be surprising, since it is precisely that which has prevented any success in all other spheres of living. Why does one live in spheres rather than fields?

For the first time in my life I have funked the challenge of a commission – the mural for the Chester Beatty Institute. In fact I had delayed so long in starting it that their patience became exhausted and they withdrew it. I simply could not face the effort of something out of routine. Neither had I the courage simply to refuse in the first place. I console myself with the knowledge that I can earn the same money far more easily at home.

Twenty-five new paintings go on show at the Marlborough next January.

Altogether I have done forty-two canvases in the last three years. I suppose that can hardly be said to show a total cessation of activity. They seem pleased with them. I do not know – as usual – though looking back I cannot see they are worse.

Odd how impossible it is to write pornography which is exciting to read afterwards – although the writing is. Yet the drawings I did years ago are very exciting.

Last week I went to see J.W. who is doing six months in Pentonville. He was well, charming, and good to look at. I look forward to his release.

8 November 1968 'It is here that are formed and set those qualities which made England's greatness possible, and which are not to be found in books any more than the Frenchman's good sense or his genius for improvization. In these peaceful courts England teaches that all agitation is vain; that one of the secrets of a happy life is to watch it pass from one's window, that running won't help you go further and that jostling is hateful.' (René Gimpel at Oxford)

12 November 1968 Gimpel: 'Botticelli's Spring could not have been done sixty miles from Florence. To survive for all time (the artist) must express all the beauty contained in a certain place and in a fixed second of eternity.'

On Rodin: 'Aubry relates that the sculptor's sensuality was so keen that in the course of a conversation his hands would caress and crush every breast and phallus within reach.'

On Soutine: 'Large sensual lips that speak as fish breathe out of water, with the same rapid, tragic beating.'

Much enjoyed Joe Ackerley's *My Father & Myself*. The economy of the style, taut, accurate, reticent. Writing for the reader, not for the pleasure of writing. If only I had read this before I allowed the edited version of my journal to be published. How I regret this indiscretion now. In spite of the testimony of the probably quite genuine pleasure it has given to a few unknown individuals who have written to say so (I have their letters) I cannot now pretend that it has any other purpose than to show off – the editing and publishing that is – not the original writing.

Chronically insecure and self-doubting I alternate between the conviction that I am worthless and can do nothing at all of value, and that I am inexhaustibly fascinating and can do nothing silly or insignificant.

17 May 1969 Some people live in high rise towers or low rise towers. Basic requirements for human existence calculated to the cubic foot. Others live in damp homely basements ten to a room. Very unhygienic. A few in mansions with six rooms per person. Or prisons, three to a cell. Or on yachts in mid ocean – 1000 uninhabited miles in all directions.

I live here, in four large airy quiet rooms, and in H.H., with seven rooms (which I share with R). I move from one to the other, as mood prompts. So I have virtually 11 rooms, in two houses, to live in. All bought with my own 'money'. All that's lacking is the life to live in them.

26 August 1969 Dinner at K.P.A. with David Hockney and Peter. Good evening. The more I see of D.H. the more he impresses me. He has all the best qualities of his generation. Modest and self confident, honest in speech, unconcerned with impressing yet considerate and well mannered, impatient with all fraudulent or compromised behaviour, ardent, curious, warm hearted, uncorrupted (and probably uncorruptable) by success – his generation have never known dire poverty I suppose. I feel so much better after such an evening. Yet I do nothing to make it. I could easily give a dinner party myself. What I like about David (among other things) is that he does what he says he will. Months ago, at P.W., talking about special issues of stamps which I did not know about he said 'Oh, but they're marvellous, haven't you seen them, I'll send you some'. And two days later I get a postcard covered with about 8s 6d worth of special issue stamps. And the last time I saw him, also at P.W., just before he was motoring to the S. of France in his convertible Morris (like mine) I said 'You ought to get a Triumph Vitesse – they're better than the Morris for long journeys'. 'Maybe I will. It's an idea. I'll go and buy one tomorrow morning. There'll just be time.' And he did.

29 August 1969 – Perama   Only 24 hours since I arrived but how differently I feel. Tensions, anxieties, depression completely vanished. In the sea this morning at S. Georgiou, lifted and buffeted by the heavy fuming sea, it occurred to me that for the first time in years (or nearly) I felt simply happy to be alive. I must remember this at home and not allow myself to be deceived (after all I did not want to come here) that the environment of the South takes charge. It is totally different from the most idyllic situations in England and cannot be substituted. A lunch of omelette, tomato and retsina in Argirades and then, after contacting P's boys – back to the sea. It is nonsense to tell myself that because I have a swimming pool at H.H. there is no need to come abroad for the sea.

23 September 1969   Dreamt I was back in Corfu, after a few days at H.H., enjoying the contrast of the warm spring air after the sunny sharp September weather here. Why bother to mention it? Because the dream conveyed a rare sense of happiness, a simple joie de vivre such as I felt the first day of bathing at S. Giorgiou and which I hardly ever feel in life.

24 September 1969   Concerto for four harpsichords by C. P. E. Bach came over the radio as I lay in bed this morning having struggled, unsuccessfully, to procure an orgasm. It sounded like a beetle which had fallen on its back.

1 January 1970   During the day, after the normal clerical and domestic chores, I go through the movements of painting, but without much zest or conviction. My mind easily wanders to other things (usually sexual). This distresses me less than it did. I feel I can and shall paint again when the urge is strong enough. I even did several drawings at H.H. last weekend. The sale of several of last year's gouaches has also helped this feeling. But this very lack of anxiety may be yet another indication of decadence.

Too much time is wasted in boredom. Wasting time, when the years of life are running out, seems an absolute wrong. Yet to seek pleasure and distraction in entertainment of one sort or another, which is common to people at my stage of life who no longer have to work full time for a living, seems an equal waste of time to lying on my studio floor during the afternoon and dozing.

Of course I would like to be like other creative artists whose passion and understanding of their craft deepens and intensifies in their middle years. I think I gain in perception – perhaps understanding. The processes and difficulties involved in painting no longer baffle and perplex me as they did. I can see quite well what is likely to happen in given situations. I can see what goes wrong and why. But I cannot bother with it for long. And it was the blind struggle to make the thing work – as though my whole identity and integrity depended on the outcome – that produced most of my best work in the past. I seem to expect success to come by routine now. It doesn't of course. But it doesn't overmuch bother me. *Da ich ein Knabe war,* and not such a young one at that, nineteen or twenty, I fell madly in love with a German girl named Gerda. We were staying with her family in Fulda. She was thirteen perhaps. Flaxen haired and lithe as a boy. All day I stared at her till my eyes bled and my heart-beats choked me. But she took no notice. The holiday finished and we came home. Her mother had given me her photograph which I'd begged of her. I wrote her letters which she did not answer. I remembered each year (at least two years) her birthday (9 September). Five or six years later, shortly before the war, she came to stay with us in London. She was engaged to be married to a young officer. One evening I was sitting at the foot of her bed, talking – I was no longer the least in love with the mature beautiful young woman – when she burst into floods of tears, flung herself at me, begged me to marry her, swore she hated her fiancé and wanted me to take her there and then. I shrunk back in alarm and embarrassment, administered formal consolation and avuncular advice. Proust could have handled such a situation in his novel.

2 January 1970 I would very much like to see someone. But who? Prunella is engaged. No answer from KPA. The Goslings away. P.W. away. To propose myself to someone like Hockney, or Procktor, whom I like, would seem an imposition. Also they are people I know in social dilution, not in concentrated confrontation. Nor do I feel like hunting for strangers. One such excursion satisfies me for a long time. I do not want to go out to a movie or the theatre (though I would go and see a blue film, sexless though I feel, if I knew where to find one). So I remain here. Yet another evening alone and no doubt with the box and its fantasies (I don't mean the TV box either). It doesn't attract me. But it didn't last night either though I enjoyed it once I'd begun. I couldn't spend an evening reading. I have painted most of the day and have no more urge for that. It is too early for bed. How many other people, I wonder, possessing the means I have, find themselves also their own prisoner.

3 January 1970 – 0400 hours I think it quite likely I shall die, not from misfortune or natural causes, but from a change of view towards these people to whom I feel beholden to remain alive (my mother, R, a handful of friends). Apart from habit, and a certain natural curiosity, the only thing which stops me from failing to wake up each morning is reluctance to cause them avoidable pain and sadness (albeit temporary). I often think about it. The necessary dose of Tuinal is always available. But having swallowed it? Knowing it was inside me and starting to work its irreversible course – what should I feel? Panic? – I think quite likely. To face the certainty of death, by one's own hand, unnecessarily. Besides, my life, though burdensome is not unbearable. I cannot honestly say I see much hope of improvement in the future. The two main fountains of life, creative activity and relationships with other people, are not flowing. True, the latter never did very well, but then I make the former compensate.

However, I may be mistaken. I am on the whole optimistic, much as I enjoy pessimistic philosophic points of view.

20 January 1970 Sir, Why are scientists and other supposedly intelligent people always trying to establish a cause and effect relationship between biological or genetic conditions and human behaviour? It is being wondered now whether the extra male chromosome recently detected in a proportion of males (notably prisoners who, of course, are conveniently available for experiments) predisposes the owner towards crime. How could it? Such 'crime' is a socially determined term and differs at different times and places. (Homosexual intercourse was a crime three years ago, but is not so, with certain exceptions, any longer.) Your correspondent is puzzled by the fact that there must be large numbers of XYY men about the place today and says 'Since most of the men presumably have no criminal tendencies, the relatively large number of men found in prison populations is particularly hard to explain'. But why 'presumably'? One is not imprisoned for possessing criminal tendencies but for committing crimes. But there are indeed a number of people about with perverse and abnormal desires, sexual and otherwise, which if acted out would certainly constitute crimes. That they do not so act out shows that men are not entirely the helpless victims of biological conditions in the way scientists would seem to like them to be (thus permitting simple explanations). They have what used to be called 'self-control' and is now usually known as 'good ego-structure'.

31 January 1970 There are people, of whom I am one, whose rôle in life seems to be surviving. They are the Survivors. They survive a 'difficult' childhood, public schools, war and other hostile environments. But when they reach the state, having survived, when no further obstacles block their paths and they are free, financially secure, sound in health, faced with a wide range of opportunities, they no longer have the strength or stamina to choose. They have no urge, no desire. All their vitality has been absorbed by the struggle for survival, and all they are now capable of doing is continuing to survive. What they originally wanted to survive for is forgotten.

26 February 1970 I remember years ago a painter asking me, Louis Le Broquy, I think it was, if I actually enjoyed painting. 'Yes, of course,' I said automatically. 'Well, I don't,' he replied.

But did I? It was sometimes a stimulating involvement, more often an anxiety-ridden pursuit of the result. I enjoyed *having done* a painting which seemed successful. It was more relief than enjoyment. A sense that, whatever might happen in the future, no one could take away the fact that I'd done *that*. And this fact is still some mild consolation in these days of the locust. But it doesn't help fill them.

I am staggered when I contemplate the daily activity of other people. Obituary notices of people roughly my age fill me with shame. Their achievements, responsibilities, unceasing activities.

16 March 1970 'And beyond him a whole landscape waiting for explanation' –

17 May 1970 How lovely could Death be, like a long summer night, quiet with dew dropping on the corners of one's cheeks and the blood beating quietly and slowly slower in the ears.

3 June 1970 Planned this morning to go and see Derek Jarman's show – not far away. Planned not only that but the weekend I would invite him to H.H. with P.P. and the lively, amusing and enjoyable things which would be said and done by all. But after half hour of this inertia takes over. I'll go next week – perhaps – I do nothing but breed pestilence. (Nor does it in any way mitigate the circumstances by dressing it in apt quotation.)

Of course it is impossible to act when all the time some part of me is watching, anticipating, censoring the action. This way lies madness, catatonic inertia, exact balance of contrary forces giving an outward semblance of calm.

I suppose it might be considered normal for anyone to have the above sequence of thoughts and fancies flash through their mind in a few seconds while they were principally engaged in something else. Whereas I go to the pain and trouble of writing them down, too slowly to keep pace with them, so that they change and recede into the past in the act of writing.

7 June 1970 Forster died yesterday apparently. A totally meaningless 3 col Ob. in *The Times*. O.M., C.H. – like Moore and Sutherland. Why?

It was not his fault. A modern Jane Austen, sharp, witty, and empathic, he did his best with a limited experience. He was idolized by the immature homosexual intellectuals of the 20's onwards, made a Father figure – (he was tougher, more independent, less sentimental than they) and much overrated as an artist (novelist). Of course he wrote well, but that's not difficult as he was literate. He also wrote simply, because he knew what he wanted to say and was not writing for effect or to conceal.

We exchanged letters some years ago. Isherwood gave him a small thing of mine (a nude boy in romantic surroundings of course) for his umpteenth birthday – much to my embarrassment at the time since I didn't know E.M.F. and imagined he would disapprove of such juvenilia. But it seems he didn't. Though the drawing was stolen (so Mark Lancaster told me) about a year ago from his rooms in King's. (F. never told me.)

So what kept him going? He was 'devoted to his mother', we are told. At Abinger. Well, I can believe it. Was he really devoted, or had he sold himself the idea at an early age (like so many queers) and was making the best of it. I am certainly not devoted to my mother and ceased to be at the age of nine when she severely let me down by not acceding to my pleas to take me away from school. She is just a burden I seem to have to wear. Forster managed better. Perhaps they shared something in common other than genes.

But after his mother died and he stopped writing, what kept him going? That I would really like to know. To know that would help me.

But perhaps keeping going is a perfectly natural human tendency and only depressives like myself find it a problem.

19 August 1970   Silence speaks volumes. Unfortunately it is very boring to listen to.

20 August 1970   Sir, The admitted severity of the sentences imposed on the rioting Cambridge students was justified by the Appeal Court on two grounds: that 'the case was far more serious than that of most disturbances of the public peace' and that proper weight should be given to the 'public interest' as well as the circumstances of the defendants. But by what scale is the case judged to be 'more serious'? Not, surely, by the cost of the damage or the extent of injuries suffered by the police and others. Unless their Lordships can explain more fully the scale of assessment used, the feeling – which appears to be shared by students generally – must remain that it was 'more serious' because less to be expected or tolerated from privileged members of a senior university. And if this is allowed to remain as seeming to have influenced the decision to give exemplary sentences, far from serving the 'public interest' the exact opposite will be achieved by giving some justification to the almost inevitable repercussions in student resentment and protest.

Religion and the arts are often classed together in the higher cultural brackets of society. There is no justification for this. No one has ever been burnt at the stake, racked, thumbscrewed or garrotted for liking or disliking any particular work of art. The same, of course, cannot be said for the Church whose record of sadistic homicide and criminal malpractice is only surpassed by that of Almighty God himself. It is not surprising that it is known as His Church. It certainly isn't mine.

It is of course 'manic' remarks like this, which so pleased me at the time, that make so much of the published Journal embarrassing to re-read. I'm surprised more critics didn't attack it at the time. Dismissal or non-reviewing is also a form of attack.

27 August 1970   I drink more and more with my midday snack – which I thoroughly enjoy and look forward to each morning. Then sleep it off until about four when I wake liverish, depressed and dull-witted. What a come down! (from what?) Continue to read at intervals and with pleasure Katherine Mansfield's Journal. (Can't you recognize the style.) Would like to copy out so many pieces that it now seems more sensible simply to buy the book. (Actually ring Harrods, after writing this, to order it – but of course it's Thursday, so there is no answer.)

Continue to take fidgety little drugs. Half drinamyl, quarter dexedrine once or twice a day. Guiltily – like I swallow my Tuinal at night. Last night I didn't, being pleasurably drunk after dining out with P., and had wretched night and wakening. But once up, was no worse than after a deep sleep.

Cannot remember when I last felt really well and zestful. When in fact I last really felt strong emotion. Boredom, self-disgust, vague physical unease and anxiety. But no real or constant symptoms. Obviously I drink too much and smoke too much. Which would account for liverishness and a generally doped feeling.

'Triumph of matter over Spirit' KM says somewhere. What are those two old protagonists. What is spirit? Have I ever believed in it? All experience is sensual experience – art, music or sex. That is all one lives for surely. Satisfaction of achievement – sensual pleasure. Same thing.

29 August 1970 – Harrow Hill The pear tree, which is loaded with fruit this year, is being slowly stripped bare by wasps. Impossible to get near. Ground is swarming with them. They fly up and down the garden like tired bullets, bang against the window, gnaw the wood on the doors. They are utterly horrid and keep me in a constant state of jitters. All doors and windows must be kept closed otherwise they are crawling everywhere. There seems nothing to do. It is a plague, like locusts. The awful thing is one knows they will be here for weeks. Half a ton of pears take a lot of eating. Weather is warm and sunny, but ruined by these pests.

'It was one of those days so clear, so still, so silent, you almost feel the earth itself has stopped in astonishment at its own beauty' – but not quite – silly Kate.

'That psychoanalysis is leading to a new outlook on life I cannot and will not admit. All analysis can do is make a valuable contribution to building up such an outlook. The latter depends on synthesis.' (Freud 1924)

This seems to me profoundly true and to explain the false, manic enthusiasm of so many who dabble in and imperfectly understand analysis. Including myself.

'Life is in any case not easy, its value is doubtful, and having to be grateful for reaching the age of seventy-three seems to be one of those unfairnesses . . .' (Freud to Pfisher)

2 September 1970 When you are about to meet for the first time a youth who you know admires you, it is impossible not to picture them as infinitely charming and attractive – such is one's irrepressible narcissism – in spite of all warnings to the contrary. In fact it is impossible not to find the idea of a nineteen-year-old boy sexually attractive. But the reality can be very different.

Reading Freud's letters, selected by his son Ernst. Three hundred out of a known 4000. This is irritating in itself. One is constantly on guard against being got at. I would prefer to do my own selection, which I have to anyway from the paltry lot E. allows us to read. Nevertheless there are continual good things – apt, shrewd observations and beautifully ironic expression. 'A crust of indifference is slowly creeping up around me; a fact I state without complaining. It is a natural development, a way of beginning to be inorganic.' (to Lou A-S)

4 September 1970 Freud on mourning: 'Although we know that after such a loss the acute state of mourning will subside, we also know we shall remain inconsolable and will never find a substitute. No matter what may fill the gap, even if it be filled completely, it nevertheless remains something else. But actually this is how it should be. It is the only way of perpetuating that love which we do not want to relinquish.' (Letter 12.4.1929)

Why was F. at the end so misanthropic? 'In the depths of my heart I can't help being convinced that my dear fellowmen, with a few exceptions, are worthless.' They can only feel he did not know enough about them or the right ones. It is not difficult to imagine the emptiness, deceit and physical ugliness of upper-middle-class Viennese Jews in 1929 – they would not be very different from upper-middle-class art lovers and intellectuals today – and were presumably the only human specimens F. knew. What would he have thought of young people today – the 50,000 at the IOW pop festival for instance – or the average student anywhere? Has there been a real improvement in human character? The result of greater self-awareness, honesty, a refusal to be blinkered by clichés? I suspect F. would not have been impressed, but seen it as cloudy romanticism (see letter to Dyer-Bennett 9.12.1928). And indeed I can see little to admire in the majority of people over 40. It is the freshness and beauty and bloom of youth that continually enchants me and that to F. would be simply an example of regression and infantilism.

It is possible perhaps that some of F.'s discoveries, the insatiable drive and omnipresent metamorphosing of the sexual instinct, for instance, which so revolted and alienated his contemporaries, also damaged his own image of humanity, which circumstances and personal limitations prevented him restoring.

Even though he may feel humanity 'worthless' he certainly never acted on this feeling. To an unknown woman who had written asking for his autograph which she could sell to a rich collector for the benefit of someone in need he writes, '. . . If by a stroke of the pen one can really do something for a worthy person in need, then one has no reason to hesitate, and one can discover something useful in human folly. Please do not omit in the interest of your protégé to drive home to the worthy lady that a specimen such as that enclosed is otherwise difficult to obtain.'

But what does one make of this (To A. Paquet, 26.7.1930)? 'I owe you special thanks for your letter; it moved and surprised me. Quite apart from the trouble you have taken to study my work, I have never before found its *secret personal intention* recognized with so much clarity . . .'

My underlining – what can he mean? What is secret, or personal in Freud's work?

To change the subject: proof of the improvement in the human salvation is that a Penguin paperback *Boys and Sex* can be bought at any book shop. Its message is in principle that sex is fun and pleasant and the more you have of it the better – autosex, homosex, hetero-sex. Never before in the history of human society has such a book been published so freely and openly (the substance no doubt was known and practised in previous societies).

In all his correspondence (including that to his wife and family) Freud seems to come nearest to declaring a real love for another human being in his letters to Romain Rolland (love = Romantic love. i.e. based on fantasy rather than knowledge). See particularly letter of May 1931. 'I have rarely experienced that mysterious attraction of one human being for another as vividly as I have with you; it is somehow bound up, perhaps, with the awareness of our being so different . . .'

This to a man he had met only once for a brief half hour.

Significantly he closes his letter with 'Farewell!' – a rejection.

Freud constantly sees himself as an old man, finished, about to pass on. (Even in 1912 – to Binswanger – 14.4.1912.) Yet in 1912 (Sept) he spent three 'lonely weeks' studying, measuring and drawing the Moses of Michelangelo in Rome. (He would have set off to do this during the week in which I was born.)

14 September 1970 – Corfu 7 am On the terrace in the low cool sun. It is the same as last year. The place takes over. I am relaxed and contented to be doing nothing all day. After first night with mosquitoes, sleep well. Each situation develops unexpectedly and with its own pleasure. The wildly friendly family who ran the café with petrol pumps at lunch on Saturday. Sampling his home-made wines through the still afternoon. The tiny waiter (seven years old) at the Kangaroo who did all the serving with immaculate skill and was furious when he wasn't allowed to add up the bill. We did it all together, with Yanni, guessing the price of things (4 ouzo, 4 bottles Retzina, four omelettes, four salads, two fish, fried potatoes, four coffees. Drachma 115)

15 September 1970 'Some writers confuse authenticity, which they ought always to aim at, with originality, which they should never bother about. There is a certain kind of person who is determined by the desire to be loved for himself alone that he has constantly to test those around him by tiresome behaviour: what he says and does must be admired not because it is intrinsically admirable, but because it is *his* remark, *his* act. Does not this explain a good deal of avant-garde art?' (W.H. Auden) Does it?

17 September 1970 Earlier yesterday (as early as Gladys's bowels would allow) we set off by caique for Kassiopi. A long voyage – three-and-a-half hours and the boat vibrated to such an extent that sitting on the chair was like sitting on a fantastic masturbation device designed by W. Burroughs. I felt sick at first – then sexually stimulated in a rather disagreeable way. But I imagined how exciting it could be to have Spiros sitting on one's lap. He didn't come. We spent the usual day. Swimming, eating, smoking, staring into the distance, thinking our own thoughts, occasionally exchanging remarks (mostly P&G of course).

I am not happy because I have no one to share with, and it is my own fault. Work is perfectly satisfactory alone. In fact loneliness is essential to sharpen the need to communicate. But not pleasures.

It was dark when we got back and Spiros joined us for dinner – he chose the rather phoney tourist café nearby which, in fact, turned on the most enchanting Greek dancing I have seen. A group of six boys, who just felt in the mood. One boy particularly, about sixteen, dark hair and laughing face, thin pale jeans 'showing everything', including the fact that he got an immense hard-on the moment he danced with a girl. This seemed not to embarrass him in the least and he made no attempt either to conceal it bashfully or display it vulgarly. It happened and was part of the general high spirits and enjoyment.

This morning is grey again and cool. The break in the weather after the first five days has never fully recovered. It is cooler, intermittent cloud and thunder, though yesterday was full sun.

1 October 1970   In 1893 Freud seriously believed that masturbation in puberty invariably led to 'neurasthenia' and later neuroses. Curiously he doesn't mention female masturbation but explains female neurasthenia as the result of insufficient fucking due to male impotence (another result of masturbation). He also thought coitus interruptus a 'most severe noxa' in producing neurasthenia. Yet the only alternative to masturbation he saw was intercourse with tarts leading to syphilis and clap. No wonder so much of the early psychoanalytical dogmas were ridiculous if they came out of such a background.

22 October 1970   Very unpleasant session with Income Tax Inspector yesterday. Hostile, polite, and Kafkaesque. They are after my blood.

Rationally I know there is little or nothing to worry about. I am not a major criminal. I have indulged in no more than normal techniques of tax avoidance when possible. But I have operated as an amateur, instead of employing professionals as most do.

But it is not the actual threat, but the appalling collapse of integrity I suffer when faced with the slightest aggression. I revert to the same frame of mind as during the Souza episode six years ago. All day I have wrestled with figures. Continuous interior dialogues explaining myself to myself. P. gave me sedatives this morning. But everything has changed. I become a cringing, terrified, victim – of what?

At least it's a change from normal depression and accidie. Adrenaline is flowing, but too soon. There is no enemy in sight. Outwardly everything is as before. The confrontation, whatever it may be, will take weeks and months to appear.

At the moment I have undergone the initial softening-up process. Most effective. Sowing seeds of guilt and anxiety which multiply hour by hour like bacteria.

8.10. How marvellously quickly time goes. Two hours and I can go to bed. Shall I describe the interview, meanwhile. I have done it so many times in silence. Once to P.W. last night. I don't really want to.

(Two drinks so far.) 8.20. Potatoes boiled, salad prepared, steak ready. Shall see R. tomorrow. I hope he will understand and be able to help (I know he will *want* to).

(Inspector X. looking at the rows of fifty Players' tins on my bench):

'I see you're a heavy smoker for a man of inexpensive tastes.'

'My partners also used to buy Players in fifty tins. They're useful for mixing paints and solvents. I agree it does represent an extravagant outlay.'

Y. & X. are seated comfortably facing me. I answer their questions easily, producing sheafs of figures. They begin to smile.

That is the crux of my problem. Inability to sustain aggression. I must make the enemy smile, like me, agree, forgive, shake hands.

They shook hands *after* the interview, in fact, which surprised me. Also helped me on with my raincoat. Of course I had expected to shake hands on entering, not suspecting hostility.

Was this to temper their rehearsed hostility? Or to mitigate it? How much is prepared on such occasions?

There were two. Y. (a brassy, sharp-edged Scot) and X. (glass-eyed and eye-casted who said nothing but watched and took notes). 'Whatever you say during this interview will be noted down and presented to the court, but you will be given the opportunity to read the précis and indicate anything you think has been unfairly reported. Is that clearly understood?'

'I would like to start by reading to you an exchange which took place in the H. of C. in 1944 relative to wilful falsification of tax returns' (those were not the actual words). 'I will hand you a copy and I would like you to follow it while I read it. I want to be sure you understand it.'

That was what Mr. Y. said.

The confrontation was designed to be hostile and intended to undermine confidence. Presumably this is part of an Inspector's training. If you plead guilty to your fiscal crimes, bequeath unasked for and unsuspected evidence (thus making their job much easier), they will (probably) settle for an amicable payment of tax in arrears.

A long, tiresome and tedious investigation increases their hostility, but also increases your chances of victory. They are better armed (technically) but have nothing to gain. You have only your slings and arrows but everything to gain. Your libidinal investment in the encounter is much higher. They are simply doing a routine job. Investigating suspect tax-dodgers. Successful prosecution brings them nothing.

So, the sensible thing to do is to fight and not surrender and plead for mercy.

But that assumes you are really guilty of something, which is not true. The guilt is imaginary and subconscious. It has nothing to do with tax returns, but concerns childhood traumas.

23 October 1970 Why suddenly a pulse of eighty-six? Have taken two Tunial and one Valium – Hoping to wake refreshed. There should be no danger.

What have I done to earn this daily agony and misery. Here in a nice house, quiet clear sky, peace, warmth, comfort.

For two years I cannot remember feeling happy, positively actively happy. There have been times when I have been free from pain, of course, drunk, doped, asleep.

Why – why – what has gone wrong?

I've never made a proper human relationship. Proper? – Supportive perhaps. I've tried to support others, but there has never been anyone I could go to in distress, in helpless disarray. No father I suppose. (Too bad, too old now.)

Yet, curiously, I don't want to die. (I have the means of doing so at hand.) If I did I would use them as one pours a drink.

I want to be happy. To enjoy life. Which is surely one of the feeblest and most pathetic remarks a man of 58 could make.

I do not know. I do not know how.

4 November 1970 Yes, yes, yes – Have just re-read from the beginning of this volume. Although so recent, I actually found parts of it entertaining. So I'm encouraged to go on. The 'Depression' lifted yesterday morning (Tuesday). An active and enjoyable day at The Slade. Followed by an enormously enjoyable autoerotic evening alone.

I really hate writing these things, yet feel I should. And honestly my only reason now is a sense of duty. A feeling that someone (in not dissimilar circumstances) may be comforted, enlightened or just entertained by such curious behaviour. Because no one else – to my knowledge – reveals such things. They record only what they think will enhance their own self-image.

12 November 1970 Tony last night. Sexual reality of fantasy after nearly two years. It does not, as heretofore, leave me with a burning desire to renew and repeat it. The feeling was mostly appreciation and gratitude – that a 25-year-old youth should give himself so completely and without reservation to be used and abused for my pleasure. But gratitude is not erotogenic. Nevertheless he had three emissions and I one, between 12 and 8 am.

One watches TV in the hope of entertainment or instruction. Four times in one evening appears a bald-headed Scot, leader, secretary, gauleiter, of the NUM to explain about the miners' strike. (Last week it was the refuse and sewage workers, next week Post Office workers perhaps.) Another station had three people singing 'New York ... is a wonderful place'. So I kick the set to pieces and phone the police who put me into a comfy straight jacket and bury me with de Gaulle.

Full moon tonight. If I lean back on my swivel-tip chair, I see it in the top right-hand corner of the window. Very clear and still.

There are things in this studio (the reflection of the stucco ceiling lays over the moon if I tip back a bit further) which have not been moved for five years. Tools, boxes, pots. Things which once were in daily use and so are still placed ready. It is like an Egyptian tomb. Thick layers of dust over things. And that smell (which I notice now each day when I come in from the outside) of stale air – tobacco tar on the walls? A smell of death and decay and staleness.

Am finishing a bottle of Clos St Jean 1964 which I opened at lunchtime. (Lunch – three slices of Rye bread with ham and watercress – two glasses of wine – then sleep on the floor till tea time.)

And cigarettes. I would guess that 150 to 200 a week have been burnt in this 'studio' over the last 10 years. 'Work out the cancer-producing benzypyrene 234 from that. 10,000 a year. 100,000 in 10 years. '100,000 cigarettes produce x pounds of soot'. What doesn't go into the lungs is washed down into the stomach with Clos St Jean. (Ordered a case of Ch. Palmer Margaux 1961 from Berry's today – most expensive I've risked so far, £2 bottle.)

1 December 1 am 1970   SLEEP. I can go on writing into the small hours but it doesn't work. The void remains. Richard, Roger, x.y.z.

There was a time long ago in similar situations when I, awake, could feel superior to those asleep. As though my wakefulness gave me some command over their sleepingness and only by gracious consent did I permit their helpless sleep. Long quiet hours in the night lying awake staring stupified at the unknown sleeping head crooked on my aching shoulder. Fearful to move or disturb or remake normal contact. Absurd feeling of absolute contact where there was none. A sleeping head, a breathing corpse. No need for speech or effort at contact. From 14 I can remember most clearly all my loved ones when asleep. Even my enemies were lovely asleep. Blank breathing mouths whose lips still were frothed with aggression. And tears, my tears dripping on a sleeper's cheek. Amazed at his not knowing. Kissing the sleeping lips which would never have accepted such assault awake.

But sleeping. The soft muscles in the neck. Loose bones. Ease your aching arm a little. Careful not to wake or restore reality. The familiar room transformed by the sleeping body. Everything strange but no longer dangerous. No sleeping thing threatens the room growing colder but the body retains its heat. Two bodies. Roughly the same temperature. At least we have blood heat in common.

9 December 1970 'The bitterness of boyhood distresses does not lie in the fact that they are large; it lies in the fact that we do not know they are small.' (G. K. Chesterton)

17 December 1970 The reason I have dropped out of society, or rather ceased to make the effort to cling on, is not that I do not enjoy company, but can no longer bear the sense of my inadequacy, my habitual overreaction, primary nervousness and fear, over-reliance on alcohol and consequent remorse and guilt. At least alone I am spared this particular bitterness.

But I'm coming to realize I'm paying too high a price for this self-indulgent quietism. For one thing the boredom and mental staleness unfits me even more for the few social occasions I still meet. I become less and less effective at the Slade, not through failure in any undertakings, but contriving to avoid undertaking anything.

At 58 the situation is not healthy and the prognosis gloomy. I live with the idea of imminent death, without believing it likely and certainly not seriously contemplating steps to bring it about. Just one of the many situations I rehearse, gaining some vicarious comfort through fantasy and momentarily forgetting the void of reality.

3 February 1971 A desire to write stimulated by my enjoyment of Mitford's Louis XIV; marvellously deft, controlled and lively style. She and Norton's translation of Saint Simon have launched me into the French 17th-century high life with much élan. Apart from the ridiculous clothes and hairstyles the people sparkle with life, energy and activities (for the most part, ones which would bore me to death or scare me out of my wits).

I do not. I keep up a mere routine. My stores of energy seem almost depleted and nothing gives me active pleasure. It is enough if I can avoid pain and anxiety states, which is not always easy, largely due to the present offensive mounted by the Tax authorities. What will happen to me if and when I have serious problems to face I cannot bear to think. Alcohol and self-stimulation occupy most evenings as usual. This routine must be now some five years old (since in fact R. moved to H.H.) and is getting as stale as everything else. A change and a break must be made, but I cannot see how or to what. H.H. affords a break, but that also is becoming routine.

What is so maddening is that with so much I cannot enjoy life more and my years are slipping away unlived and unloved.

Of course I am not alone in this. I notice how often even in 17th-century France the rich and successful succumb to 'melancholy' in middle age – for no apparent reason. It is certainly wrong to imagine 'depression' is a contemporary illness, only its name and etiology have changed.

On my grave I think I would like this epitaph:

> Je vais où va toute chose
> Où va la feuille de rose
> Et la feuille de laurier.

Remarkably similar to Rimbaud's

> Gracieux fils de pau
> Promène toi la nuit
> En movant doucement cette cuisse
> Et cette second cuisse
> Et cette jambe de gauche.

5 February 1971 It is shameful and humiliating to have to reveal, yet again, my complete inability to face up to situations involving hostility and aggression. The second confrontation with the Revenue over my tax returns last Tuesday has reduced me to the same state of panic anxiety in which my instinctive urge is to throw myself on their mercy, confess all, and beg for forgiveness. Of course their technique in questioning is designed precisely for this effect, as my accountant points out, and the worst that can happen, so he assures me, is that I shall have to pay them some money. But rational reassurances, while helpful, do little to loosen this absurd knot of panic which precludes any peace of mind except during the hours when I'm unconscious. The neurotic constellation, which has enabled me to make some success in creating a substitute friendly and con-trollable world in my art, also ensures my utter inability to deal with life's ordinary problems in a rational way. Aggression never provokes me to the natural desire to fight back. I always want to run away.

16 March 1971 The only Truths you know are what you remember of experiences lived through. Do not let other people's ideas make you doubt what you know. (Ideas of the clever fall like apples from trees.)

23 March 1971 'The terrible, by a law of the human mind, always touches on the verge of the ludicrous' (Coleridge). True or not true? The massacres of My Lai for instance, German concentration camps.

Perhaps a 'healthy' mind has to find an element of absurdity in the end to escape the tyranny of reality (laughter in *Lear*, for instance). The 'unhealthy' mind, which over-identifies, is slowly broken down by contemplation of horror. Depressing effects of continually reading daily newspapers which concentrate on the unpleasant. Yet most people presumably want this or the papers wouldn't serve it. Or do papers only think people want it, and since people certainly want daily papers, are forced to read what is written and in fact are slowly corrupted thereby?

26 May 1971 I was awoken by the frantic gnawing of a mouse in the room last night. I kept hoping it wasn't a rat, the noise seemed so loud. I threw paperbacks in the direction it seemed to come from. It was about 5 o'clock. I was dreading the morning because of my court case. But being woken so early the feelings of panic were less acute than I had expected. When I finally got up about 7.45 there was a large pile of fluff lines up along the bottom of the door. Presumably it had been trying to get out with the haul which it must have been quickly collecting all through the night from all over the room. The floor under the bed was quite clear.

The case did not go too badly. I defended myself and got the bench discussing whether I should or should not have reported the accident in the light of the facts I gave. (I had stopped, but had not exchanged particulars with the driver who had run into me, because he hadn't asked for them and he was in such a towering rage that I only wanted to get away.) It turned out I should. I heard the lady magistrate say, 'I don't mind how small the fine is, but of course the licence must be endorsed.' I was fined £2. It was over and done-with in half an hour. I had taken one tranquillizer in the bus and then, at the last minute, half drinamyl.

Depression a little less acute now, but it has been almost constant for months.

Am reading Delacroix's Journal, properly, for the first time with some pleasure. How alike we are in some respects, except that he was 24 when expressing feelings familiar still to me at 59.

'What are most real are the illusions that I create with my painting. The rest is shifting sand.' In different words I expressed exactly this idea in my Journal and it was singled out by one critic (E. Lucie-Smith) as being 'rather betraying'.

'I have two, three, maybe four friends. So I have to be a different man with each of them or, rather, to show to each the face he recognizes. It is one of the greatest calamities that one can never be known and sensed completely by one and the same man; and when I think of it, I believe that here is the sovereign evil of life – it is this inevitable loneliness to which the heart is doomed.'

7 June 1971 – Edinburgh Coming down from the Castle near the Mount 'Could I presently beg your pardon sir if you're not too busy?' One could hardly want to be importuned more elegantly – a cross between Nijinsky and Marlon Brando – tough, slav, Scots.

Marvellous lighting of Princes St and the Castle and the deep, forested gully thick with green and rhododendrons beneath which invisible trains run. What a good idea. Very civilized city visually. The rest I don't know.

The couple in the portico of the *Scotsman*. Girl with her hands relentlessly in the boy's crutch. He kissing then taking another drag from his cigarette parked on the ledge of the window. Taking her hands away but she insisting, not caressing him but insistently rubbing him. Then without a word or gesture they part – he across the road, she into a bus. No backward glance, no farewell, no parting.

July 1971 – 4.05 am How different if one has the sense of belonging – to an old family for instance – of being a part of something rather than an isolated thing alone. (I'm thinking of the Nightingale family – the Smiths.) I never had a 'family' in that sense. Just a mother. No one else.

22 September 1970 – Harrow Hill It was a week ago last Monday that I collected PW from hospital and brought him here. Robert and Phillip and Rib came on Sunday. David Hockney for lunch on Monday. R and I have been preparing on average ten meals a day (lunch and dinner), which has really been quite enjoyable. At least it is lively.

31 September 1971 I ask only two things – to achieve a loving relationship with R (since it is too late now to believe it can be done with anyone else) and rediscover a real drive for painting.

It was in October 1944 that the Germans arrived in Malton. When I read what I wrote about that evening and night of the great gale I am moved almost to tears by the emotional tension of the writing. I cannot believe it was me. I cannot identify myself with the person who wrote these things. I think I must have cribbed them, yet I know I did not. It is like meeting in a dream and half-recognizing someone one once knew but had forgotten. Such complete discontinuity of identity is frightening. Was I my 'true self' then, or now? Or does the true self not exist, except in fragments? I remember at the time I was still much influenced by Lawrence whose *Seven Pillars* I was reading when I started this Journal. Though I disliked much of the book, and today find it unreadable, I was fascinated by the dry, terse, self-conscious exactness of the prose, like an auto-autopsy. Instinctively I adopted that style.

2 October 1971   Sir, The Arts Council stand convicted of cowardice in the face of the enemy and gross betrayal of one of their beliefs, namely that the electrocution of catfish is a valid aesthetic experience – (I don't mean for the fish). I hope therefore that the panel will lose no time in offering themselves for public electrocution in place of Mr H's exhibit – SM pulling the switch. Only in this way can honour be restored and all the important issues met: Mr M's aggression, the RSPCA's concern for the welfare of fish and the insatiable lust for novelty of the art-loving public. It would also have the additional merit of relieving the RSPCA of the burden of visiting art shows and give them more time to picket Billingsgate Market where it is well known that abominations of cruelty are daily practised on the fish.

P.S. I do not wish to imply that the voltage used should be lethal. A short, sharp shock, such as is used in convulsive therapy to relieve other symptoms of acute hysteria and mental malfunctioning, is all that is necessary to satisfy the requirements of Art and Honour.

26 November 1971 – Harrow Hill   Desperate for something to do I start again reading in Arnold Bennett's Journals which I had put down some months ago out of boredom. And I come upon a passage where he has been re-reading the earlier note books and finds them 'very good' (in parts). Such confidence staggers me, so I read back the earlier pages myself. Yes they are good. Why? they say almost nothing about himself, except that he suffers from frequent 'liver attacks', but he gives clear sharp cameos of other things and people, particularly Paris life in 1904.

What is boring is being continually told how many thousand words he has written before or after lunch. It is more interesting to know what he had for lunch (Bifsteak and soufflé potatoes cost 6d). It should not be imposssibly difficult to write like that once I'd got into the habit. The demon is sloth.

Apart from a little gardening in the morning, the days are almost entirely dissipated in trivial reading, eating, drinking and sleeping. R. is relaxing and pleasantly companionable these days, but no use hoping for intellectual stimulus there. It's the lack of this that makes me so irritable at times I think (I absolutely light up if I get hold of an adult book or article to read, which is rare). Typical of so much 'intelligent' writing now are Hoggart's Reith Lectures. The subject – communication – should be interesting, but the turgid, lifeless, convoluted prose is barely comprehensible to me. I read sentences over and over and barely grasp what he's trying to say and wonder if it's my mind which is going soft.

As for Bennett's words – one of these pages holds 300 I reckon, so if I write ten at a stretch (which is not unknown) that brings me level with his output. Not so extraordinary after all. Come to think of it, I don't think I've read a single book by Bennett. Being unfashionable at the time my snob culture reading started (with Woolf – Lawrence – Joyce – Eliot, etc) he was easily dismissed – with his contemporaries – as being just not worth while. And since the act of reading has always been slow and irksome with me I welcomed any excuse for not reading a productive author.

30 January 1972 Some painting this morning – not much more than technical tidying up of some landscape panels. Read the Sunday papers – poisonous rivers, polluted seas, overpopulation – madness – kidney disease – liver flukes and their diabolical practises – the coming Revolution – incurable unemployment. From a warm room I look onto a cold world and wish for a companion.

Sunday Times publishes the first of a series of get fit exercises. Did half of them but gave up from laziness more than exhaustion.

31 January 1972 Remarkable film on penguins last night. Looking, as they do, like slapstick comedians in evening dress, they also live the most unattractive sort of life possible in frozen antarctic wastes, blizzards, stormy seas and predators, yet never fail to look charming, rather helpless and comic. How we project ourselves onto animals. Impossible not to believe they think and feel as we do. Only reptiles and insects seem inhuman and incomprehensible and some of them are quite like people I know.

Later the *Winterreise* – marvellously played by Britten (invisible), abominably sung by Pears (all too visible in fancy travel clothes). The piano alone made it worth keeping with. Turned the light down so the screen was blank.

11 February 1972 Interviews in the afternoon. 1.45 to about 6.00. Bill at his most tiresome. One moment raspingly aggressive, the next talking in whispers so gentle and genteel as to be almost inaudible. Appearing to defer all decisions to other people while in fact maintaining complete control. Yet it's impossible not to like him, almost to love him, because of his fundamental warmth and good will. But his manners can be outrageous.

13 February 1972 Half Drinamyl and a glass of sherry makes all the difference. Started new small panel about 11.30. Continue to two with sherry. Then some salami and toast. Remains of last night's wine (G. Echezaux 1959 – Berry Bros). Now 3.10. Rather drunk but much happier. Sun shining. Power restored. New painting started. Long siesta.

14 February 1972 Good evening at P.W. last night. Edward Albee and young friend, Keith Milow, Robert and Rib. Albee extremely agreeable. Quiet, modest, intelligent, relaxed. Excellent company. Much impressed that he was familiar with my published journals. Wanted to know if the photographs of Pagham were 'discretely' selected. Tried to explain the complete 'innocence' of those days (and complete sexual suppression) so hard to comprehend today.

18 February 1972 Dinner with Alan and Jennifer Ross to meet William Feaver who wants to write about me. I liked him: modest, unpretentious intelligent youth – looks like a student, rather scruffy. Writing very entertaining but 'too clever by half' to be taken really seriously. Though his article on Bacon certainly demolished the reverential accolade which has been built up round him and said some sharp, accurate and penetrating things which certainly needed saying.

28 February 1972 Morning at Slade and round the galleries. Nothing memorable except Meadows's sculpture at the R.A. Show. Here at last was something with human thought and feeling and real sculptural sensibility. The equal of anything by Moore. Some sort of locked-in hermetic feeling in Sanderson, but it didn't come across. The rest mostly good fun. Large environmental stuff. Once seen for ever forgotten.

Passed a swish gallery in Bruton Street next to Reid & Lefèvre and spotted an early landscape of mine inside (57/8). Went in. It looked good. Better than I'm doing now. Yet I could not at all remember having done it. When or where. Would like to have it back. Asked the price. About £500. Had been borrowed from Kalman.

29 February 1972 12.15 am   To Hayward Gallery in the afternoon to see Rothkos. Feeble stuff. Large decor. Boring to paint and look at. Not surprising he killed himself if that was all there was to do. No problems. Couldn't go wrong. Some good T.V. tonight. Drunk practically a bottle Beaune '64. Arsenal v Derby City. V. Good. No score. 'Space beteen Words.' 'Thick as thieves.' All good. Much better entertainment than most theatres and far less trouble.

2 March 1972   Long and pleasant evening with Pru last night. But increasingly inability to remember names of anything. Strong feeling of being a bore all the time. Compulsive drinking makes it worse.

6 March 1972   Since meeting him I have been reading all Feaver's articles in *London Magazine*. He is certainly the most perceptive and entertaining critic writing today. Possibly because he is not backing anything – but rather taking the mickey. Which is refreshing after the unbearable portentous journalese which accompanies most art products. His style, though, is too compressed, too striving for the witty line, too monotonous in bulk.

22 March 1972   Up at 7.30 after two Tuinal. Manic morning. Painting well. Extraordinary change. Why?

6.20: Best day's painting I've had for over a year. Probably the results are no better than at other times. But I've felt that wonderful elation of being involved. Of struggling with a problem I understand and which I know is soluble. It is not necessary to succeed in solving it to enjoy the struggle. The inner drive once more. The welling up of creative urge. The desire to make something again. Four new panels and started a fifth. Two are practically finished, or well under control. A bit picturesque but quite well made. Problem, as usual, is to find the forms which paraphrase reality of object and feeling without being merely descriptive. If only I could get this sort of activity going at H.H. Might try tomorrow. Take up the new panel and continue there.

Very strange dreams this morning of caressing a naked girl. Pressing against her cunt and exciting her. She was with another youth who has faded. She had flaxen hair platted down her back. Very slim with no breast that I remember. But a warm mouth which I kissed. She moaned and made copulating movements against my soft penis. Then

Dennis Rix in my old studio at Hamilton Terrace. He looked exactly like Aubrey but taller and thinner. He had some scars around the socket of one eye and the bridge of his nose.

6 April 1972 – Uzès Lunch with David and Mai in their fabulous setting. Sleep in the sun under the olive in warm sun. Cool in the evening. Gastric flora taking on the local bouquet, a very aromatic dry thyme. Driving around in the car, pleasant new Renault. Hotel Terminus here. Strange reception. No rooms, sorry, full right up, but wait a moment. Let's see what we can do. Then shown into two perfectly good rooms. Rather Balzacian. Reverse plumbing. Collapsing floors. Crumbling cement. Likelihood of electrocution from switches. Room 22 Frs. Noisy.

Climatically the landscape is good to be in. But visually I could do nothing with it. Far too much light to begin with. No contrasts. No colour except local tints. Mimosa, iris, wisteria.

25 April 1972 Reading (*London Mag*) Roy Fuller. Georgic II 'But where are the painters whose technique their whole/Ambition, will make the marvellous plausible,/Enamoured of appearance?'

Well my dear Roy, what we once thought marvellous, now seems less so. The Pageant of Nature with her marvellous effects – suns setting, birds nesting, buds bursting, insects popping – are no longer the vital sources for the painter even though he may well still be 'enamoured of appearance'. The facts have already been recorded and the appearances long ago celebrated. What more is there to say? How in our age, watching the technological destruction of our planet, can we be enamoured of the beauty and bounty of Mother Nature. The back room boys know all about her tricks now and can perform them quite convincingly in the laboratory. She's been stripped of her mystery (the essential ingredient in worship) and shown, like all mothers to their grown-up children, to be far less omnipotent than she seemed. What once seemed marvellous is now reduced to evidence supporting a theory.

Mutant genes and meson particles may be plausible but lack an enamouring appearance. Of course we cannot shed our childhood's desire to be overwhelmed. Mountains, tempests, vast seas and driving winds still have the power to restore us to our human status. Making us forget the simple meteorological explanations and predictions of such splendid seeming phenomena. But ambition? Ambition to the artist still remains the same: to bring order and clarity into the confused evidence of his senses. The visual image, to be plausible, must encompass more than a love of the look of things.

While writing this I remembered Roy's earlier book which I bought during the war and re-read recently with unexpected pleasure. *A Lost Season*. To prolong the sound of his voice I found it and took it to read with my cold meat and salad. I noticed I had written on the flyleaf the date of my re-reading. 12 March 1961.

27 April 1972 Although I had planned to go to H.H. today the morning was so grey and cold that I decided to spend another day painting here. I did not achieve much. The catalogue arrived of Barbara's [Hepworth] new show at Marlborough Fine Art. As usual little small things are beautiful and the large monumental bronzes hopeless. But what energy and industry. I remember feeling the same talking with her in St Ives. A tightly wound spring of tension. But without a trace of self-doubt, self-questioning. Everything always going forward. Big projects in the morning, small ones in the afternoon. Ben just the same. And now, in her 70s, success everywhere and all the promotion machinery of MFA behind her. I felt trivial and depressed as a consequence.

But of course my 'art' commenced as an escape from 'life' for which I lacked all equipment, and proceeded throughout the fairly productive '50s to '60s on the basis of sublimated sexual energy. Now there is no more libido to sublimate. I just lack the intelligence to know how to select and utilize my abilities. Also in painting, as in living, I need always a strong stylistic influence. I model my behaviour and my opinions on those people who impress me. There happen to be no painters today who impress me. I've never had any real relationship with what other people appear to see as my own style. To me it has never been more than the existence of my failure to be someone else. And certainly not something to live up to or cultivate.

I very much wish I were part of a society. A social group. Club, University. Among people of equal and congenial minds. My solitude is simply the result of having extricated myself from every group in which I found myself because of the stifling, thwarting atmospheres in which I felt it impossible to think my own thoughts.

I don't know anybody quite like myself. They probably exist but I don't know them. Anyone who lives quite such an impoverished life (except very old people, of course, who have memories). But with me it has always been like this. Fifty years of it. According to the records it probably looks quite different. The places I've been to. The things I've done. People I've met. Some fame, success. But it amounts to nothing. I am still locked in – with my non-self. My memoirs could be written in one sentence: I've spent my life looking for myself. True, I've found other things in the process but not the one thing which would give them meaning – a sense of my own identity – different from others.

3 May 1972 Started the II vol. of Russell's Autobiography with the marvellous growing conviction that here is a man with whom I am almost totally in sympathy.

5 May 1972 'Time, they say, makes a man mellow. I do not believe it. Time makes a man afraid, and fear makes him conciliatory, and being conciliatory he endeavours to appear to others what they will think mellow. And with fear comes the need for affection, of some human warmth to keep away the chill of the cold universe.' (Russell, 1931.)

10 May 1972 Back from the Hayward party for Bernard Cohen. Slade set plus Whitechapel and the Meyers etc. Last night also a party at Redfern. P. Proktor, Pru, Mario, Denvir, Rodrigo M., Pollock (impossible), Hockney, Raymond Mortimer, Alan Ross, etc.
Monday J. Synge alone to discuss possible show at Redfern. Dinner at Huntsman, tiring evening with no great hope or prospect (of course R the will give me a show). Tonight Leslie Waddington, to whom I have not spoken for ten years, also renewed his invitation to show with him. I feel more inclined that way, except that the Gallery worries me. Too like a surgery. Too impersonal. R. more cozy. But, I feel, less really able or efficient. (Much impressed that L.W. should have renewed his invitation after so long.)

16 May 1972 Russell on Tolstoi: 'What is valuable is his power of right ethical judgement and his perception of concrete facts; his theorizings are of course worthless. It is the greatest misfortune to the human race that he had so little power of reasoning.'
On G. B. Shaw: 'I admit he is forcible. I don't admit he is moral. I think envy plays a part in his philosophy in this sense, that if he allowed himself to admit the goodness of things which he lacks and others possess he would feel such envy that life would be unendurable. Also he hates self-control and makes up theories with a view to proving that self control is pernicious.'
Dear Mike (Whose letters after months arrived yesterday)
It was good to hear from you again. When I last wrote to Sheffield I seem to remember asking you some rather sharp, and perhaps

impertinent questions, which didn't surprise me remained un-answered. If you found them encouraging, so much the better, though I hate the thought that they conveyed obligations of gratitude. (All interpersonal communications which come with this prepaid intent should be rejected.) The problem of unposted letters I well under-stand. It's the super-ego blocking the line (you can't say that – what will he think of you – he won't understand). Also one has to know what one means by 'contact' (which you say you value). I remember a bit of the countryside around Sheffield. It starts and stops quickly with none of the dreary compromise of 'garden cities' (at least not then, but things change).

Is 'communal living' different there than elsewhere – apart from the fact that northern communities seem on the whole warmer, more spontaneous, less defensively critical than the south? What did you actually do up there? Make drawings of grasses or abandoned steel works?

Buber I couldn't get on with – admittedly I didn't try very hard, I was put on to him by David Gascoyne years ago as the most important writer of the century. I can't understand that sort of loaded, turgid, pedantic, symbolist, abstract language. I've not got the mind. I prefer Russell whose autobiography I've just read. Marvellous things there (but only in the 1st two vols), particularly the letters – on religion to Lowes Dickinson and others on the problems and pleasures of living generally. As for Jung I go for Freud who stays with the facts (unpleasant though they may be) in so far as we know them, and like Russell holds to an ethical belief that truth is worth knowing. There is something too cozy and self-comforting in the cloudy metaphysics of Jung and Buber. Who have they actually helped to live more fulfilled lives? Jungian analysis is like an annual total submersion in Wagner's Ring. Probably you would like Yeats's vision – a favourite along with W. Reich (Der Funktion des Orgismus) with many students now in need of a quick solution to the problem of living.

21 May 1972 – Harrow Hill Sunny and pleasant days in the garden. Odd jobs. Any ideas of painting or seeing people which I frequently bring with me and think about on the drive up, evaporate after half a day. I settle back into a contented vegetative routine. True I take no amphetamines as I usually do in London. I sleep more, drink less, but feel more lethargic. Perhaps it is the air.

22 May 1972 On the same day that Michaelangelo's Pietà in S. Peter's was mutilated by a young man with a hammer I read of Acconci's 'exhibition' at Sonnabend. This consists of a sloping ramp covering half the floor area of the gallery beneath which the artist crawls on two afternoons each week and masturbates, while listening to the footsteps of visitors walking about over his head. He cannot be seen, but readers of *Forum* are shown a photograph of him lying on his side beneath the sloping ramp with his trousers round his ankles and quite clearly handling his penis. The report states that the act is prolonged as much as possible to ensure maximum ejaculation of semen. The title of the piece is called 'Seedbed'.

Well – I remember one day alone at H.H. soon after the studio had been completed ejecting some semen onto the new floor boards to stain them and, as it were, baptise the room. But it didn't occur to me it was creating a work of art. Apparently I was wrong. I also possess an 8 × 10 piece of towelling, dating from the early '60s which is stained an ochre yellow from 100 ejaculations of my own semen. I made a point of ejaculating always onto the same piece of cloth, folding it up, and putting it away until the next time. What would be the value of such an object in the current art market? And since I now ejaculate mostly under the stimulus of E.T. the area of carpet between my legs has already received some 20 to 30 ejaculations. But it doesn't show very clearly on the carpet. Perhaps I should start again by placing the piece of towelling at the appropriate spot.

3 June 1972 My life seems purposeless and completely idiotic. Yet I cannot think of anyone else whose life I would like in exchange. The purpose of life is supposed to be self-realization – self-fulfilment – but this begs every question. How does one know what self is until it's realized. We have ambitions, dreams, fantasies of what we'd like to be, but mostly these are compensations. Unrealizable because out of character. How do you know when you've realized something. You have a public image. You are assessed in a certain way. A man of means who has achieved something. But what?

John Piper has been given a C.H. Highest social honour. I think him a less good painter than I, but an infinitely nicer and more able man. More active. More in the swim. Done more. Been about longer in the right circles. (He would not have gone down to S. Wimbledon to see the new house of a working-class orphan who will never be anyone in the public eye.) Or if he did he would fit it in quickly and ably between other more important appointments.

Perhaps I spend my time with the wrong people. I was more or less offered the position of Professor of Painting at the RCA a few weeks ago. Naturally turned it down because I have no ambitions that way. Am too old for change. Felt I would be completely inadequate to fulfil such a post, yet if there was a real risk of my inadequacy I would not have been offered it by people (Esher) who are not sentimental fools. But I can neither see nor believe in myself in powerful social positions. I hide behind apparently friendly father figures (WMC [William Coldstream] – WT).

I've withdrawn from the active material world of daily living – like a monk, a Buddhist. A Krishna lover. But without dedicating myself to higher power. Consequently I am left really alone. Living solely with my stomach, genitals, memories, intellect. A one-man band with all the instruments strung around me playing in an empty but temperate desert.

11 June 1972   Did my reports, expenses, and sent them off. Conscious of being tired and of eye strain. The total number of students at the four places was about 150 and each student would have been showing not less than twenty works and often thirty including drawings. That makes a total of between 3000 and 4500 works, each of which has to be looked at carefully and assessed critically. Perhaps that is why my eyes feel strained. I think I could now conjure up, sufficiently clearly to describe, not more than 20 works in all. And I would quite likely recognize about 1000 if I saw them again. Though this figure is purely a guess.

13 June 1972   Slade day with somewhat acrimonious staff/student meeting this afternoon. But what is it all about? Mostly personalities showing off. Cohen always with some ready-wrapped aggression to throw around. He dislikes not being No 1 in any situation. The students for the most part grumbling inarticulately that they can't get instant gratification for their every whim. The staff, for the most part, deeply committed to inertia and the status quo while paying ready lip-service to radical suggestions. The exercise might be valuable if it ended with mutual respect for the different positions, but in fact everyone is just confirmed in their prejudices. The Slade is run by WMC. The students are selected on the personal whims and quirks of the staff. Students expend most of their energies on fighting the system. The result is that the present Diploma Show is of a generally lower standard than the four shows in Scotland where students accept a rigid though not oppressive system of academic training.

27 June 1972   In between bouts of heavy gardening with R. – mostly cutting hedges and thinning out dead wood – am reading *Journal of a Disappointed Man* – I see I bought this in 1941 and wrote my name in it. Probably it was one of the two or three books I took with me when I was called up. Whether I got any solace from it I can't remember. Yet I undoubtedly take after him – (he in turn finds his duplicate in Marie Bashkirtseff whom of course I haven't read). In fact Barbellion has read (at 24) a good deal more than I. But oh the heterosexual pranky jokes and bantering aggressive friendships. Very typical of the time. Paralyzing fear of being thought queer. He is boringly hypochondriacal. He seems to have every possible symptom of terminal illness in succession, but still one doesn't know what his 'ill-health' consists of. A maddening man, but compulsively readable for some reason (his book was very popular) and very good when being objective. He is also very astute. After relating an evening of self-imposed solitude and acute depression and boredom he finishes, 'When I had dramatized my misery, I enjoyed it, and acute mental pain turned into merely aesthetic malaise'.

30 June 1972   To help him over 'bad' patches B. took arsenic and strychnine 'in tablet form' every so often. I thought they were poisons like (I suppose) barbiturates, and alcohol and amphetamines. Which we take today.

2 July 1972   Finished Barbellion's Journal. Which makes my earlier comments properly ridiculous, or at least unjust. The final pages when he is dying and knows he is dying have a dignity on which all comment is superfluous. The book must be unique.

Perhaps there is something to be said for having the capacity to endure boredom rather than flee into some distraction like the cinema, TV or playing patience. But it's very tiring. B. took the most elaborate precautions to preserve his journal and feared its possible loss or destruction more than anything else. I suppose that is understandable if you see it as your sole achievement. It would hardly matter to me at all now if mine were destroyed (except perhaps for some of the unpublished erotic passages). But I should go on writing it as I know of no other way of filling in idle hours. Perhaps if I took more trouble. But then it would cease to be a Journal but become a conscious work of literature. In which case I would prefer to write about something other than myself who I no longer find particularly interesting.

3 July 1972 Got Maurice Bowra's Memoirs from the Library. What a bore. Correct, upper class, and orthodox in everything. No feeling of a real person. Lifeless, monotonous style. Certainly shan't read it.

23 August 1972 12.50 am White light and silence everywhere. Harvest moon. A bigness which wipes out all small things. The white corn against white sky. No sound. Absolute purity and stillness. Two silent bats. I hate to turn on the light to write this.

8 January 1973 It seems absurd that sexual activities should loom so large and importantly at 60. Perhaps it's not uncommon (male menopause?). It is known that men revert to masturbation frequently after 60. At least in my idleness I shall try and keep this Journal daily. I want to make it as factual as possible, i.e., recording what I did, not what I felt or thought. Arnold Bennett records briefly the bilious headaches, neuralgia, insomnia, before getting down to the facts. How, living in France, he could settle for bread and milk dinner every night is beyond belief. His wife and mistress (?) would sit down to 150 snails gathered in their garden that afternoon.

22 January 1973 Checking my entry in the International *Who's Who* I see my leisure interests are noted as 'eating and drinking with friends, bathing in the Ionian Sea'. I wonder when I said that? Probably after returning from Corfu. What I should say is 'Drinking alone, sexual self-pleasuring with autoerotic devices.' But I shan't.

Passing strangers in the street I am often struck, and slightly appalled, by the realization that each one of them is just as important to himself, is as much the centre of his Universe, as I am of mine. Other people to me are potential sources of aid or obstruction. They never feel quite real since they are clouded over with my projections. Intellectually I accept the autonomy and equal importance but I cannot experience this – feel it. Usually I feel myself slightly ill at ease or threatened in their presence, unless they are old friends, in which case I assume they exist to protect and help me. I am not very happy when asked suddenly to help them. My instinctual reaction is to feel imposed on. Naturally I try to conceal this from fear of turning them into enemies. In a situation of danger I don't think I would risk my own safety to help a stranger, though I might if I felt that a public display of selfishness and cowardice would expose me to even greater danger. This comes, perhaps, from not living in a coherent society but an incoherent mass of people. When I am in love with someone (if I ever was) the situation is different. Then their well-being and existence is as important to me as I am to myself. I could sacrifice myself for a loved one. But not for a stranger.

This protective sense of simulated self-sufficiency, which I was driven to adopt in childhood, explains perhaps why I have so few friends. Or lovers.

The last really creative bout was 1967/68 culminating in the Marlborough Show in December 1968–January 1969. Since then I have done about thirty paintings, mostly small, simply by pushing. Not many really took off. A few did. I don't think they are any the worse – so far as I can tell. But the involvement has been less and consequently the pleasure of doing them.

In fact, of course, the dominant feeling under which I have always worked has been anxiety – will I bring it off? – rather than pleasure in the doing. I think now I am simply shying off situations of stress and tension. The possibility of just painting for pleasure is inconceivable.

To enlarge on this: to begin with there was the conception, felt and half perceived in the mind, of the painting. Not a clear visual conception but a strong emotional anticipation of the feeling I should get having done it and looked at it. This could have the intensity of sexual desire and was certainly connected with eroticism to some degree because of my choice – or rather compulsion – towards certain subjects involving male bodies. Once having committed myself and breached the blank canvas, from then on it was a desperate struggle to gain the far shore. Very little sustained pleasure occurred during this time. Moments of hope and euphoria followed by blank defeat. The result was some sort of compromise between what I wanted to achieve and what I was capable of doing. It passed the main tests but it wasn't what I'd hoped. In retrospect the initial conception fades. One cannot hold on to the intention but sees only the result. The conception in fact is almost instantly confused and contaminated as soon as one starts painting. The results can often seem quite good, but in an impersonal way. As though they had been done by someone else.

What seemed to keep an artist like Bennett going (I am still reading the Journals) was obedience to schedule. The fact that the schedule was usually self-imposed was no excuse for breaking it. If he decided to be in bed by a certain time he would leave a play or opera he was enjoying in order to be on time. When he started a new novel he decided when it ought to be finished and it was finished. So many words per day, so many words per book, divide one into the other and you get the time it will take to write it. There is something splendid about this but also something absurd. As though he did not dare to allow himself any freedom but must need to be his own slave and master at the same time. Early journalistic training perhaps – employee mentality from which one cannot escape. I have it, but am more delinquent and self-indulgent which probably only makes things worse for me. I don't gain more freedom. I merely incur more guilt.

23 January 1973 After lunch and a short snooze, to stave off a threatening cloud of depression I drove to the West End and walked to see the Titian Diana and Acteon in the N.G. Crowds of young people in the Gallery who interested me more than anything on the walls. I could see nothing in the painting but a tired, cliché-ridden bit of clever picture-making. It is not *about* anything. The landscape setting is a 19th-century operatic backcloth. Diana is posed in order that her right bared breast with central nipple faces squarely to the spectator. Her 'bow' is a heavy length of carved mahogany which couldn't possibly be bent, or even if it could there was no bow string. The quiver of arrows being in the small of her back quite out of reach. She is neither a hunter nor a goddess. Just a model posing. Acteon is so badly drawn and painted as to be scarcely credible. He wears a sort of ass's head between his shoulders and might have come from a 3rd-form's production of *Midsummer Night's Dream*. The dogs (they are certainly not hounds) paw at the figure. One has a face which resembles a baby bear. Considering the drama and mystery latent in the subject it is the most abysmal failure of the imagination. I consider my collage gouache, which I did hurriedly for Buckle's scheme, greatly superior. And I am not exactly prone to liking my own work.

29 January 1973 Reading *The School of Venus* I get a vivid idea of how intensely pleasurable heterosexual intercourse must be. And I much regret I have never known it. Nor is it easy to be sure which sex I would prefer to be. Physically perhaps the woman, but temperamentally the man. I mean I wouldn't want to wait passively while the man fucks me. But the simultaneous pleasuring of two bodies in intercourse – the wide range of possible ways of coupling, each with its different distinct quality of sensation – there is nothing equivalent in the homosexual world.

28 September 1973 The knocking of Longford continues. To my relief. It is obvious that society is not going to try once more and ban pornography – though if they would discourage and prevent the display and sale of 'false' pornography – such as one sees in all the

Soho windows – that would be a great benefit. But no one has yet come forward to extol the benefits of pornography.

'Sir. As a middle-aged, homosexually-orientated pervert, obliged, through personal inhibitions and timidity, to content himself with an exclusively imaginary sex life, the availability of porn is of the greatest benefit to my well being and mental health, as well as affording hours of harmless sexual enjoyment. Before it was available (to me) compulsive and chronic masturbation was severely taxing on my powers of imagination as well as sexually unfulfilling and boringly frustrating. Now, I can live a full and satisfying sex life, albeit with myself alone. The worst that can be said about such a programme is that one comes to prefer it to interpersonal sexual activity. But since this is nearly impossible to achieve anyhow and when it was actively sought and sometimes found, never satisfactory, the loss is negligible. To deprive someone so addicted of the wonderland of sexual pleasure would be senselessly cruel and likely to result in severe nervous breakdown or a desperate pursuit of satisfaction through criminal activity.'

I suppose, if M. were no longer alive and I had no profession and image to maintain in the public eye, I might conceivably send such a letter to *The Times*. But then it is even less likely to be printed.

21 October 1973 Reading *Clayhanger* with much enjoyment, I wonder if Bennett had actually seen a boy stripped naked and birched, or whether the brief but terrible description was purely imaginary. Date 1835, place the workhouse at Burnsley. Boys of seven worked 18 hours a day in the potteries.

24 October 1973 The Schwitters show. Some of the most beautiful art objects I've seen in years. I came away tingling. Stared with envy and desire to emulate. Mostly done between 1923–29. Had I seen these instead of Brangwyn, what sort of artist should I be? Great desire to start some constructions but – the self-defeating doubts and questions which will wear down my desire. All my miseries and depression stem from the inability to act out desires when they are felt. The times I do – such as in painting – I become whole again.

4 November 1973 When I read of Auden returning to Christ Church and meeting distinguished people with some of whom he was at prep school, I feel an envy and bitterness which is almost suffocating. I seem right outside life. My 'friends' – P.W., K.P.A., Pru are really only peripheral contacts. I value them certainly – but their company is demanding and I always part from them, not with regret as from a real friend, but relief that the strain of maintaining contact is temporarily over. I come back to my aloneness – which is not enough.

I pick up Mann's letters and read (1954) 'without work, that is, without active hope, I wouldn't know how to live. Every time I feel this way, all I can do is to remember that only recently I managed to turn out something quite talented and successful, and that distraction and fatigue, which are not necessarily permanent, are responsible for my present plight.'

24 November 1973   John Berger on the box. Having won the £5000 for *G*. Well – he's too smooth. Too much the professorial orator for me to believe in. Effective? yes. He knows how to hang on the ball. (The BBC interviewer was quite outsmarted.) Yet – he claimed to be after the truth (who doesn't) and not mind if the 'truth' is difficult to comprehend (Thomas Mann was also after the truth but strove to make his books witty and entertaining). I suspect that J.B. lacks a sense of humour. Takes himself too seriously. A pundit. He overbids his hand. *Hang it all, Robert Browning, there can be but one Sordello.*

19 December 1973   Painting snow scenes. Quite well. Bad morning awakening as usual – panic, depression – but day quite active. Much aware all the time of my 'enlarged liver'. Wish I'd never been told since it will not make me deny myself the indulgences without which life would not be worth living. But I do not feel really well – nor really ill. Certainly I feel best after drinking. Maximum daily consumption is three sherries midday, four martinis, one bottle of wine. Often wine lasts one-and-a-half days, two bottles in three days. L.P. Hartley drank two bottles of vodka a day (but he died last week – of what? P.W. may tell). Anyway he did not presumably die in agony.

27 January 1974   Dinner party with the Goslings. Mary Rose and Hugh and their beautiful 18-year-old son Mark, Peggy Ashcroft, Jonathan, Bob and V. The nicest evening I have spent for months and the nicest dinner party for years. Very skilfully done. Drinks with cold snacks downstairs at the table. Then change places and dinner is served (poussin, veg, cheese, baked apple). Upstairs for coffee and port. Peggy left first. Then Hugh and Mary Rose dropped me off on their way round to Sussex. Much taken by Mark. Lovely evening, which I wish did not have to end.

20 March 1974 Reading the Gide–Valéry correspondence. They met in 1890 both about 21. Rimbaud died the next year. Cézanne and Picasso were painting. What an age to be alive in. Of course there may be circles of similar quality of intelligence today, but if so I do not know them. The nearest I get is a dinner party with John Lehmann, Roy Fuller and Charles Osborne – which is not very near. (A bit nearer might be a dinner party at P.W. with, say, Leppard, Shaffer, Rylands; but with homosexuals always an element of queer camp reduces even intelligent people to triviality.) Sleep deeply now every afternoon after sandwich lunch with two/three glasses sherry and two/three glasses wine. Best time of the day. Read *The Times* and quietly drop off. Marvellously quiet always in this house. Try and take a little walk in the afternoon to shorten the siesta and make a break before the evening. No phone goes (though people claim they are 'always' ringing me). Very glad they don't. Don't want contacts. Am not at all lonely. Lack only zest, drive, a joy in living. Feel like this notebook – 'Narrow, feint and ruled'.

Legs and thighs of footballers. Watched this evening trying to discover whether a padded crotch covered their genitals. Like to see them play naked – or better strip off naked after the match and stand still. Examine them minutely. Such stamina, skill and vital charm. Incredible that people can see, think, react as quickly as they do. Marvellous people. I bow down in deference.

13 April 1974 'People believe that something fundamentally true comes out when a person lets himself go.' (Valéry). Well, so it does. When the gentlemanly restraints and customary self-possession are broken, a person reveals aspects of himself, normally concealed, which certainly are 'fundamentally true'. Which is not to say they are of any value or benefit to anyone. They are just true. But V. is a stickler for etiquette and good form. He condemns Gide for publishing an anecdote, which while no means to his disfavour was nevertheless told in private, as between friends, and thereby offending against V's concept of friendship (though not against friendship in abstract he is quick to add). He guards himself against a relaxed friendship with G, seeing always the page of the Journals on which it will later be stylishly reported.

It may be part of the fundamental immaturity of homosexuals that makes them want to reveal themselves to the world at large. To tell the whole truth. (Are we not all as children told to tell the whole truth?) Or it may (be) a matter of temperament. V. was naturally reserved. He despised the public and gave them only what he thought they deserved. G. had the romantic's notion of loving the world – while being careful to keep from beneath its trampling feet. V. was more grown up. More mature. Yet he underestimates the value to others of being allowed to glimpse the human and vulnerable side to great public figures. I think that if one is a public figure one owes it to others to let them see one's weaknesses and failures. It consoles and reassures them. The distance was not so great as they thought. However, one is not entitled to reveal the privacies of others.

Really my life is absurd. There is nothing to keep one living except painting and guilt. (Am I therefore a better painter than those who live also?)

14 May 1974 How soothing to read through the names of château-bottled claret. But my half-bottle of Ch. Beychevelle '64 from Hedges and Butler does not seem very distinguished. Maybe I should drink Ch. Ausonne '61 at £17.50 a bottle or Ch. Petrus '66 at the same price.

24 May 1974 Perhaps I shall be remembered in the end as a sort of de Sade of auto-erotic finesse.

1 June 1974 Disturbing day with bad mail. Income Tax questions. Lease questions. Laughton wanting some more information about past sales of pictures. Spent three hours of the morning trying to keep hold (half drynamyl). Then got down to some gouaches which went quite well. But why am I pestered from all sides with problems which I cannot handle. Other people have secretaries, wives – someone. All these people I am paying to look after my present problems simply add to them. Every week letters from Laughton, Kirby, Glover & Co, Cheifitz, Moore Stevens, Duveen & Walker, Waddington.

5 June 1974 The Tax thing is really incomprehensible. Laughton seems impressed by the orderliness of all my records yet gives the impression it would be better for me had I been less so. Suggested I might deny I had kept any records of works done or sold. The 19th-century image of the helpless moronic genius which is what the Revenue cast me as. Or want to. All this would not matter, it would all be fun (like the Watergate affair appears to be on TV) if I were properly alive, with some zest, some desire to win and live. But I don't care. If I were taken out before a firing squad in Wigmore Street I would not protest. At least the initiative would come from someone else and the end quickly.

27 July 1974 Three o'clock in the morning. Hours of discomfort. Death passes and repasses over me like an enemy aircraft which senses your presence and is after you. Unusually calm, I bear witness with humble pride to what I have been and to what I have done. Now has come the moment to stop joking. Open, you gates of eternity. 'Before death – The maximum energy is demanded of you at a moment when the energy has become absolutely useless.' (Montherlant).

30 September 1974 Auden died yesterday in Vienna. Will Townsend dead. Am strangely affected by these things although neither were close friends. The sudden disappearances of things once taken for granted, like the small cosy Victorian villas out on the Southend Road which I pass going to H.H. One by one they disappear. What do I live for? Habit, fear and a sense of obligation.

3 October 1974 Auden. The thing Bill mentioned particularly on Monday was his enthusiasm for things. His energy and unflagging enthusiasm and zest for life. At 66. Well – I haven't. But then he was outgoing. Not an introvert. But his enthusiasm could also be extremely tiresome and boring because he held forth the whole time (that evening a year ago in the restaurant with P.W. and Auden, Spender and two others at the next table. You couldn't hear yourself think for the noise he was making and flicking cigarette ash all over the food ... The Chanterelle it was. Last time I saw him. Rather frightening to look, like some large aggressive reptile.).

Only when working, alone here or occasionally at the Slade, do I feel alive. The rest of the time is sleep or a semi-drunken doze. The days are too long for what I can put into them. Common complaint. At least I do not kill time (with meaningless routine activities). I suffer its weight like a large stone pressing into my belly. (I claim no credit for this, an element of ritual is probably a good thing.)

16 October 1974 Good Slade morning with all my new students (except the lady with the metallic green eyelids who is clearly self-sufficient) all charming friendly and lovely youths. I think I did not altogether fail them. The quality of young people today. The sheer human quality – gentle, uncomplaining, understanding. Wish I could remember their names, though it doesn't matter. Tacit human presence – just two of us in a small room together for thirty minutes. Talking and in some sort of contact. Relaxed and informal. Honest – or trying to be.

How different life might be. No-one would believe that someone with my 'success' could live so impoverished a life. So bound to routine, boredom, a mother, a middle-aged neurotic. If only (bad phrase) but if only I had hooked onto someone like Pru or Elizabeth Ayrton. Some grown up adult. Instead of two neurotic incompetent infants (aged 92 and 49).

12.12 am. I write because there is no one to talk to, and it is blissfully quiet. But I would like someone to talk to other than a hypothetical posterity. I would like one of my five new students to talk to now. Quiet, relaxed, slightly drunk. A Socratic soirée? Silly.

17 October 1974 P.W. wanted me to go to dinner tomorrow with Albee. 'I know he likes you.' Since I hardly know him there is no reason why he should like or dislike me. He never answered a letter I wrote him in N.Y. about a year ago. So I guess the attraction is not irresistible. But P.W. wanted to make up a 'dinner party'. When I said I was not free Friday but was free yesterday or today he made excuses that the company would not be suitable, i.e., the pieces were already in place. One is just part of a sort of jig-saw.

29 October 1974 Reading Madox Ford's *The Good Soldier*. Promises to be entertaining in a dryly ironic way after you get used to the irritating rib-nudging style. Three evenings of Scrabble is enough. How I hate the beginning of these long evenings. Only five o'clock and already pitch dark and not yet time for a drink.

31 October 1974 10.45 pm. Merlyn Evans dies on Tuesday. 63. Long enough. He died quickly in a fall going from the RCA to the Waddington party for MacWilliam. Pru told me about it this morning over the phone. Wrote to Mary. But what can one say? Funeral on Tuesday at Golders Green which I shall try and avoid going to. Let the dead bury the dead. What's the point – only if I thought Mary would be really pleased to see me there. Instructions in *The Times* as to where flowers may be sent. Didn't like that. Total waste, except profit for the florists.

6 November 1974 Slade. Not one single student kept his tutorial appointment. Increasing sense of isolation and being cut off from life. Stayed till 3.30, missing Merlyn's funeral which I wanted a reason for doing. Could see no point in meeting a lot of people I know and would like to see in conditions where it would be unsuitable to express pleasure in doing so.

11 November 1974 Programme on Poulenc on TV this evening, 9.05. We had nearly finished dinner and I wanted to watch. Ramsay joins me, reluctantly. Oboe and bassoon trio – *mouvement perpétuel*, which I used to practice when I was 17. R. yawns, fidgets and goes to bed. Then comes *Les Biches*. Stills of the original cast, Lifar, Nemchinova, the *adagietto*, which Harold Colebrook first played to me in 1933. All the unbearable longing for those years – the magic – the torment and frustration. The revival at Covent Garden. Parkinson dancing the page boy. A whole world of longing, lost. R. couldn't share it. It could have been something we might talk about. Something which meant so much to me, because a part of me in my youth. And to hear it again here, in this meaningless house, this prison which I have made to die in. Why couldn't it work out just this once? This one evening. Nemchinova (Parkinson) dancing on a bare stage in Poulenc's house in France and the adagietto played by his aged friend on the piano. I know that music like I know the taste of my own tears. The adagietto. Lifar at 16, when I first saw him in 1929. Blood streaming down his legs after dragging himself across the rough boards of Covent Garden at the end of *Fils Prodigue*. Sweat streaming down his lynx-like face and bare shoulders. That was my first glimpse of a world to which I knew I belonged but never really entered. Lifar grew old (he is roughly my age) fat and querulous. The prodigal son has been danced by others, but nothing can recreate the staggering wonder of that Saturday afternoon when I first saw him in 1929 (special leave was given me to come up from Hornsey). And I can share it with no one. M. took me, of course, but understood nothing.

The half hour or so of that programme which I watched alone tonight with Poulenc was the happiest I have spent for years. Also the saddest, because the happiness was only in the memory, or imagination. It never really happened. It was unreal.

13 November 1974 From the news media we seem faced with imminent economic and social collapse and total chaos. Yet all is quiet. Cars run. Food can be bought. Bombs explode elsewhere. Fires burn. I am probably more physically comfortable at the moment than Montaigne in his attic. What's more I have a car in the garage, and 'could' drive anywhere in Europe starting now. 'Could' if I had the desire and initiative. Instead I finish a bottle of Vougeot '61, half-anxious about the morrow. Not that I have anything to do except keep living and avoid pain.

Bill Coldstream kindly asked after my mother today when I took several glasses of rather acid Vin Rosé in his room with a group of students who had been assembled for no very clearly identifiable reason. His act went well. Like Olivier in *The Entertainer*. Impossible to know what he really thinks or feels. Perhaps he doesn't allow himself the time. An extrovert (I suppose). Continuously involved with other people. Impossible to imagine he has ever spent the sort of solitary evenings I spend.

Constantly I wonder how unique and extraordinary I am. Whether I alone have invented my little auto-erotic E.T. machine (an invention which might surely be put on the level of the discovery of anaesthetics) or whether such devices are all over the place. If they are, since their benefits to middle-aged masturbators are so superlatively effective and rewarding, it is surprising one has not heard about them. The nearest thing, in the market, of course, is the electrical vibrator, which bears no comparison. It is infinitely inferior.

26 November 1974 Looked at some pictures of Jackson Pollock. Some are still good. Though I could do better. Scale, energy and nerve is all one requires.

0105. Cleaned the telephone. First time in 21 years. Enjoy little late-night nonsenses like this which also are practical.

I have smoked 20 cigarettes since getting back this afternoon and drunk a bottle of Muscadet as well as four/five gins and feel very fine now. But I shall pay for it tomorrow. How do you balance this up? The alternative seems to be to feel bad all the time. The opposite is impossible except for those who live by 'higher things' – such as God, vegetarianism, teetotalism, monogamism etc.

3 November 1974 H.H. once again, looking at *The Times* reproduction beside my desk and am ravished by the face of the boy Egyptian King Tutankamoun.

If I had to choose one work from the long history of human artifacts I would choose that gold mask, the onyx eyes, tear-stained gold cheeks. The extraordinary way it looks at you, through you. Sad, childlike about the mouth. Austere, but understanding, encouraging one to go on trying. The one most beautiful human image I know. If that were the image of God I would kneel and worship him.

The only thing comparable is the dark-haired onyx-eyed butcher boy at the Co-op who stood so patiently, with folded arms, on Saturday, waiting in the queue to pay for three bars of Fry's Crunchie. How I would like to stand him, side by side, with the mask of T.

20 November 1974 What was Rimbaud's cock like? What a pity such things are completely undocumented. (I'm not interested in Verlaine's. He shouldn't have one.)

16 December 1974 *H.H. Tutankamoun.* I stare for hours at the onyx-lined eyes of T. The gold mask beside my desk here. It is the nearest to religious worship I know. And it is worship. I pray to him and love him and would carry out his commandments if I knew what they were, if he'd lived long enough to make them known. But he didn't. He died at 16, 5000 years ago, an Egyptian pharoah, a young boy. The goldsmith who made his death mask certainly knew and loved him. Of course *The Times* photographer has helped – but he cannot create what was not there – he can only revere – which he has done superbly (who was he – does he know the ikon he has made?) Am I the only *Times* reader who keeps staring, year after year, at this wonderful boy's face – those sad, understanding eyes. How superior to any image of Jesus. How much more worth kneeling down to and worshipping. If there was a Tutankamoun religion I would belong. Perhaps it is just for me. Full but pursed lips. Waiting perhaps to open and receive, not sure. Possibly spit venom. One must know how to approach a king. But the eyes are unmistakable. They are fuller of compassion and understanding than any I know. Nothing in Christian iconography comes anywhere near them.

That is what is so strange. An image 3000 years BC which displays Christian ideas far more clearly than anything which was done AD. The Christ image was always of suffering; torture: one had to *pity* Jesus and 'love' him for his sacrifice.

The Egyptian just looks at you with infinite understanding. He asks nothing. He judges not, nor censors. He looks with your eyes and you look back. And there is an indescribable understanding and sympathy and love.

Though in the sharp lines of the nostrils and edges of gold upper lips is no promise of help.

You are more beautiful than anything in the Classical world. If I could make anything as beautiful as you I would be happy and justified.

Understanding and compassion. And you lived and died quietly – not saying anything we know – not doing much – lived only half of the life of Jesus. Founded no religion. Caused no wars or misery. No one was tortured to death in your name (so far as we know). You make rather nonsense of Christianity.

19 December 1974   In 1545 painters were concerned with 'the combat of Lust and Reason'. Difficult to see which is which.

15 January 1975   Apropos Rimbaud: At the end of 'Antique' from *Les Illuminations*, Mercure edition of 1947 is given:
Promène-toi, la nuit, en mouvant doucement cette cuisse, cette seconde cuisse et cette jambe de gauche.
I think there should be a conjunctive 'et' here [ie between 'cuisse' and 'cette'], to separate the five soft sibilants (which sound squashy) and to indicate the effort of moving ('et' can be spoken with an intake, a gasp of breath) first the right thigh – then the left leg.

En mouvant doucement cette cuisse, et *cette seconde cuisse*, et *cette jambe de gauche* (Marvellous to use 'seconde' instead of the more obvious 'autre'.)

Tes boules precieuses, remuent. Your precious balls move about, stir, draw up – what had he in mind?

Had he observed the testicular retraction of his own sex during masturbation? – or Verlaine's? – or someone we don't know about – an Abbéville kid perhaps?

Or was he remembering the sight of youths' testicles swinging from side to side, forwards and back, as they walk, quite innocently, into the shower, or changing room, towards you at school?

And what particular antique figure had he seen? In the Louvre? (I can't remember any), in Abbéville? The best are in the B.M. and Athens.

But, of course, he was in London at that time (1872) at 139 Wandsworth Bridge Road SW6 – (I think). So he would certainly have seen the Elgin marbles.

How I would like to have seen Rimbaud naked at 17. But that is best left to imagining. There would not have been any anatomical difference between R. and the numerous boys I met in Soho seventy years later in 1942. And not many spoke French. Boulanger, I remember, with his pearly nipples and silk skin, soft and sleepy. (He was shot full of hot metal six months later.) To destroy something as beautiful as Boulanger's body (he was a French Canadian of 17) is a crime beyond understanding – I mean beyond any justification.

17 January 1975   Two Japanese were seated opposite me on the tube coming back from Euston. One with the Samurai face of a warrior, vicious, virile, frightening in its animation, the almond eyes and eyebrows from a Hokusai print. The other, rather plump, a listener, watched me watching the other, who jabbered incessantly, quite unaware of the environment.

I allowed myself a short sexual fantasy involving him but it did not produce much satisfaction. His beauty was like that of a wild cat. Lotus lips, hawked eyebrows, olive skin, widespread thighs. Nothing much showing between. But if he were seized and stripped naked, strung up by his wrist to a high bar and whipped sharp and quick between his thighs it might be possible to break open the marble self-satisfaction of his countenance.

11 February 1975 Bill Coldstream. This is his last year, and the last session we shall have together. I shall miss him. With all his over-talkativeness and sometimes tiresome long-windedness, everyone is the better off for having known him. To me, personally, he has given a consistent supportive encouragement, almost flattery, and I have gained a little self-confidence through being with him. He never knocks anyone, or makes them feel foolish, or tries to outsmart them. He makes people feel better than in fact they are. He is excessively modest about his own achievements and activities, is always telling jokes about himself. (Yet so many, who do not know him, think of him as a power maniac.) He has taught me a lot. How to de-fuse tense situations – to make the silly remark at the sensible moment. When to be a clown. But never to put down someone who feels the necessity to be a 'great man', also not being taken in by it. Very shrewd, perceptive and with a warm insight.

14 June 1975 In my youth art was a fantasy, an escape. A compulsion-created alternative to a real world with which I could not come to terms. Now the need is less compulsive, reality less irksome – my withdrawal more advanced. I no longer want to meet people very much. A few old friends give me some intellectual stimulus. I find little interest in the cultural activities of the time. Or rather I feel little curiosity to find out more about them. There is certainly no painting today which excites me at all. Fifteen or twenty years ago there was. Guston was perhaps the last real challenge.

When I think about painting at all I think of doing a romantic, enigmatic, figurative composition somewhere in the style of Piero and Giorgione. Figures with faces. But it would need planning, and then laborious painting out. None of the sometimes exciting plunges into the white canvas with no preconcepting. All that too often ends the same way.

10 October 1975 When Pru showed me all those letters to *The Times* about the proposed Wealth Tax which artists had been asked to sign I wondered why no one had asked me. My address is known. I don't think it can be assumed I'm dead since *The Times* has carried no obituary. Perhaps it is just tacitly assumed I no longer matter.

22 October 1975 CANCER ERA BEGINS. The possible, or indeed likely, proximity of death does not worry me.

But I do want to make a graceful exit. Not in pain or prostration. And alone, alas, because I can see how good it would be to die holding someone's hand. But I do not know anyone to whom this would be agreeable.

Since I have lived mostly alone it seems agreeable to die alone. I can see that it would have worked out better in other ways. But they didn't come my way.

27 October 1975 The fact that I no longer have to make any decisions and cannot take any responsibility for what happens to me, my mother, or anyone else is some consolation. Decision-making nearly always induces panic. My desires are never very clear-cut and are often conflicting. A very limited field of choice suits me better than wide horizons of opportunity. I claim no merit in this timid attitude to life, but I never acquired the weapons of a warrior. I have something of the shrewdness and cunning of small mammals.

12 November 1975 Bill Coldstream called in for about 15 minutes this afternoon and made me laugh so much that my whole inside ached and I had to rest afterwards. Unfortunately nothing he said would seem in the least funny if written down as everything relies on his dry ironical delivery and extraordinary powers of mimicry. This time it was Stephen who had sent Bill a passage from the Journal Alan is currently publishing in the *London Magazine* in which some disclosures were made about Bill's sexual interests when a youth. Bill had related all this at a luncheon party when he was thoroughly in his cups and S. had noted it all down. Bill rings Alan and begs him not to publish it without cuts, largely on account of Winifred. A pity. I would love to know what Bill had said.

How this man can have 'enemies' in the art world, or be thought a power maniac is beyond me. No one is more modest, unpretentious, kind, understanding and un-self-seeking. The reason he was 'on' so many boards, committees, and whatnot is simply that he has a keen sense of public obligation and is extremely efficient. His manner can, at times, seem a little astringent and dismissive, but this is usually because he is preoccupied with something else at the time and is not very good at turning on the superficial social charm. He can also talk too much (though it is nearly always worth hearing) and he is not a good listener. He likes an audience better than being one. Though he can also be infinitely patient with the inarticulate when he senses they have something which it is important to them to say.

24 July 1976 – Harrow Hill Stay up the whole week. Rectal pains dominate the day. Do little other than lie on my back.

13 August 1976 Rosamond Lehmann at Patrick's. A good evening. Patrick always makes things work between people. Rosamond is softly intelligent and very gentle. We separate only on the question of an 'after-life' which she passionately believes in – a life in which one sees again one's loved ones (particularly her daughter). P. does too. I cannot begin to believe in it. Immortality of the soul is without a trace of meaning to me. What is 'soul'? An invention of people who dislike the idea of oblivion. Oblivion holds no terrors for me. Life is a temporary experience in a vast landscape of death. Death is where we come from and in a short time return. The huge, inorganic world of rock and water. Life is a tiny dream in an eternity of non-life. I do not mind this. Let's go and eat (8.45).

The problem will always be taking the final dose at night – when I feel reasonably content. It is the morning when I want to prolong the oblivion of sleep. Suppose one took the dose in the morning – no alcohol in the blood stream – would it work? Could one just go back to bed and sleep into eternity?

But it's ridiculous to leave so important a matter as suicide to a question of mood. If the decision to end one's life is made, then it must be done in the most practical and efficient way possible. To leave it to 'how one feels' at the moment of action is absurd. After all, it's a permanent decision. It cannot be reversed.

This extraordinary dry hot summer continues. Every day the same. The car hood has not been raised since March. It's boring but uncomplicated. One takes the weather for granted, which is rare here.

8 September 1976 My ideal of death would be a ceremonial suicide in the presence of my friends. P.W., Pru, K.P., Bob, Veronica. (I have to exclude R. because it would be beyond his capacity.)

We would have a meal here at Belsize Park. Then with P.W.'s help I would take the necessary pills, alcohol, change into my night attire and go to bed. The others would be drinking, laughing, perhaps playing some music by my bedside. Plenty of booze. As I get dozy I would take my leave of being, one by one, with sadness but not despair. And not lonely. It would be a ritualized affair, civilized and well conducted.

11 September 1976 Rather severe pain on getting up, did some shopping and dozed as usual. 'Life After Death' which K.P.A. lent me is just a history of guesswork surrounding that subject about which no one has any knowledge whatsoever and is consequently crashingly boring. True in ESP there is some evidence of a life of sorts going on, but even those who get in touch can tell you nothing of what sort of life. One thing is clear. If everyone who has died still has some sort of life somewhere it must be distinctly congested. I prefer to believe in oblivion – or a return to the state one was in before conception and birth.

24 September 1976 Have now got radiation sickness and cystitis on top of everything else. Feel like hell. No appetite.

17 October 1976 Patrick came to give me a vitamin injection again this morning. He does this each week. He was smart and debonair as usual. Fits of panic when I feel I cannot endure this long drawn-out torment any longer. But what can I do but endure it like others have to? It's much worse if the radiation is in the thorax according to P. So I suppose I can be thankful for that.

11 May 1977 Should do my Income Tax accounts but cannot bring myself to make the effort. Get slightly drunk each midday on Guinness and sherry. Induces some half sleep in the afternoon. The reason I sit at the window now each evening is to see some life going on. Am an old man before my time. Not yet 65. Pension papers arrived the other day. Life gets more and more like a Samuel Beckett play. No wonder he won the Nobel Prize. Though for exactly what I am not clear.

8 September 1977 I thought in bed last night about Boulanger, the French Canadian I picked up in the York Minster one night about 1944 and took him home to bed. He was with a friend who had a date with a girl and asked me if I would look after him. They were both very drunk. I got him home by taxi and gently undressed his half-sleeping body. Never have I seen anything more beautiful. His skin was the texture of rose petals, his nipples mother-of-pearl. His navel set like a pearl in his belly. His legs were straight and strong but not bulging with muscle. His hands and feet were perfectly formed. He was 16. I lay for hours with the light on gazing with rapture at his perfect loveliness. He lay half-sleeping heavy with drink. His lips half parted showed the edge of his white teeth. I kissed him many times but got no more response than from a statue. His body smelled of warm new bread. His name was Boulanger which seemed appropriate. We had no sex. It was enough for me to look at him. Then later in the morning it got cold and I drew up the covers and held him in my arms, warm and supple, breathing gently against each other's cheeks. Some weeks later I met his friend again in the York Minster and asked after him. I was told he'd been blown to pieces on the Anzio Beachhead.

One of the most flattering things which has happened to me over the past few years is to have three of my Rimbaud gouaches bought by Prof. Hackett. I first met him at Victor Waddington's party where I was showing the first of the drawings – *Antique*. I was introduced to him and of course had no idea who he was. Much to my surprise he asked me if *Antique* has any reference to Rimbaud's poem of that name. I replied that it had and managed to quote fairly accurately the lines which had particularly inspired me. A few minutes later I noticed a red spot go on the frame and he had bought it. Shortly afterwards he sent me his small monograph on Rimbaud and I realized that not only was he Professor of French at Southampton University but a Rimbaud specialist who had written several books on the subject. His understanding seemed exactly like my own. When subsequently he bought two more of the later gouaches last year from Leslie I felt that my instinctive reactions to Rimbaud were not as wayward and bizarre as I feared they might be.

4 November 1977 9.30 am   The capsules have been taken with some whisky. What is striking is the unreality of the situation. I feel no different. R. returned to H.H. yesterday. But suddenly the decision came that it must be done. I cannot drag on another few years in this state. It's a bright sunny morning. Full of life. Such a morning as many people have died on. I am ready for death though I fear it. Of course the whole thing may not work and I shall wake up. I don't really mind either way. Once the decision seems inevitable the courage needed was less than I thought. I don't quite believe anything has happened though the bottle is empty. At the moment I feel very much alive. P.W. rang and asked me to dine with him tonight. But I had already made the decision though not started the action. I cannot believe I have committed suicide since nothing has happened. No big bang or cut wrists. 65 was long enough for me. It wasn't a complete failure I did some [At this point the words lapse into illegibility and stop].

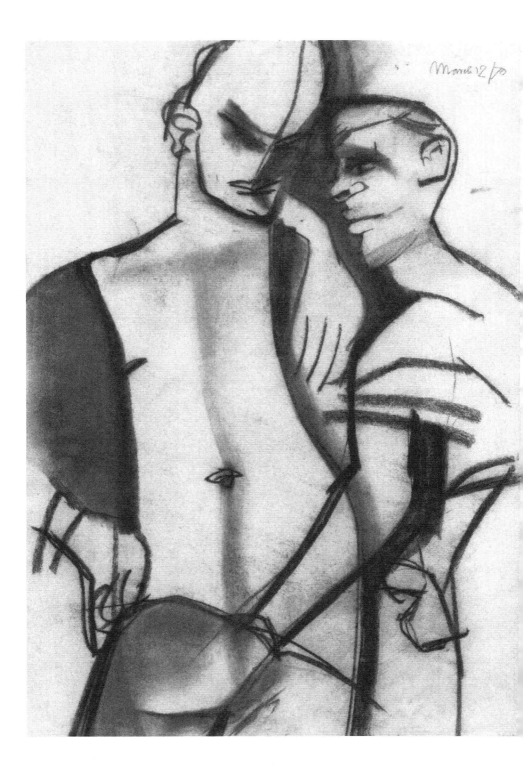

Index